ELECTRONIC BRAIN

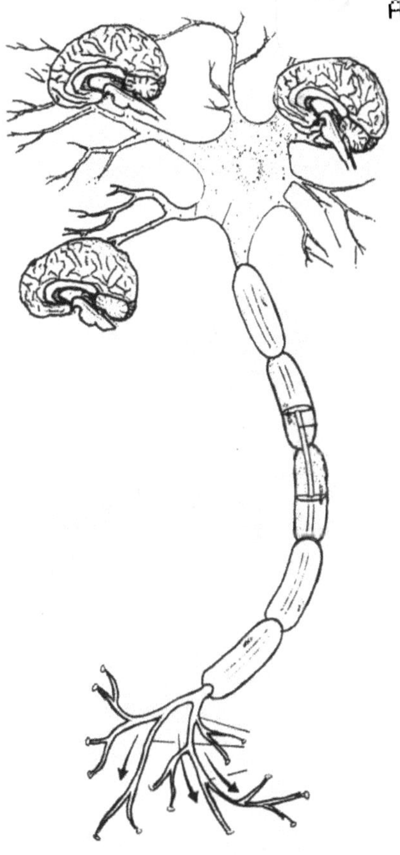

ISSUE 2

ISBN: 978-1-968958-05-3

Editor – Jean-Paul L. Garnier

Cover Art – Intermingled by Zara Kand

First Edition | 2026

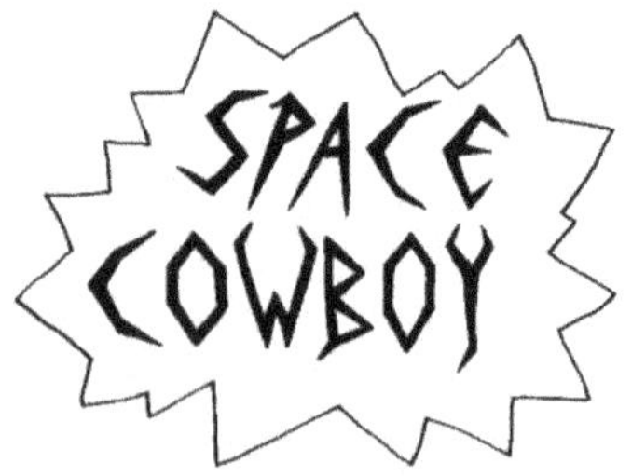

Space Cowboy Books

61871 29 Palms Hwy.

Joshua Tree, CA 92252

www.spacecowboybooks.com

Table of Contents

LUST & GRIEF

These are two aspects of our inner worlds that we all experience yet are reluctant to discuss openly, even though we may experience them simultaneously. Do we avoid these subjects out of shame or merely the difficulty of speaking about them out loud? Is part of the reason America's puritanical background? *Electronic Brain* aims for open and honest communication about difficult subjects and to plumb the depths of the human experience, no matter how uncomfortable. Our relationships with sex and death are a necessary part of being alive, yet we often stifle honest communication in fear of repercussion or out of shame. This is inherently unhealthy and can prevent an individual from processing grief in such a way as to come out the other end stronger and unscathed.

Art and literature are, of course, two healthy ways in which we express our complicated relationships with our feelings of lust and grief. Some of the greatest artworks ever created deal with these subjects, such as Bach's Chaconne. This piece of music is one of the most beautiful expressions of grief ever set down to paper. And while our expression of these subjects might be deeply private, this does not preclude that we can transmute such difficulties into works of incredible beauty. Desire and sadness often hold hands, and at times they may exalt each other, forming rapturous founts of emotional expression.

Not every work in this issue expresses these subjects blatantly, nor need they. Some of the works contained herein may not, for you, fit squarely into any category – and that is okay, for *Electronic Brain*'s mission is to cross thresholds, to openly delve into all aspects of human culture and its wide variety of possible expressions. In keeping with our mission, you will find: plays, comics, musical scores, fiction, interviews, and works which are not easily defined. For fans of speculative fiction, many of these works will not appear to be a part of the genre at first. But sexual fantasy is, after all, still fantasy. And history that was planned for, but didn't occur, is alt-history. What does it say about us when material of this nature makes us uncomfortable? And when art makes us uncomfortable, should we look away, or ask ourselves why our discomfort has arisen? What can we learn about ourselves by looking? I don't have an answer to that question for you, but I do wholeheartedly believe that you should ask yourself before looking away.

   Disagree, agree, have a comment? Send it in and we may print it in the next issue.

Jean-Paul L. Garnier
Joshua Tree, CA
2026

Scan for Bonus Audio - https://spacecowboybooks.bandcamp.com

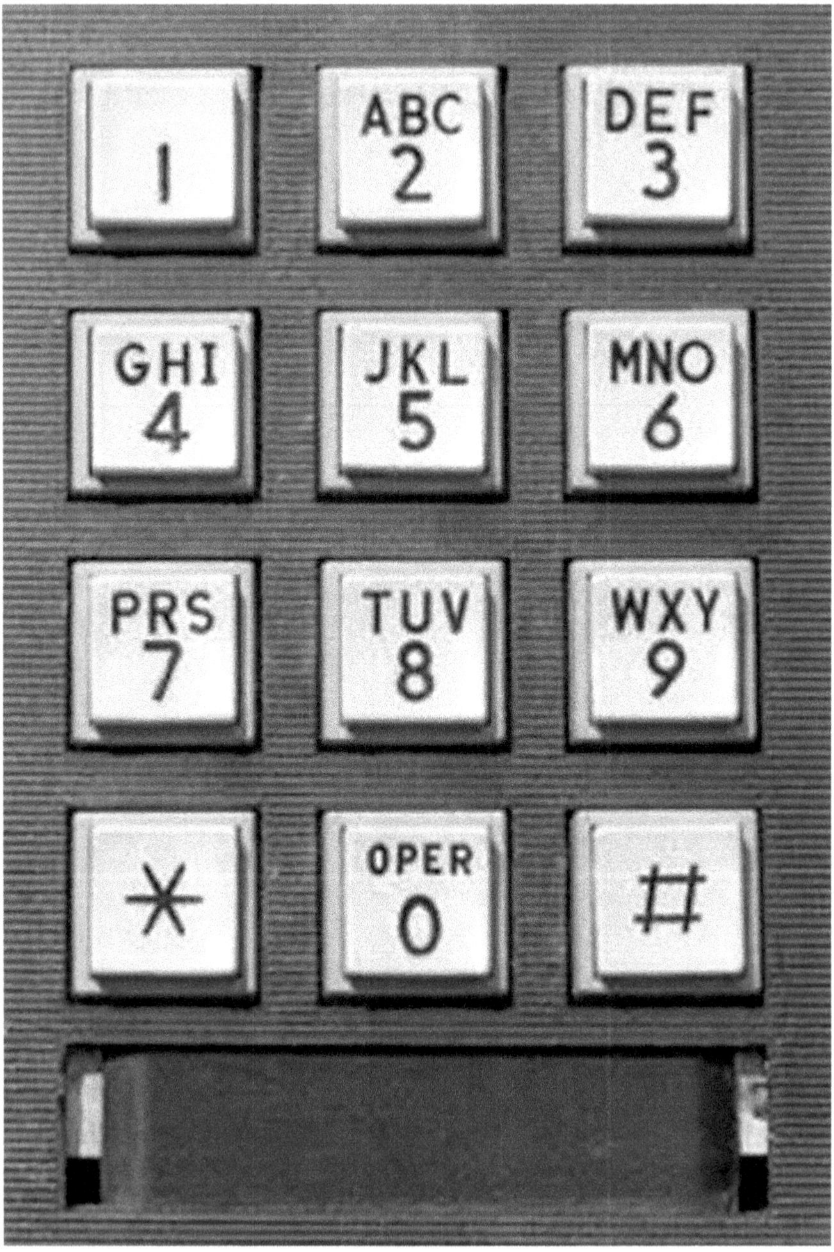

1
ABC
2
DEF
3
GHI
4
JKL
5
MNO
6
PRS
7
TUV
8
WXY
9
*
OPER
0
#

ANTIGRIEF HOTLINE
By Pablo Ramírez & Jenna Hanchey

Adapted from "Hello, This is Automatic Antigrief: What Problem Can I Solve for You Today?" by Jenna Hanchey, originally published in *Nature*

·

ALEX: 30s-40s; has recently lost their mother. Gender-Fluid Casting.
Customer Service Representative: Is trying to ensure that ALEX is 100% satisfied. Gender-Fluid Casting.
MOM: A simulation of ALEX's mother. Female-presenting Casting.

SCENE: Calling Customer Service

ALEX is peering into a picture frame on the mantel, and then at the wilted plants next to it. They raise a hand toward the picture frame when MOM enters.

>MOM
>AH! I remember that day. It was August 29, 1989 and we were traveling to...

>ALEX
>No, it's just that the plants need watering...

>MOM
>You were wearing a light blue sweater and a pair of jeans...

ALEX
Mom, stop function.

MOM abruptly stops and returns to an ambivalent and stoic
stance. MOM appears to be idle.

ALEX returns to the mantle where they begin to light a candle
when MOM starts up again.

MOM
Careful! Fire is hot! You could burn yourself! In
the case of a first-degree burn, place the burn
under cool water then coat the area with
petroleum jelly...

ALEX
Mom, stop function.

MOM stops mid-sentence and returns to their idle position.
ALEX moves to sit on the couch. MOM follows them and sits
down next to them. For a moment, ALEX and MOM are at
peace.

MOM
(Abruptly and loudly)
Let's play a game!

ALEX
What?!—

MOM
We can play dominoes, or Euchre, or even
Monopoly.

ALEX
I don't want to play a game—

MOM
Let's play chess!
(MOM reaches behind her and pulls out an old
chessboard)
Ugh, a spider!

ALEX turns to their MOM and notices the small spider on the
chessboard. MOM places the game on the coffee table in front of
them and moves to swat the spider with her hand.

ALEX
Mom! No!

MOM stops.

ALEX
(To the spider)
Runaway, little guy!
(Gently blows air at the spider)
(To MOM)
There. It's gone! Also, you could've used the
swatter, it's right next to you.

MOM
Let's play a game!

ALEX
I don't want to—

MOM
I remember when you were young and you were
always asking me to play games with you. 'Mom,
Mom! Play with me, pleeeeease'—

ALEX
(Softly)
Stop...

MOM
And I would. Whether it was hide and seek or
'doctors.' Do you remember when you tried to—

ALEX
(Forcefully)
Mom! Stop.

MOM
And you shoved the pencil up my nose and I
sneezed!

ALEX
Mom, stop function!

MOM stops and returns to an idle position. ALEX and MOM sit
on the couch quietly. ALEX places their head in their hands.
After a moment of silence, MOM begins to set the chessboard
up.

MOM
Let's play a game!

ALEX
You know what?
(Alex pulls out their phone and dials a number.)

I've had it.

ALEX sits awkwardly on the couch. They are on hold with customer service for AntiGrief. Hold music can be heard playing before the customer service representative answers the call. MOM continues to set the board. CUSTOMER SERVICE REPRESENTATIVE answers the phone. They are a disembodied voice.

> CUSTOMER SERVICE REPRESENTATIVE
> Hello?

> ALEX
> Hi.

> CUSTOMER SERVICE REPRESENTATIVE
> Thank you for calling AntiGrief: One stop shop for all of your grieving needs. With AntiGrief, healing is only a simulation away. Am I speaking with Alex?

> ALEX
> Yes.

> CUSTOMER SERVICE REPRESENTATIVE
> Perfect. Welcome, Alex. I am your customer service representative and I will be assisting you this evening.
> (Beat)
> Are you calling about our Memory Keepers novelty function? Never lose a memory again!

> ALEX
> No, thank you, I'm not.

CUSTOMER SERVICE REPRESENTATIVE
Or are you calling about our limited 'Chatting it
Up' package? You can video chat with a sim of
any deceased family member!

ALEX
No, it's not that!

CUSTOMER SERVICE REPRESENTATIVE
Well, I'm sure you want to know about our
newest service! Aroma-stalgic! It is the latest in
aroma therapy. Simply load in your memory bank
and the Aroma-stalgic will fill your home with
familiar aromas! Like the play dough from your
pre-k classroom! Or the bowl of fruity cereal that
you had every morning before school! Or your
mom's freshly baked chocolate chip cookies!

ALEX
No! No, thank you!
(Beat)
Actually, I already have the At-Home Live-Sim
Quantum Deluxe Package.

ALEX stares at MOM who has been playing chess by herself this
entire time.

CUSTOMER SERVICE REPRESENTATIVE
(Excitedly)
OOOOOOHHH!
(Beat)
(Seriously)
Oh. Are you experiencing a problem with your
sim today?

ALEX
Well. It's not a problem exactly. It's just that I
don't even know why I do it sometimes.

CUSTOMER SERVICE REPRESENTATIVE
Do what?

ALEX
So, I'll be home, watching Creative Cooking and
trying to design those fancy interactive sims to
overlay the protein packs, You know, just like
they do on TV?

CUSTOMER SERVICE REPRESENTATIVE
Mmhmm

ALEX
But then, before I even realize what's happened,
she's there.

CUSTOMER SERVICE REPRESENTATIVE
Your sim?

ALEX
My mom.
(Beat)
I mean, I know I granted all the permissions for
the app, but it's just a little surprising how quickly
it works. I don't even register thinking about her
until she's already with me.

CUSTOMER SERVICE REPRESENTATIVE
Are you unhappy with the sim? Would you like us
to remove it from your account?

ALEX
No! No. Don't get me wrong—it's great to talk to
her. It's like a dream come true. I'm really glad
she changed her mind and we got it set up when
we did—

CUSTOMER SERVICE REPRESENTATIVE
Your mother's personality upload was rather
recent.

ALEX
Right.

CUSTOMER SERVICE REPRESENTATIVE
Cause of death?

ALEX
A shuttle accident.

CUSTOMER SERVICE REPRESENTATIVE
How long after the upload did she pass?

ALEX
Two months later.

CUSTOMER SERVICE REPRESENTATIVE
I'm sorry. That is rather abrupt.

ALEX
It's okay. I love having her here. I think. It all
happened so quickly, afterward, that I almost
didn't even realize she was gone. And the sim is
perfect! The sensory notes are indistinguishable
from reality. When I hug her, I can feel her firm
shoulders and soft waist. I can smell the lavender

oil she always used in her hair. I can tell the
difference between her free-and-easy laugh and
her slightly-sardonic one.
(Laughs)
I appreciate that she's still giving me her subtle
brand of advice from beyond the grave...

MOM disappears.

> CUSTOMER SERVICE REPRESENTATIVE
> We appreciate your positive review of our
> services! So. Is there a problem I can help you
> with? Where is it occurring?

> ALEX
> No...maybe...I don't know. The "problem" isn't
> with your character map of her, or my own
> implants that register the sensory details.

> CUSTOMER SERVICE REPRESENTATIVE
> You know, we can change the input for an extra
> fee—

> ALEX
> Yes, yes. I know. Thank you, but that's not what
> I'm calling about.
> (Beat)
> (Picks up the fly swatter from the table and plays
> with it absent-mindedly.)
> I don't actually know how to describe the
> problem, okay? It's like—I want to know the
> reason I summon Mom's sim before she appears.
> (Scratches their back with the fly swatter.)
> I have this feeling that I'm missing something—

And when I look up.... She's standing by the window, watching the birds like she used to, or sitting in her favorite easy chair reading a book.

CUSTOMER SERVICE REPRESENTATIVE
Ah! I see. You're wondering why your sim displays new releases. Ads are a part of your particular package.

ALEX
No…yes. I remember that ads are part of the deal. I'm not asking why she's reading Elon Musk's fifth memoir, but—What called her there in the first place?

CUSTOMER SERVICE REPRESENTATIVE
(Slightly frustrated)
Our sims are intuitive, Alex, which means that they are able to sense when you want to see them. Once they sense your longing, they appear. You see your mother's sim because you want to see her.

ALEX
Yeah, I get that I must have wanted to see her. Maybe the problem is that I don't feel the wanting. She's always just there. Answering the questions I didn't ask about what I should do on my next date, commiserating about that story from work that I haven't even told her yet. And she retells the memories I apparently want to hear in exactly the same manner.

CUSTOMER SERVICE REPRESENTATIVE
Yes! Our Sensorial Precision System offers 100%
factual accuracy!

ALEX
I'm aware of your 100% rating. That's really cool.
What I'm saying is it doesn't sound like her. My
mom was never 100% factually accurate.
(Beat)
And that's actually good, because it breaks the
illusion that it is her long enough for me to
remember she's dead and gone and this image of
her isn't real. That's it, I guess. Those are the
moments I get closest to what it is I'm looking
for—the moments when the pit of my stomach
drops, and I get this swooshing feeling, like a
black hole has opened in my soul and threatens to
pull all that's left of me inside it. As if I'm
standing at the precipice waiting to jump. And for
one glorious instant, there is a depth to my
existence. My whole being is caught between the
elation of unfulfilled longing and a horror of
having gotten exactly what I wished for.
(Beat)
And just like that, it's gone again.
(Sardonically)
I guess you could say the problem is that the app
works too well.

CUSTOMER SERVICE REPRESENTATIVE
Splendid! We at AntiGrief love hearing such
positive reviews from our valued customers. Do
we have your consent to post your comment on
our NeuroSite?

ALEX
(Sighs)
Sure.

CUSTOMER SERVICE REPRESENTATIVE
Great! Was there anything else we could help you
with?

ALEX
Yes. As I was saying, I think what I really mean
is...I miss what it feels like to miss her. Does that
make sense?

CUSTOMER SERVICE REPRESENTATIVE
Yes. With AntiGrief, your sim will appear
whenever you start to miss them. Soon all of your
feelings will just fade away.

ALEX
Right. I get that that's the whole point of the
program.
(Beat)
I just don't feel as happy about it as you seem to
think I should; as everyone seems to think I
should. Because I'm not happy. I'm not anything.
I want to feel again. And if you can't help me,
maybe I'll just—I don't know—delete the whole
thing!

CUSTOMER SERVICE REPRESENTATIVE
(Tactically)
Have you considered our "Pause" feature?

ALEX
"Pause" feature?

CUSTOMER SERVICE REPRESENTATIVE
For a small payment each month you can pause
our features. Once you're ready to rejoin the
AntiGrief experience, simply start your plan again
at no extra cost.

ALEX
And...she'd always be there, waiting for me?
When the pain gets too much, when the feelings
start to overwhelm me, I could just turn it back
on?

CUSTOMER SERVICE REPRESENTATIVE
Of course! Remember that we have a satisfaction
rating of 100%.

ALEX
It's not that I don't trust your 100% satisfaction
rating. I just...
(Begins to cry)

CUSTOMER SERVICE REPRESENTATIVE
Alex, is everything alright?

ALEX
No! Everything's not alright!

CUSTOMER SERVICE REPRESENTATIVE
What's the matter? What's wrong?

ALEX
Me! What's wrong is ME! It's not the sim, or your
program, or your impossibly high satisfaction
rating! What I don't trust are my own feelings!
And what I choose to do with them!

MOM appears. She is sitting next to them on the couch.

> ALEX
> (Cont.)
> There she is. Right on time, I suppose.

ALEX and their mother share a tender moment as they stare softly into each other's eyes.

> CUSTOMER SERVICE REPRESENTATIVE
> Alex? Are you there? Alex?

> ALEX
> Sorry, what was that? I got distracted for a moment.

> CUSTOMER SERVICE REPRESENTATIVE
> Are you—I mean, is there anything else that we can help you with today?

> ALEX
> No, uh, I think we're done here. Thank you. I'll be ok.
> (Beat)
> Right now, I need to go talk with my mom.

The phone call ends. ALEX turns towards their mother again and they hold each other's hands.

> ALEX
> (Noticing the small spider again)
> Oh my god! What are you still doing in here?

MOM reaches for the fly swatter and moves to kill it.

ALEX
Mom! No!

ALEX takes the fly swatter from MOM. They use the fly swatter
to gently pick up the spider.

ALEX
(cont.)
Come on, Mom. Let's take her home.

•

The Party Must Go On: For Pablo
By Jenna Hanchey

Pablo and I tinkered with this script for over a year after we originally adapted it from one
of my previously published stories. We finally decided to submit it at our last meeting in
February 2025, sitting outside and enjoying the Arizona sunshine, a week before he passed
away. A few days after he died, I received the acceptance—on what would have been his
33rd birthday.

I don't have words to describe the shining star that Pablo was in this world. His creativity
was boundless and beautiful, and so full of care: for others, for the world, for imagination,
for life itself. He made so many brilliant works of art, and so few of them got the chance to
reach the world. I am incredibly honored and grateful that I got to be a part of one that did.
It's fitting that it's a piece about grief: about, as he writes below, grappling with the
awareness of absence.

In his other published work, "'We're Gonna Party': a poetic review on Joshua Chambers-
Letson's *After the Party: A Manifesto for Queer of Color Life*," Pablo writes:

I do not want the party to end.

Sifting through invitation lists,

I find myself waiting for folkx to arrive.

And so I grapple with the awareness of absence,
I swerve with the entanglements that
Helped originate the alternate worlds
That queer people of color seek in order to survive.
And so, the party must go on.

For Pablo, for all the queer people of color we lose while they still have so much left to be
and become and give, so much art yet to reach the world, the party must go on.

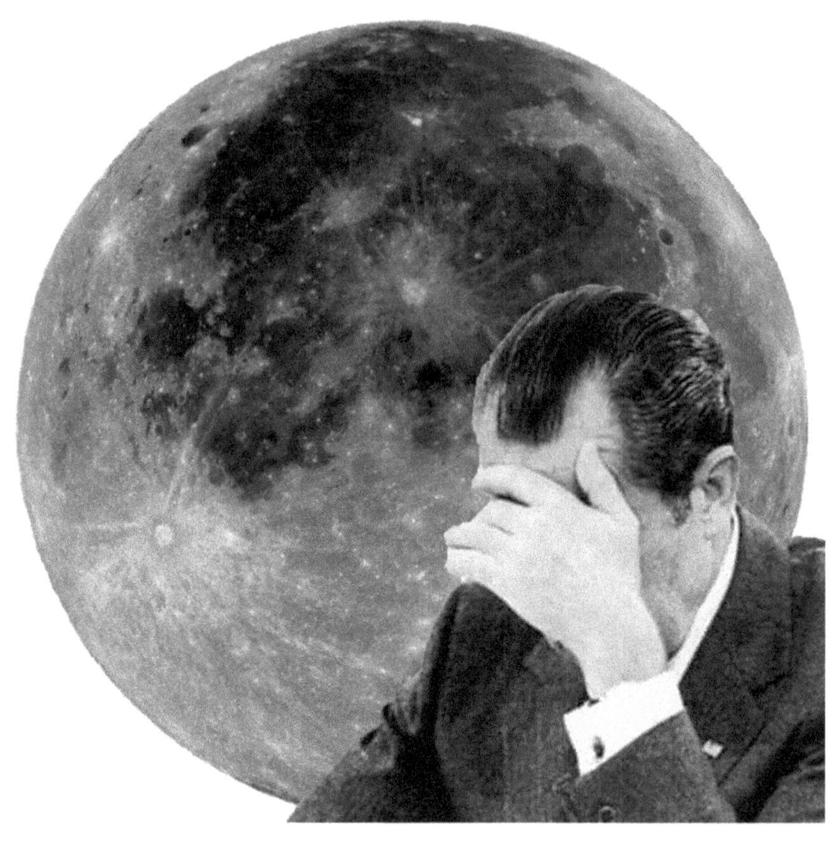

From: Bill Safire July 18, 1969.

IN EVENT OF MOON DISASTER:

Fate has ordained that the men who went to the moon to explore in peace will stay on the moon to rest in peace.

These brave men, Neil Armstrong and Edwin Aldrin, know that there is no hope for their recovery. But they also know that there is hope for mankind in their sacrifice.

These two men are laying down their lives in mankind's most noble goal: the search for truth and understanding.

They will be mourned by their families and friends; they will be mourned by their nation; they will be mourned by the people of the world; they will be mourned by a Mother Earth that dared send two of her sons into the unknown.

In their exploration, they stirred the people of the world to feel as one; in their sacrifice, they bind more tightly the brotherhood of man.

In ancient days, men looked at stars and saw their heroes in the constellations. In modern times, we do much the same, but our heroes are epic men of flesh and blood.

Others will follow, and surely find their way home. Man's search will not be denied. But these men were the first, and they will remain the foremost in our hearts.

For every human being who looks up at the moon in the nights to come will know that there is some corner of another world that is forever mankind.

PRIOR TO THE PRESIDENT'S STATEMENT:
The President should telephone each of the widows-to-be.

AFTER THE PRESIDENT'S STATEMENT, AT THE POINT WHEN NASA ENDS COMMUNICATIONS WITH THE MEN:

A clergyman should adopt the same procedure as a burial at sea, commending their souls to "the deepest of the deep," concluding with the Lord's Prayer.

[A SAD, SAD FACE, AND SADDEST EYES THAT EVER]

By Sappho
Translated by Bliss Carman

A sad, sad face, and saddest eyes that ever
  Beheld the sun,
Whence came the grief that makes of all thy beauty
  One sad sweet smile?
In this bright portrait, where the painter fixed them,
  I still behold
The eyes that gladdened, and the lips that loved me,
  And, gold on rose,
The cloud of hair that settles on one shoulder
  Slipped from its vest.
I almost hear thy Mitylenean love-song
  In the spring night,
When the still air was odorous with blossoms,
  And in the hour
Thy first wild girl's-love trembled into being,
  Glad, glad and fond.
Ah, where is all that wonder? What god's malice
  Undid that joy
And set the seal of patient woe upon thee,
  O my lost love?

CREATING ON THE STREET – AN INTERVIEW WITH MICHAEL ALAN ALIEN

Michael Alan Alien is a visual and performance artist based in New York City, notorious for his audacious approach to creativity. Alongside partner Jadda Cat, Alien hosts private performances known as 'The Living Installation,' wherein audiences witness materials spontaneously transformed into breathing artworks, humans as their canvas. Always flamboyant, sometimes a bit grotesque, these characters often spill out onto the streets, disrupting the monotony of everyday life. His 2D works are equally stimulating, deconstructing the way we process image.

Zara Kand

ZK: *What initially prompted your venture into both performance and visual art?*

MA: As a kid growing up in New York City, I was always a bit of a prankster, the class clown. I love mischief, and I was always drawing. Those characteristics never left me. Every day in class, I would just draw the whole time. I would be the kid that was drawing, but in the early 80s where I grew up, there weren't many kids doing art. The NYC I grew up in was poor and struggling, with no education in the arts. Being an artist was not discussed as a professional career. In time, as I got older and continued to be the oddball out making art every day, people started telling me, 'You're doing visual art. You're an artist.' I had started working in the nightclub scene as my first job, and I got more eyes on me drawing and seeing my work. At 16 years old, I was running a nightclub, which is a whole other interview. But by having that job, being exposed to greater NYC, I learned that I was an artist.

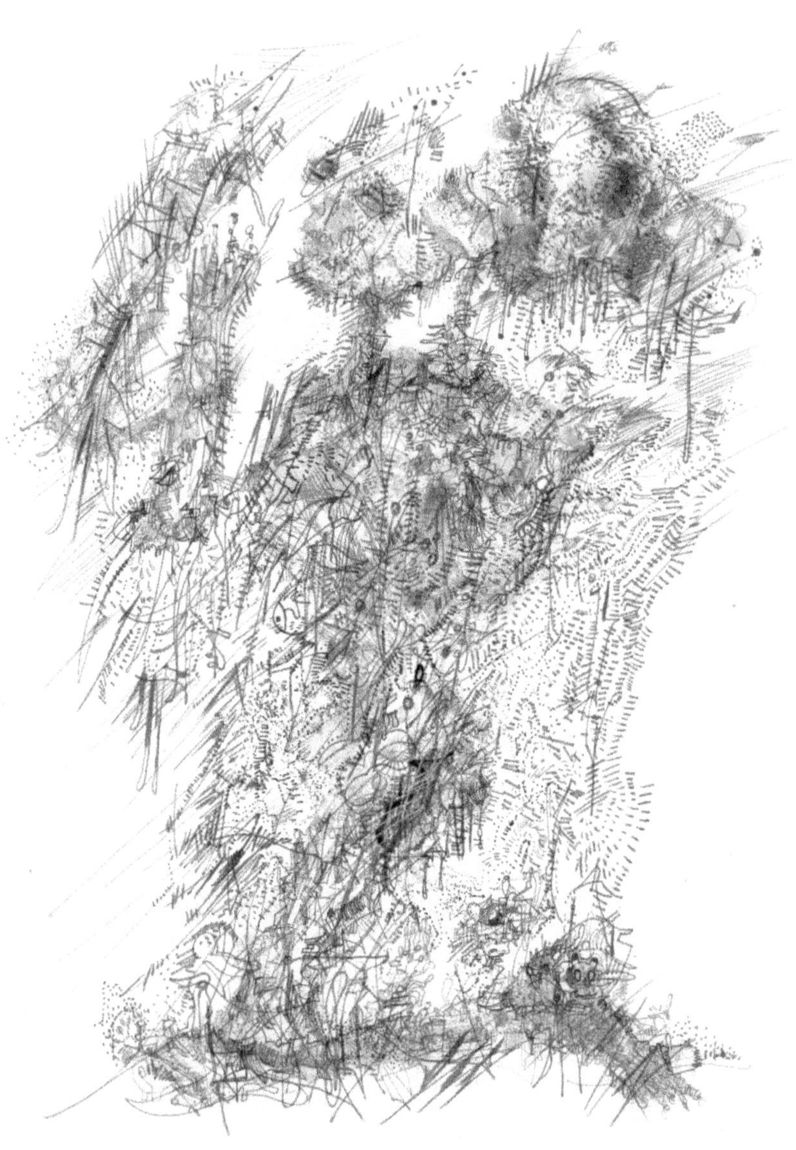

ZK: *'The Living Installation' must require a lot of not giving a fuck about what other people think. Was it difficult breaking through that barrier at first, in terms of caring about how people on the street might react to such absurdist expression?*

MA: Yes, 'The Living Installation' is pretty much about having a very silly time and it's also very daring, but at the end of the day, it really doesn't matter what anyone else thinks besides yourself. You have to remind yourself that you're only inside your own head. You'll never know what anyone else truly thinks, nor does it matter, but it does matter to make a stand and keep public art going in NYC, as it is becoming extremely gentrified and subcultures are becoming extinct. I've been doing this for a very long time, and I think it's important that every city has a culture to make it great. NYC does come from funky, wacky, crazy art people. People come here from all over the world hoping to see it, but not as many artists are showing and creating on the street anymore. It's never easy because the world has changed and everyone is on their cell phone. The culture has shifted where people are just too interested in taking selfies or capturing content for their social media, but the fight has to continue for urban art to thrive. It's just part of New York. That will never end as long as I'm here. Who cares what anyone thinks? Have fun. Change the way they think by being you.

ZK: *What kind of effect have these performances had on your audiences?*

MA: Different effects for different people. For some people it has changed their life. They have new ideas, make new meaningful friendships, and they feel a bit more free in a pretty *controlled* world. 'The Living Installation' once was called the Draw-A-Thon before it developed into what it is now. Not too many crazy drawing events existed outside of art school in New York until my event. Then I saw all these pretty bad drink-and-draw events pop

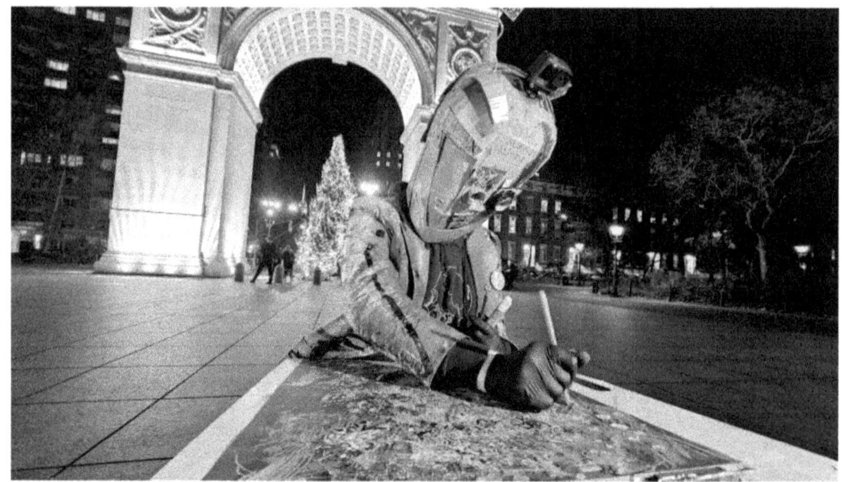

up that were just trying to make money. I did help start an alternative life drawing & painting initiative throughout NYC. Many, many people have been inspired, whether they care to say it or not, but you know this has been a really changing thing. I also think it is keeping this kind of raw, crazy style going that is inside of many people.

ZK: *Your drawings and paintings also feel very uninhibited, as if you're channeling something. What's going on in your head during these painting & drawing sessions?*

MA: Thank you. I think at the end it's always hard to truly explain what is going on inside your mind in a way that translates properly, but I am channeling and I'm truly free. I would say I'm completely connected to the paper and canvas, and I'm not trying to edit or make something a certain way. It's definitely not contrived, and it's very free, based on my creative system that I've created for many, many years of different marks, different lines, different dots, different materials. It's also important to understand how many different materials I'm using to create an overlapping experience. The layering process is similar to spray painting a wall. When I spray paint a wall, I use color over color over color.

When I'm painting, I'm not thinking of what the next layer will be. I'm just putting marks and materials over each other, creating a very confusing, vital piece that no one could really understand how it's done, which is what I love. I love not knowing, but not knowing and putting that out there to extreme existentialism, giving people something to look at where they need to apply themselves and come up with their own answers within the work that I've created. These pieces are designed to change in time. You look at it in the morning and see one thing, then you see it at night and it's totally different based

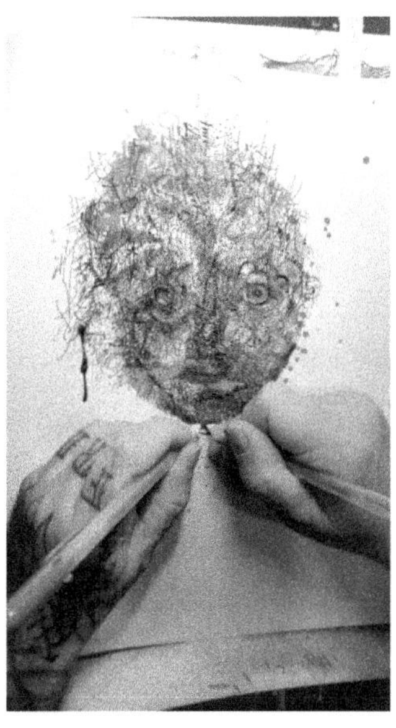

on your mood or the shifting light. The work itself is a mind game. I have a hard time looking at art that just gives me a clear picture. I feel like we're in a different timeframe now. We need to think and look at things from multiple perspectives. This is multiple perspective painting and drawing.

ZK: *You execute your visual art ambidextrously, which is rather uncommon. Have you always drawn this way, or did that involve a learning curve?*

MA: During the pandemic, I looked back at some of our videos because I was at home with my lady, Jadda Cat, and I was like, "Wait, look, I'm using two hands," and she was like, "Yeah, you always do that." I guess I never really thought about it, but I became more aware when we started documenting my process. I remember painting large walls outdoors in the late 90s and using two hands to spray paint the crap out of the wall, and everyone else would take hours, but I was done in 10 minutes.

ZK: *I understand you've experienced some personal losses of late. Does creative expression help you to process these feelings of grief?*

MA: Yes, it does. It's the best therapy and way to channel. With grief, you must take what's inside and put it into something instead of it eating you alive. Once you do, you then can help others as well.

ZK: *In your bio, you mention preserving the "raw creative essence of old New York." Can you elaborate on this, and why this is important to you?*

MA: Well, first off, I'm born and raised here. Second off, my family struggled economically so my upbringing comes from a perspective that is not normally seen in art. I do think that my 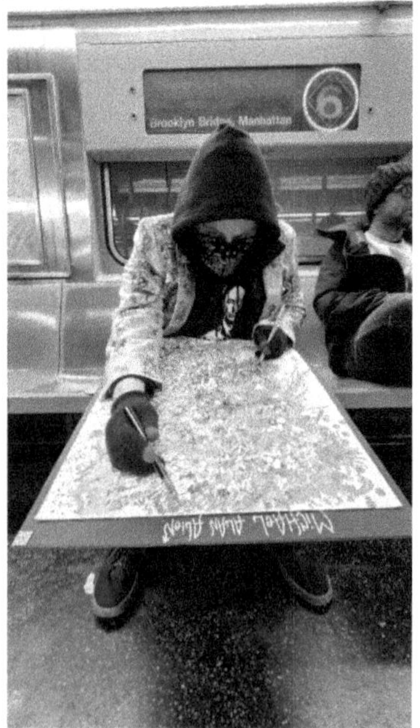 perspective should be seen in the gallery and museum setting, because that setting is often only from the elite class or someone who has connections within the art world. It can be quite closed off, so a lot of my work is about hopefully changing this and giving people a different perspective because we are in NYC. This is the place - correct - but this narrative is constantly leaving out the people from here, especially from my generation. We hear of so many artists, but we rarely hear of the artists born here, and if we do, they usually come from money. We rarely hear of working-class artists that make it big, or below-poverty-level artists that make it big, even though these people are those who make the city.

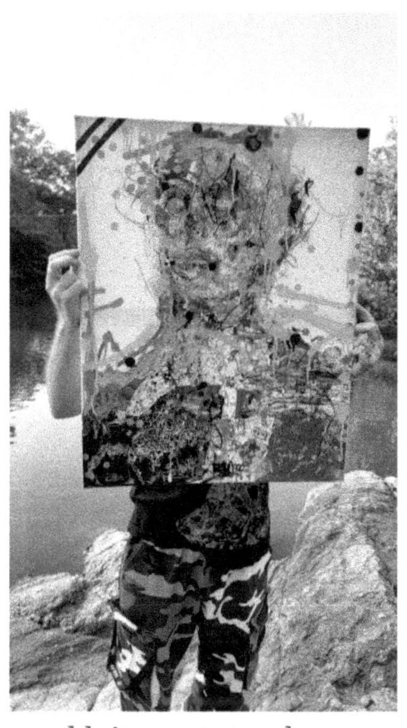

The people who have suffered, endured New York through many years, through its great and bad times, and I think that is really what can paint a picture where you can understand a city through the youth. The people who have heard the sounds and seen it all can then show you the paintings that really show the city. I think it's super important. I think it's sad that it's not really something that is a topic for museums. That's the first part of this equation, to create some equality. The second part is my language. This is the art that I've made from growing up here. I wouldn't want to change my way. I wouldn't want to change my view of how I create. It's very natural.

ZK: *It seems that although you've been doing 'The Living Installation' for many years now, only recently has it garnered substantial public interest. Do you have any advice for artists struggling with exposure or self-doubt?*

MA: I'm not so sure about that. 'The Living Installation' has always been in the press. It was featured in the New Museum, throughout many articles through all its years running. It's always been hard, but I did it weekly from 2004 till now. There's been quite a lot of articles on it, from the Village Voice to the New York Times to The Sun, etc. There should be much more news on it. It's always been news, but it's not a mainstream piece. This is very punk DIY. Luckily, we did get press but it's still all very underground. Many people have no idea. It's a big world out there.

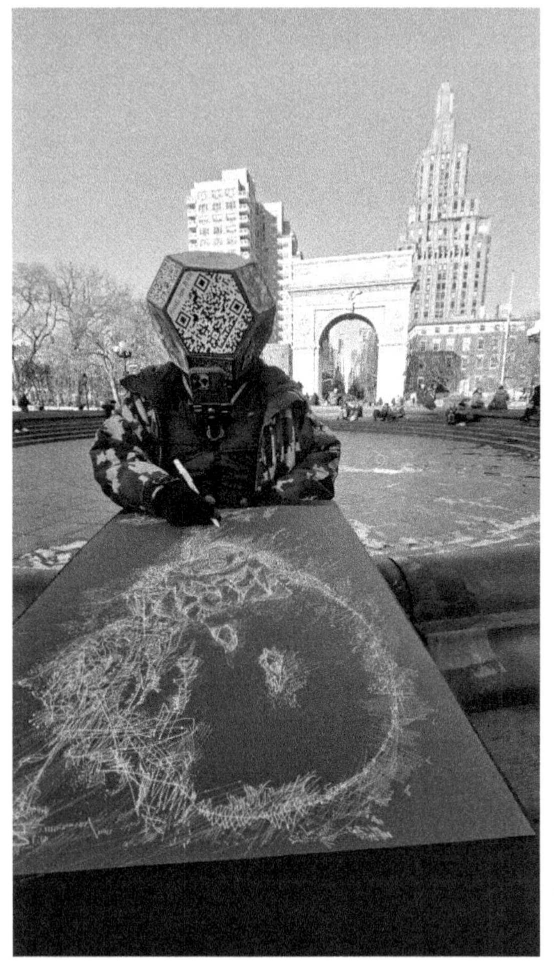

My only advice is you have to do something every day. People forget what happened years ago, so you have to just keep doing it every day. Live it. That's the only way. People always ask me, 'How do I get any news?' I say, 'I have no idea. I got lucky, honestly. I don't even know how they found me,' and then I just do the next thing. I have no clue what I'm doing, but I do know that I do something every day.

ZK: *Any exciting creative goals for the years ahead?*

MA: I've made over 9,000 detailed drawings and paintings. I've sold quite a bunch of them, but I do know I have at least 6,500 at my studio that I'm trying to archive. It's quite the process, and I'm also making videos on each group of them, and I'm gonna put these long-format videos up on YouTube. My goal is within a year I could get at least 50 of these long-format videos published so people can see and understand my work more. It is a truly meticulous and explorative process.

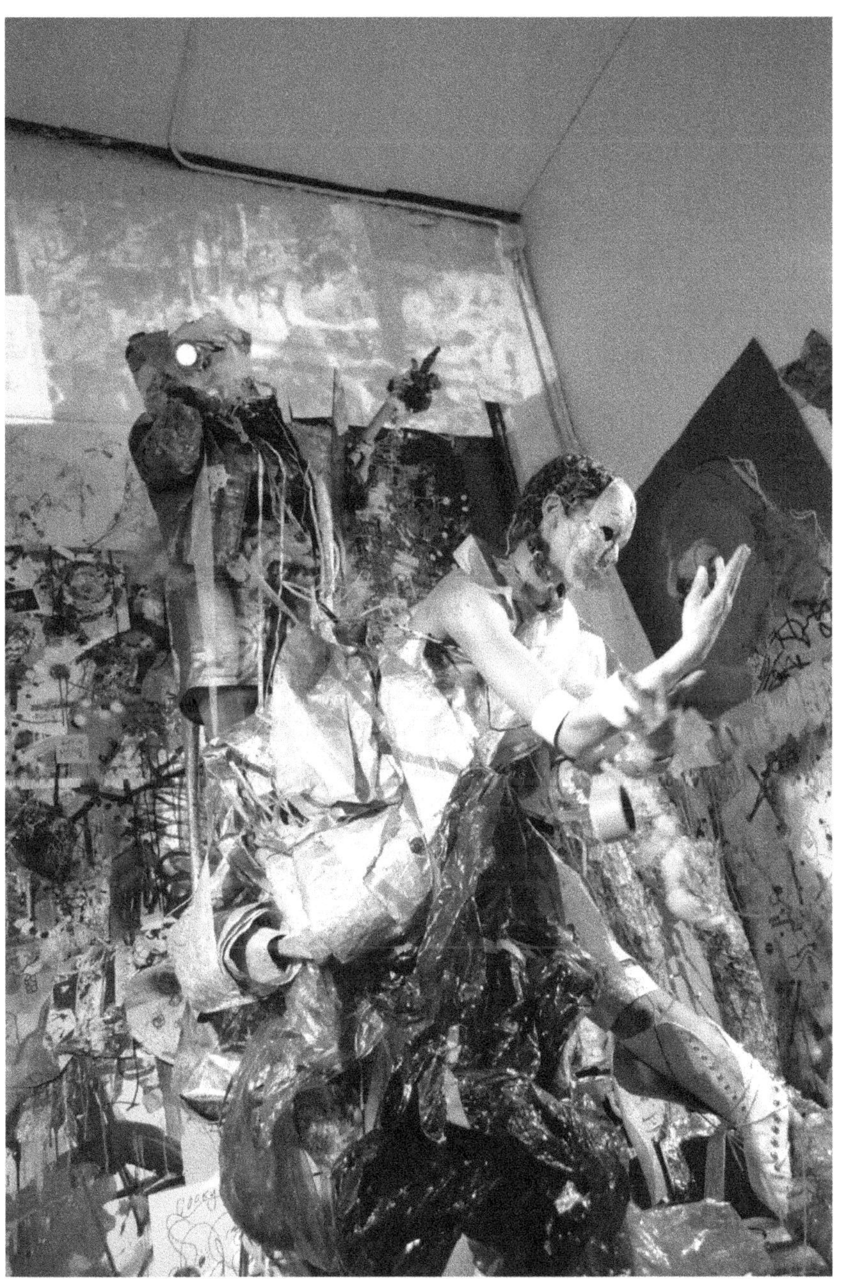

Electronic Brain Etude:
A Binaural Arpeggio Loop in Six Parts
INTRODUCTION

<u>Purpose</u>

Binaural beats are created when the listener hears tones of slightly different pitches in each ear, usually when wearing stereo headphones. They are divided into five categories (Delta, Theta, Alpha, Beta, Gamma) based on their effect and how far apart the two frequencies are.

By separating the parts of musical piece into left and right one can create different binaural beats that vary simply based on voicing the chords in a progression differently. In other words, small changes in chord voicings can create differences in the types of binaural beats the listener would hear.

Binaural beats are used by many for various wellness purposes, and using this methodology can help you create your own musical pieces with binaural beats – even if you don't read music. Using a sequencer, you can program the notes from the detail for each measure to replicate these effects.

<u>Effects</u>

Binaural beats are perceived to have the following effects:
Delta - Sleep and relaxation
Theta - Meditation and creativity
Alpha - Focused calm
Beta - Alertness and concentration
Gamma - High-level cognitive function

<u>Instrumentation</u>

Because they are common musical terms, I labeled some of the parts based on terms for vocal ranges. These do not have to be voices. You can use almost any instrument to play the notes in the piece to create the binaural beats.

Electronic Brain Etude:
A Binaural Arpeggio Loop in Six Parts
CONSOLIDATED PARTS

Drone Left: A0
Drone Right: F#0

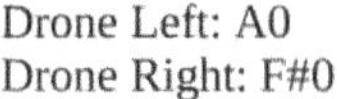

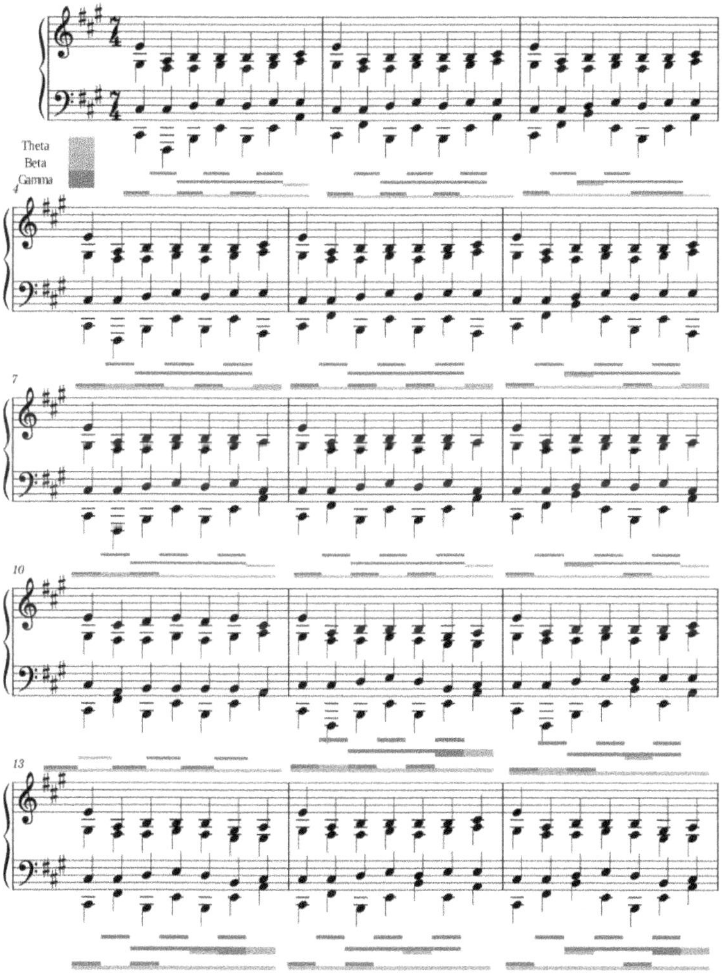

Electronic Brain Etude:
A Binaural Arpeggio Loop in Six Parts
MEASURE 1 BINAURAL MAPPING

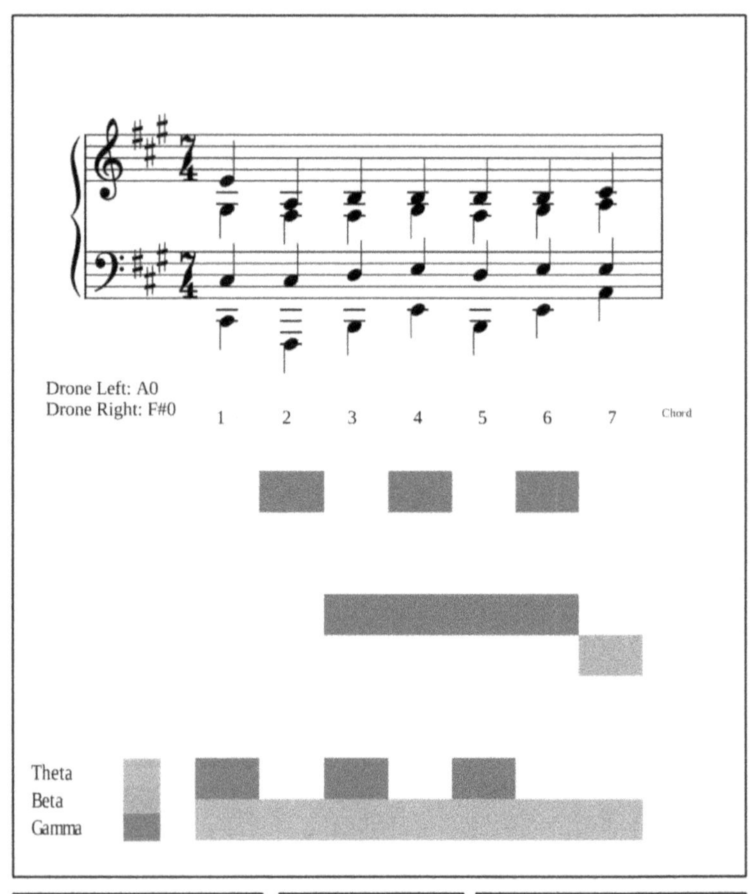

Chord Progression	Binaural Ranges	Intervals
C#m-F#m-Bm-E-Bm-E-A	Delta: 0.5-4Hz	S-A: Soprano/Alto
	Theta: 4-8Hz	S-B: Soprano/Bass
Parts	Alpha: 8-13Hz	S-DR: Soprano/Drone-Right
1-Soprano/High (L)	Beta: 13-30Hz	T-A: Tenor/Alto
2-Alto/MedHigh(R)	Gamma: 30-42Hz	T-B: Tenor/Bass
3-Tenor/MedLow(L)	(Absolute Values)	T-DR: Tenor/Drone-Right
4-Bass/Low(R)		DL-A: Drone-Left/Alto
5-Drone-Left(L)		DL-B: Drone-Left/Bass
6-Drone-Right(R)		DL-DR: Drone-Left/Drone-Right

Electronic Brain Etude:
A Binaural Arpeggio Loop in Six Parts
MEASURE 1 BINAURAL MAPPING

Chord	Part #	Side	Part Name	Note	Freq (Hz)	Interval Name	Interval Val	Freq Diff (Hz)	Binaural Type	
1-C#m	1	Left	Soprano (S)	E4	329.63	S-A	C#3-E4	121.98		
1-C#m	2	Right	Alto (A)	G#3	207.65	S-B	C#2-E4	260.33		
1-C#m	3	Left	Tenor (T)	C#3	138.59	S-DR	F#0-E4	306.51		
1-C#m	4	Right	Bass (B)	C#2	69.3	T-A	G#3-C#3	-69.06		
1-C#m	5	Left	Drone-Left (DL)	A0	27.5	T-B	C#2-C#3	69.29		
1-C#m	6	Right	Drone-Right (DR)	F#0	23.12	T-DR	F#0-C#3	115.47		
1-C#m						DL-A	G#3-A0	-180.15		
1-C#m						DL-B	C#2-A0	-41.8	Gamma	
1-C#m						DL-DR	F#0-A0	4.38	Theta	
2-F#m	1	Left	Soprano (S)	A3	220	S-A	F#3-A3	35	Gamma	
2-F#m	2	Right	Alto (A)	F#3	185	S-B	F#1-A3	173.75		
2-F#m	3	Left	Tenor (T)	C#3	138.59	S-DR	F#0-A3	196.88		
2-F#m	4	Right	Bass (B)	F#1	46.25	T-A	F#3-C#3	-46.41		
2-F#m	5	Left	Drone-Left (DL)	A0	27.5	T-B	F#1-C#3	92.34		
2-F#m	6	Right	Drone-Right (DR)	F#0	23.12	T-DR	F#0-C#3	115.47		
2-F#m						DL-A	F#3-A0	-157.5		
2-F#m						DL-B	F#1-A0	-18.75	Beta	
2-F#m						DL-DR	F#0-A0	4.38	Theta	
3-Bm	1	Left	Soprano (S)	B3	246.94	S-A	F#3-B3	61.94		
3-Bm	2	Right	Alto (A)	F#3	185	S-B	B1-B3	185.2		
3-Bm	3	Left	Tenor (T)	D3	146.83	S-DR	F#0-B3	223.82		
3-Bm	4	Right	Bass (B)	B1	61.74	T-A	F#3-D3	-38.17	Gamma	
3-Bm	5	Left	Drone-Left (DL)	A0	27.5	T-B	B1-D3	85.09		
3-Bm	6	Right	Drone-Right (DR)	F#0	23.12	T-DR	F#0-D3	123.71		
3-Bm						DL-A	F#3-A0	-157.5		
3-Bm						DL-B	B1-A0	-34.24	Gamma	
3-Bm						DL-DR	F#0-A0	4.38	Theta	
4-E	1	Left	Soprano (S)	B3	246.94	S-A	G#3-B3	39.29	Gamma	
4-E	2	Right	Alto (A)	G#3	207.65	S-B	E2-B3	164.53		
4-E	3	Left	Tenor (T)	E3	164.81	S-DR	F#0-B3	223.82		
4-E	4	Right	Bass (B)	E2	82.41	T-A	G#3-E3	-42.84	Gamma	
4-E	5	Left	Drone-Left (DL)	A0	27.5	T-B	E2-E3	82.4		
4-E	6	Right	Drone-Right (DR)	F#0	23.12	T-DR	F#0-E3	141.69		
4-E						DL-A	G#3-A0	-180.15		
4-E						DL-B	E2-A0	-54.91		
4-E						DL-DR	F#0-A0	4.38	Theta	
5-Bm	1	Left	Soprano (S)	B3	246.94	S-A	F#3-B3	61.94		
5-Bm	2	Right	Alto (A)	F#3	185	S-B	B1-B3	185.2		
5-Bm	3	Left	Tenor (T)	D3	146.83	S-DR	F#0-B3	223.82		
5-Bm	4	Right	Bass (B)	B1	61.74	T-A	F#3-D3	-38.17	Gamma	
5-Bm	5	Left	Drone-Left (DL)	A0	27.5	T-B	B1-D3	85.09		
5-Bm	6	Right	Drone-Right (DR)	F#0	23.12	T-DR	F#0-D3	123.71		
5-Bm						DL-A	F#3-A0	-157.5		
5-Bm						DL-B	B1-A0	-34.24	Gamma	
5-Bm						DL-DR	F#0-A0	4.38	Theta	
6-E	1	Left	Soprano (S)	B3	246.94	S-A	G#3-B3	39.29	Gamma	
6-E	2	Right	Alto (A)	G#3	207.65	S-B	E2-B3	164.53		
6-E	3	Left	Tenor (T)	E3	164.81	S-DR	F#0-B3	223.82		
6-E	4	Right	Bass (B)	E2	82.41	T-A	G#3-E3	-42.84	Gamma	
6-E	5	Left	Drone-Left (DL)	A0	27.5	T-B	E2-E3	82.4		
6-E	6	Right	Drone-Right (DR)	F#0	23.12	T-DR	F#0-E3	141.69		
6-E						DL-A	G#3-A0	-180.15		
6-E						DL-B	E2-A0	-54.91		
6-E						DL-DR	F#0-A0	4.38	Theta	
7-A	1	Left	Soprano (S)	C#4	277.18	S-A	A3-C#4	57.18		
7-A	2	Right	Alto (A)	A3	220	S-B	A2-C#4	167.18		
7-A	3	Left	Tenor (T)	E3	164.81	S-DR	F#0-C#4	254.06		
7-A	4	Right	Bass (B)	A2	110	T-A	A3-E3	-55.19		
7-A	5	Left	Drone-Left (DL)	A0	27.5	T-B	A2-E3	54.81		
7-A	6	Right	Drone-Right (DR)	F#0	23.12	T-DR	F#0-E3	141.69		
7-A						DL-A	A3-A0	-192.5		
7-A						DL-B	A2-A0	-82.5		
7-A						DL-DR	F#0-A0	4.38	Theta	

Electronic Brain Etude:
A Binaural Arpeggio Loop in Six Parts
MEASURE 2 BINAURAL MAPPING

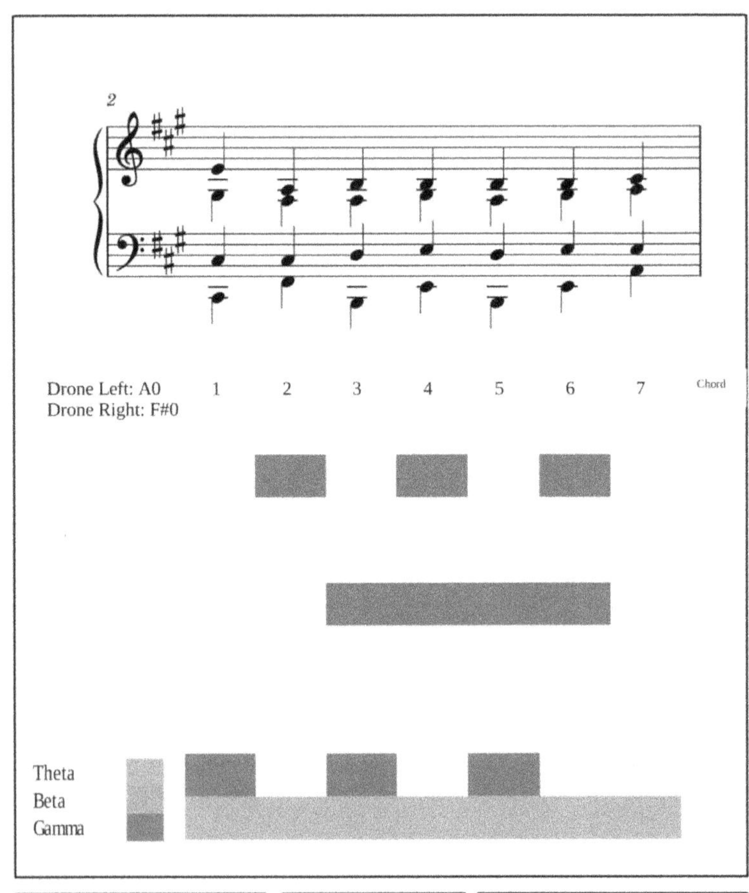

<table>
<tr><td>

Chord Progression
C#m-F#m-Bm-E-Bm-E-A

Parts
1-Soprano/High (L)
2-Alto/MedHigh(R)
3-Tenor/MedLow(L)
4-Bass/Low(R)
5-Drone-Left(L)
6-Drone-Right(R)

</td><td>

Binaural Ranges
Delta: 0.5-4Hz
Theta: 4-8Hz
Alpha: 8-13Hz
Beta: 13-30Hz
Gamma: 30-42Hz
(Absolute Values)

</td><td>

Intervals
S-A: Soprano/Alto
S-B: Soprano/Bass
S-DR: Soprano/Drone-Right
T-A: Tenor/Alto
T-B: Tenor/Bass
T-DR: Tenor/Drone-Right
DL-A: Drone-Left/Alto
DL-B: Drone-Left/Bass
DL-DR: Drone-Left/Drone-Right

</td></tr>
</table>

Electronic Brain Etude:
A Binaural Arpeggio Loop in Six Parts
MEASURE 2 BINAURAL MAPPING

Chord	Part #	Side	Part Name	Note	Freq (Hz)	Interval Name	Interval Val	Freq Diff (Hz)	Binaural Type
1-C#m	1	Left	Soprano (S)	E4	329.63	S-A	G#3-E4	121.98	
1-C#m	2	Right	Alto (A)	G#3	207.65	S-B	C#2-E4	260.33	
1-C#m	3	Left	Tenor (T)	C#3	138.59	S-DR	F#0-E4	306.51	
1-C#m	4	Right	Bass (B)	C#2	69.3	T-A	G#3-C#3	-69.06	
1-C#m	5	Left	Drone-Left (DL)	A0	27.5	T-B	C#2-C#3	69.29	
1-C#m	6	Right	Drone-Right (DR)	F#0	23.12	T-DR	F#0-C#3	115.47	
1-C#m						DL-A	G#3-A0	-180.15	
1-C#m						DL-B	C#2-A0	-41.8	Gamma
1-C#m						DL-DR	F#0-A0	4.38	Theta
2-F#m	1	Left	Soprano (S)	A3	220	S-A	F#3-A3	35	Gamma
2-F#m	2	Right	Alto (A)	F#3	185	S-B	F#2-A3	127.5	
2-F#m	3	Left	Tenor (T)	C#3	138.59	S-DR	F#0-A3	196.88	
2-F#m	4	Right	Bass (B)	F#2	92.5	T-A	F#3-C#3	-46.41	
2-F#m	5	Left	Drone-Left (DL)	A0	27.5	T-B	F#2-C#3	46.09	
2-F#m	6	Right	Drone-Right (DR)	F#0	23.12	T-DR	F#0-C#3	115.47	
2-F#m						DL-A	F#3-A0	-157.5	
2-F#m						DL-B	F#2-A0	-65	
2-F#m						DL-DR	F#0-A0	4.38	Theta
3-Bm	1	Left	Soprano (S)	B3	246.94	S-A	F#3-B3	61.94	
3-Bm	2	Right	Alto (A)	F#3	185	S-B	B1-B3	185.2	
3-Bm	3	Left	Tenor (T)	D3	146.83	S-DR	F#0-B3	223.82	
3-Bm	4	Right	Bass (B)	B1	61.74	T-A	F#3-D3	-38.17	Gamma
3-Bm	5	Left	Drone-Left (DL)	A0	27.5	T-B	B1-D3	85.09	
3-Bm	6	Right	Drone-Right (DR)	F#0	23.12	T-DR	F#0-D3	123.71	
3-Bm						DL-A	F#3-A0	-157.5	
3-Bm						DL-B	B1-A0	-34.24	Gamma
3-Bm						DL-DR	F#0-A0	4.38	Theta
4-E	1	Left	Soprano (S)	B3	246.94	S-A	G#3-B3	39.29	Gamma
4-E	2	Right	Alto (A)	G#3	207.65	S-B	E2-B3	164.53	
4-E	3	Left	Tenor (T)	E3	164.81	S-DR	F#0-B3	223.82	
4-E	4	Right	Bass (B)	E2	82.41	T-A	G#3-E3	-42.84	Gamma
4-E	5	Left	Drone-Left (DL)	A0	27.5	T-B	E2-E3	82.4	
4-E	6	Right	Drone-Right (DR)	F#0	23.12	T-DR	F#0-E3	141.69	
4-E						DL-A	G#3-A0	-180.15	
4-E						DL-B	E2-A0	-54.91	
4-E						DL-DR	F#0-A0	4.38	Theta
5-Bm	1	Left	Soprano (S)	B3	246.94	S-A	F#3-B3	61.94	
5-Bm	2	Right	Alto (A)	F#3	185	S-B	B1-B3	185.2	
5-Bm	3	Left	Tenor (T)	D3	146.83	S-DR	F#0-B3	223.82	
5-Bm	4	Right	Bass (B)	B1	61.74	T-A	F#3-D3	-38.17	Gamma
5-Bm	5	Left	Drone-Left (DL)	A0	27.5	T-B	B1-D3	85.09	
5-Bm	6	Right	Drone-Right (DR)	F#0	23.12	T-DR	F#0-D3	123.71	
5-Bm						DL-A	F#3-A0	-157.5	
5-Bm						DL-B	B1-A0	-34.24	Gamma
5-Bm						DL-DR	F#0-A0	4.38	Theta
6-E	1	Left	Soprano (S)	B3	246.94	S-A	G#3-B3	39.29	Gamma
6-E	2	Right	Alto (A)	G#3	207.65	S-B	E2-B3	164.53	
6-E	3	Left	Tenor (T)	E3	164.81	S-DR	F#0-B3	223.82	
6-E	4	Right	Bass (B)	E2	82.41	T-A	G#3-E3	-42.84	Gamma
6-E	5	Left	Drone-Left (DL)	A0	27.5	T-B	E2-E3	82.4	
6-E	6	Right	Drone-Right (DR)	F#0	23.12	T-DR	F#0-E3	141.69	
6-E						DL-A	G#3-A0	-180.15	
6-E						DL-B	E2-A0	-54.91	
6-E						DL-DR	F#0-A0	4.38	Theta
7-A	1	Left	Soprano (S)	C#4	277.18	S-A	A3-C#4	57.18	
7-A	2	Right	Alto (A)	A3	220	S-B	A2-C#4	167.18	
7-A	3	Left	Tenor (T)	E3	164.81	S-DR	F#0-C#4	254.06	
7-A	4	Right	Bass (B)	A2	110	T-A	A3-E3	-55.19	
7-A	5	Left	Drone-Left (DL)	A0	27.5	T-B	A2-E3	54.81	
7-A	6	Right	Drone-Right (DR)	F#0	23.12	T-DR	F#0-E3	141.69	
7-A						DL-A	A3-A0	-192.5	
7-A						DL-B	A2-A0	-82.5	
7-A						DL-DR	F#0-A0	4.38	Theta

Electronic Brain Etude:
A Binaural Arpeggio Loop in Six Parts
MEASURE 3 BINAURAL MAPPING

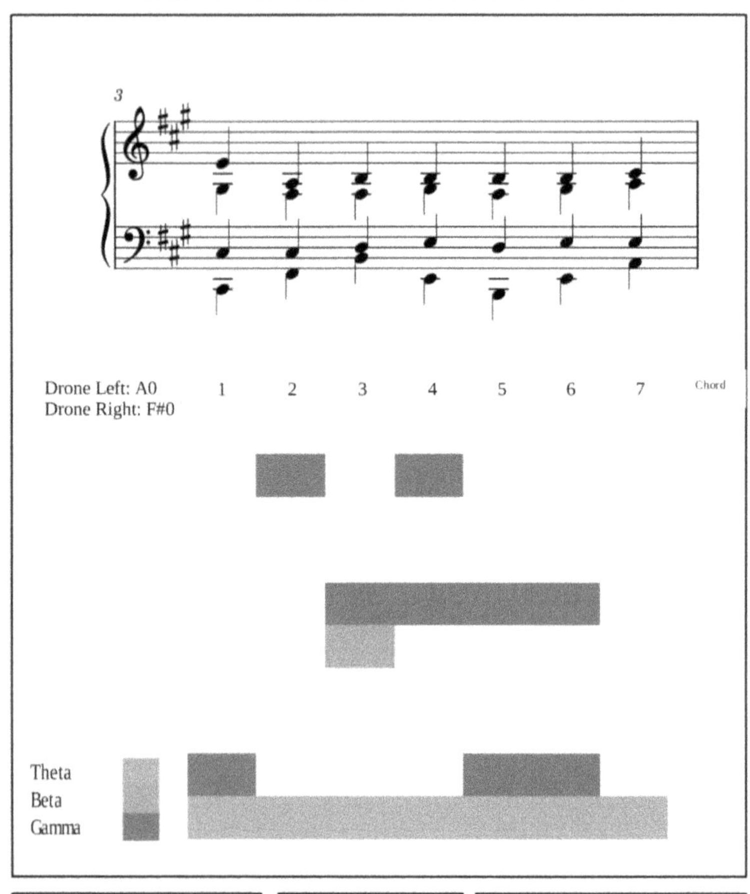

<table>
<tr><td>

Chord Progression
C#m-F#m-Bm-E-Bm-E-A

Parts
1-Soprano/High (L)
2-Alto/MedHigh(R)
3-Tenor/MedLow(L)
4-Bass/Low(R)
5-Drone-Left(L)
6-Drone-Right(R)

</td><td>

Binaural Ranges
Delta: 0.5-4Hz
Theta: 4-8Hz
Alpha: 8-13Hz
Beta: 13-30Hz
Gamma: 30-42Hz
(Absolute Values)

</td><td>

Intervals
S-A: Soprano/Alto
S-B: Soprano/Bass
S-DR: Soprano/Drone-Right
T-A: Tenor/Alto
T-B: Tenor/Bass
T-DR: Tenor/Drone-Right
DL-A: Drone-Left/Alto
DL-B: Drone-Left/Bass
DL-DR: Drone-Left/Drone-Right

</td></tr>
</table>

Electronic Brain Etude:
A Binaural Arpeggio Loop in Six Parts
MEASURE 3 BINAURAL MAPPING

Chord	Part #	Side	Part Name	Note	Freq (Hz)	Interval Name	Interval Val	Freq Diff (Hz)	Binaural Type
1-C#m	1	Left	Soprano (S)	E4	329.63	S-A	G#3-E4	121.98	
1-C#m	2	Right	Alto (A)	G#3	207.65	S-B	C#2-E4	260.33	
1-C#m	3	Left	Tenor (T)	C#3	138.59	S-DR	F#0-E4	306.51	
1-C#m	4	Right	Bass (B)	C#2	69.3	T-A	G#3-C#3	-69.06	
1-C#m	5	Left	Drone-Left (DL)	A0	27.5	T-B	C#2-C#3	69.29	
1-C#m	6	Right	Drone-Right (DR)	F#0	23.12	T-DR	F#0-C#3	115.47	
1-C#m						DL-A	G#3-A0	-180.15	
1-C#m						DL-B	C#2-A0	-41.8	Gamma
1-C#m						DL-DR	F#0-A0	4.38	Theta
2-F#m	1	Left	Soprano (S)	A3	220	S-A	F#3-A3	35	Gamma
2-F#m	2	Right	Alto (A)	F#3	185	S-B	F#2-A3	127.5	
2-F#m	3	Left	Tenor (T)	C#3	138.59	S-DR	F#0-A3	196.88	
2-F#m	4	Right	Bass (B)	F#2	92.5	T-A	F#3-C#3	-46.41	
2-F#m	5	Left	Drone-Left (DL)	A0	27.5	T-B	F#2-C#3	46.09	
2-F#m	6	Right	Drone-Right (DR)	F#0	23.12	T-DR	F#0-C#3	115.47	
2-F#m						DL-A	F#3-A0	-157.5	
2-F#m						DL-B	F#2-A0	-65	
2-F#m						DL-DR	F#0-A0	4.38	Theta
3-Bm	1	Left	Soprano (S)	B3	246.94	S-A	F#3-B3	61.94	
3-Bm	2	Right	Alto (A)	F#3	185	S-B	B2-B3	123.47	
3-Bm	3	Left	Tenor (T)	D3	146.83	S-DR	F#0-B3	223.82	
3-Bm	4	Right	Bass (B)	B2	123.47	T-A	F#3-D3	-38.17	Gamma
3-Bm	5	Left	Drone-Left (DL)	A0	27.5	T-B	B2-D3	23.36	Beta
3-Bm	6	Right	Drone-Right (DR)	F#0	23.12	T-DR	F#0-D3	123.71	
3-Bm						DL-A	F#3-A0	-157.5	
3-Bm						DL-B	B2-A0	-95.97	
3-Bm						DL-DR	F#0-A0	4.38	Theta
4-E	1	Left	Soprano (S)	B3	246.94	S-A	G#3-B3	39.29	Gamma
4-E	2	Right	Alto (A)	G#3	207.65	S-B	E2-B3	164.53	
4-E	3	Left	Tenor (T)	E3	164.81	S-DR	F#0-B3	223.82	
4-E	4	Right	Bass (B)	E2	82.41	T-A	G#3-E3	-42.84	Gamma
4-E	5	Left	Drone-Left (DL)	A0	27.5	T-B	E2-E3	82.4	
4-E	6	Right	Drone-Right (DR)	F#0	23.12	T-DR	F#0-E3	141.69	
4-E						DL-A	G#3-A0	-180.15	
4-E						DL-B	E2-A0	-54.91	
4-E						DL-DR	F#0-A0	4.38	Theta
5-Bm	1	Left	Soprano (S)	B3	246.94	S-A	F#3-B3	61.94	
5-Bm	2	Right	Alto (A)	F#3	185	S-B	B1-B3	185.2	
5-Bm	3	Left	Tenor (T)	D3	146.83	S-DR	F#0-B3	223.82	
5-Bm	4	Right	Bass (B)	B1	61.74	T-A	F#3-D3	-38.17	Gamma
5-Bm	5	Left	Drone-Left (DL)	A0	27.5	T-B	B1-D3	85.09	
5-Bm	6	Right	Drone-Right (DR)	F#0	23.12	T-DR	F#0-D3	123.71	
5-Bm						DL-A	F#3-A0	-157.5	
5-Bm						DL-B	B1-A0	-34.24	Gamma
5-Bm						DL-DR	F#0-A0	4.38	Theta
6-E	1	Left	Soprano (S)	B3	246.94	S-A	G#3-B3	39.29	Gamma
6-E	2	Right	Alto (A)	G#3	207.65	S-B	E2-B3	164.53	
6-E	3	Left	Tenor (T)	E3	164.81	S-DR	F#0-B3	223.82	
6-E	4	Right	Bass (B)	E2	82.41	T-A	G#3-E3	-42.84	Gamma
6-E	5	Left	Drone-Left (DL)	A0	27.5	T-B	E2-E3	82.4	
6-E	6	Right	Drone-Right (DR)	F#0	23.12	T-DR	F#0-E3	141.69	
6-E						DL-A	G#3-A0	-180.15	
6-E						DL-B	E2-A0	-54.91	
6-E						DL-DR	F#0-A0	4.38	Theta
7-A	1	Left	Soprano (S)	C#4	277.18	S-A	A3-C#4	57.18	
7-A	2	Right	Alto (A)	A3	220	S-B	A2-C#4	167.18	
7-A	3	Left	Tenor (T)	E3	164.81	S-DR	F#0-C#4	254.06	
7-A	4	Right	Bass (B)	A2	110	T-A	A3-E3	-55.19	
7-A	5	Left	Drone-Left (DL)	A0	27.5	T-B	A2-E3	54.81	
7-A	6	Right	Drone-Right (DR)	F#0	23.12	T-DR	F#0-E3	141.69	
7-A						DL-A	A3-A0	-192.5	
7-A						DL-B	A2-A0	-82.5	
7-A						DL-DR	F#0-A0	4.38	Theta

Electronic Brain Etude:
A Binaural Arpeggio Loop in Six Parts
MEASURE 4 BINAURAL MAPPING

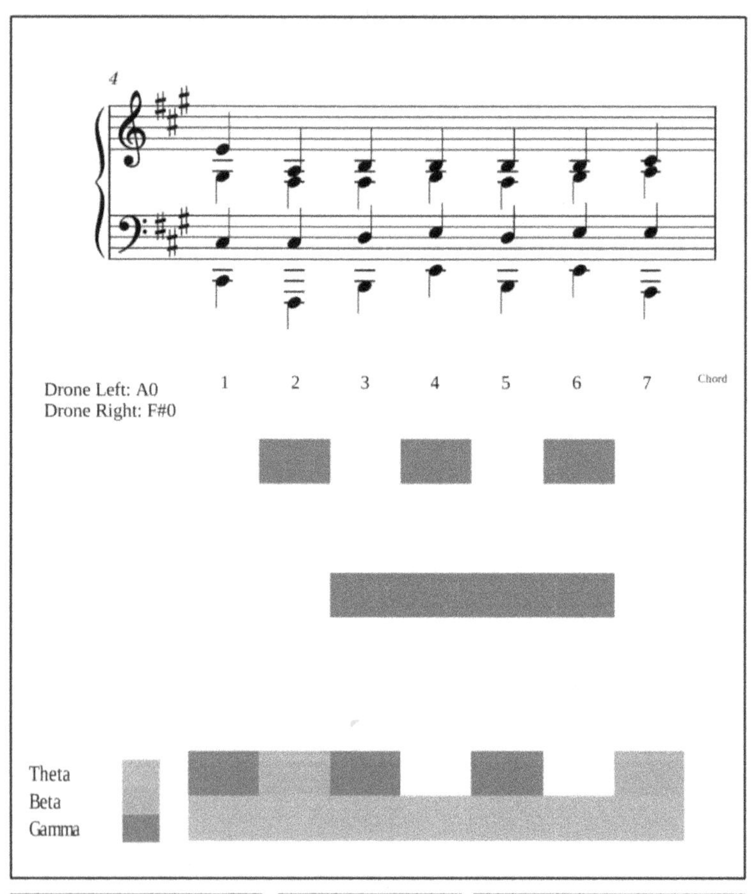

Chord Progression
C#m-F#m-Bm-E-Bm-E-A

Parts
1-Soprano/High (L)
2-Alto/MedHigh(R)
3-Tenor/MedLow(L)
4-Bass/Low(R)
5-Drone-Left(L)
6-Drone-Right(R)

Binaural Ranges
Delta: 0.5-4Hz
Theta: 4-8Hz
Alpha: 8-13Hz
Beta: 13-30Hz
Gamma: 30-42Hz
(Absolute Values)

Intervals
S-A: Soprano/Alto
S-B: Soprano/Bass
S-DR: Soprano/Drone-Right
T-A: Tenor/Alto
T-B: Tenor/Bass
T-DR: Tenor/Drone-Right
DL-A: Drone-Left/Alto
DL-B: Drone-Left/Bass
DL-DR: Drone-Left/Drone-Right

Chord	Part #	Side	Part Name	Note	Freq (Hz)	Interval Name	Interval Val	Freq Diff (Hz)	Binaural Type
1-C#m	1	Left	Soprano (S)	E4	329.63	S-A	G#3-E4	121.98	
1-C#m	2	Right	Alto (A)	G#3	207.65	S-B	C#2-E4	260.33	
1-C#m	3	Left	Tenor (T)	C#3	138.59	S-DR	F#0-E4	306.51	
1-C#m	4	Right	Bass (B)	C#2	69.3	T-A	G#3-C#3	-69.06	
1-C#m	5	Left	Drone-Left (DL)	A0	27.5	T-B	C#2-C#3	69.29	
1-C#m	6	Right	Drone-Right (DR)	F#0	23.12	T-DR	F#0-C#3	115.47	
1-C#m						DL-A	G#3-A0	-180.15	
1-C#m						DL-B	C#2-A0	-41.8	Gamma
1-C#m						DL-DR	F#0-A0	4.38	Theta
2-F#m	1	Left	Soprano (S)	A3	220	S-A	F#3-A3	35	Gamma
2-F#m	2	Right	Alto (A)	F#3	185	S-B	F#1-A3	173.75	
2-F#m	3	Left	Tenor (T)	C#3	138.59	S-DR	F#0-A3	196.88	
2-F#m	4	Right	Bass (B)	F#1	46.25	T-A	F#3-C#3	-46.41	
2-F#m	5	Left	Drone-Left (DL)	A0	27.5	T-B	F#1-C#3	92.34	
2-F#m	6	Right	Drone-Right (DR)	F#0	23.12	T-DR	F#0-C#3	115.47	
2-F#m						DL-A	F#3-A0	-157.5	
2-F#m						DL-B	F#1-A0	-18.75	Beta
2-F#m						DL-DR	F#0-A0	4.38	Theta
3-Bm	1	Left	Soprano (S)	B3	246.94	S-A	F#3-B3	61.94	
3-Bm	2	Right	Alto (A)	F#3	185	S-B	B1-B3	185.2	
3-Bm	3	Left	Tenor (T)	D3	146.83	S-DR	F#0-B3	223.82	
3-Bm	4	Right	Bass (B)	B1	61.74	T-A	F#3-D3	-38.17	Gamma
3-Bm	5	Left	Drone-Left (DL)	A0	27.5	T-B	B1-D3	85.09	
3-Bm	6	Right	Drone-Right (DR)	F#0	23.12	T-DR	F#0-D3	123.71	
3-Bm						DL-A	F#3-A0	-157.5	
3-Bm						DL-B	B1-A0	-34.24	Gamma
3-Bm						DL-DR	F#0-A0	4.38	Theta
4-E	1	Left	Soprano (S)	B3	246.94	S-A	G#3-B3	39.29	Gamma
4-E	2	Right	Alto (A)	G#3	207.65	S-B	E2-B3	164.53	
4-E	3	Left	Tenor (T)	E3	164.81	S-DR	F#0-B3	223.82	
4-E	4	Right	Bass (B)	E2	82.41	T-A	G#3-E3	-42.84	Gamma
4-E	5	Left	Drone-Left (DL)	A0	27.5	T-B	E2-E3	82.4	
4-E	6	Right	Drone-Right (DR)	F#0	23.12	T-DR	F#0-E3	141.69	
4-E						DL-A	G#3-A0	-180.15	
4-E						DL-B	E2-A0	-54.91	
4-E						DL-DR	F#0-A0	4.38	Theta
5-Bm	1	Left	Soprano (S)	B3	246.94	S-A	F#3-B3	61.94	
5-Bm	2	Right	Alto (A)	F#3	185	S-B	B1-B3	185.2	
5-Bm	3	Left	Tenor (T)	D3	146.83	S-DR	F#0-B3	223.82	
5-Bm	4	Right	Bass (B)	B1	61.74	T-A	F#3-D3	-38.17	Gamma
5-Bm	5	Left	Drone-Left (DL)	A0	27.5	T-B	B1-D3	85.09	
5-Bm	6	Right	Drone-Right (DR)	F#0	23.12	T-DR	F#0-D3	123.71	
5-Bm						DL-A	F#3-A0	-157.5	
5-Bm						DL-B	B1-A0	-34.24	Gamma
5-Bm						DL-DR	F#0-A0	4.38	Theta
6-E	1	Left	Soprano (S)	B3	246.94	S-A	G#3-B3	39.29	Gamma
6-E	2	Right	Alto (A)	G#3	207.65	S-B	E2-B3	164.53	
6-E	3	Left	Tenor (T)	E3	164.81	S-DR	F#0-B3	223.82	
6-E	4	Right	Bass (B)	E2	82.41	T-A	G#3-E3	-42.84	Gamma
6-E	5	Left	Drone-Left (DL)	A0	27.5	T-B	E2-E3	82.4	
6-E	6	Right	Drone-Right (DR)	F#0	23.12	T-DR	F#0-E3	141.69	
6-E						DL-A	G#3-A0	-180.15	
6-E						DL-B	E2-A0	-54.91	
6-E						DL-DR	F#0-A0	4.38	Theta
7-A	1	Left	Soprano (S)	C#4	277.18	S-A	A3-C#4	57.18	
7-A	2	Right	Alto (A)	A3	220	S-B	A1-C#4	222.18	
7-A	3	Left	Tenor (T)	E3	164.81	S-DR	F#0-C#4	254.06	
7-A	4	Right	Bass (B)	A1	55	T-A	A3-E3	-55.19	
7-A	5	Left	Drone-Left (DL)	A0	27.5	T-B	A1-E3	109.81	
7-A	6	Right	Drone-Right (DR)	F#0	23.12	T-DR	F#0-E3	141.69	
7-A						DL-A	A3-A0	-192.5	
7-A						DL-B	A1-A0	-27.5	Beta
7-A						DL-DR	F#0-A0	4.38	Theta

Electronic Brain Etude:
A Binaural Arpeggio Loop in Six Parts
MEASURE 5 BINAURAL MAPPING

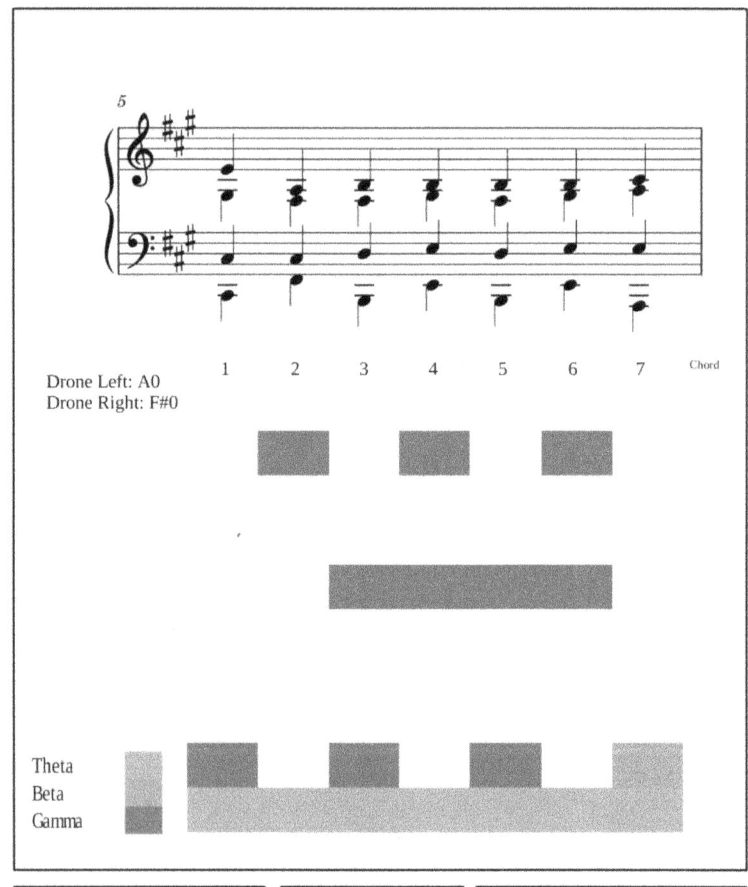

<u>Chord Progression</u>
C#m-F#m-Bm-E-Bm-E-A

<u>Parts</u>
1-Soprano/High (L)
2-Alto/MedHigh(R)
3-Tenor/MedLow(L)
4-Bass/Low(R)
5-Drone-Left(L)
6-Drone-Right(R)

<u>Binaural Ranges</u>
Delta: 0.5-4Hz
Theta: 4-8Hz
Alpha: 8-13Hz
Beta: 13-30Hz
Gamma: 30-42Hz
(Absolute Values)

<u>Intervals</u>
S-A: Soprano/Alto
S-B: Soprano/Bass
S-DR: Soprano/Drone-Right
T-A: Tenor/Alto
T-B: Tenor/Bass
T-DR: Tenor/Drone-Right
DL-A: Drone-Left/Alto
DL-B: Drone-Left/Bass
DL-DR: Drone-Left/Drone-Right

Electronic Brain Etude:
A Binaural Arpeggio Loop in Six Parts
MEASURE 5 BINAURAL MAPPING

Chord	Part #	Side	Part Name	Note	Freq (Hz)	Interval Name	Interval Val	Freq Diff (Hz)	Binaural Type
1-C#m	1	Left	Soprano (S)	E4	329.63	S-A	G#3-E4	121.98	
1-C#m	2	Right	Alto (A)	G#3	207.65	S-B	C#2-E4	260.33	
1-C#m	3	Left	Tenor (T)	C#3	138.59	S-DR	F#0-E4	306.51	
1-C#m	4	Right	Bass (B)	C#2	69.3	T-A	G#3-C#3	-69.06	
1-C#m	5	Left	Drone-Left (DL)	A0	27.5	T-B	C#2-C#3	69.29	
1-C#m	6	Right	Drone-Right (DR)	F#0	23.12	T-DR	F#0-C#3	115.47	
1-C#m						DL-A	G#3-A0	-180.15	
1-C#m						DL-B	C#2-A0	-41.8	Gamma
1-C#m						DL-DR	F#0-A0	4.38	Theta
2-F#m	1	Left	Soprano (S)	A3	220	S-A	F#3-A3	35	Gamma
2-F#m	2	Right	Alto (A)	F#3	185	S-B	F#2-A3	127.5	
2-F#m	3	Left	Tenor (T)	C#3	138.59	S-DR	F#0-A3	196.88	
2-F#m	4	Right	Bass (B)	F#2	92.5	T-A	F#3-C#3	-46.41	
2-F#m	5	Left	Drone-Left (DL)	A0	27.5	T-B	F#2-C#3	46.09	
2-F#m	6	Right	Drone-Right (DR)	F#0	23.12	T-DR	F#0-C#3	115.47	
2-F#m						DL-A	F#3-A0	-157.5	
2-F#m						DL-B	F#2-A0	-65	
2-F#m						DL-DR	F#0-A0	4.38	Theta
3-Bm	1	Left	Soprano (S)	B3	246.94	S-A	F#3-B3	61.94	
3-Bm	2	Right	Alto (A)	F#3	185	S-B	B1-B3	185.2	
3-Bm	3	Left	Tenor (T)	D3	146.83	S-DR	F#0-B3	223.82	
3-Bm	4	Right	Bass (B)	B1	61.74	T-A	F#3-D3	-38.17	Gamma
3-Bm	5	Left	Drone-Left (DL)	A0	27.5	T-B	B1-D3	85.09	
3-Bm	6	Right	Drone-Right (DR)	F#0	23.12	T-DR	F#0-D3	123.71	
3-Bm						DL-A	F#3-A0	-157.5	
3-Bm						DL-B	B1-A0	-34.24	Gamma
3-Bm						DL-DR	F#0-A0	4.38	Theta
4-E	1	Left	Soprano (S)	B3	246.94	S-A	G#3-B3	39.29	Gamma
4-E	2	Right	Alto (A)	G#3	207.65	S-B	E2-B3	164.53	
4-E	3	Left	Tenor (T)	E3	164.81	S-DR	F#0-B3	223.82	
4-E	4	Right	Bass (B)	E2	82.41	T-A	G#3-E3	-42.84	Gamma
4-E	5	Left	Drone-Left (DL)	A0	27.5	T-B	E2-E3	82.4	
4-E	6	Right	Drone-Right (DR)	F#0	23.12	T-DR	F#0-E3	141.69	
4-E						DL-A	G#3-A0	-180.15	
4-E						DL-B	E2-A0	-54.91	
4-E						DL-DR	F#0-A0	4.38	Theta
5-Bm	1	Left	Soprano (S)	B3	246.94	S-A	F#3-B3	61.94	
5-Bm	2	Right	Alto (A)	F#3	185	S-B	B1-B3	185.2	
5-Bm	3	Left	Tenor (T)	D3	146.83	S-DR	F#0-B3	223.82	
5-Bm	4	Right	Bass (B)	B1	61.74	T-A	F#3-D3	-38.17	Gamma
5-Bm	5	Left	Drone-Left (DL)	A0	27.5	T-B	B1-D3	85.09	
5-Bm	6	Right	Drone-Right (DR)	F#0	23.12	T-DR	F#0-D3	123.71	
5-Bm						DL-A	F#3-A0	-157.5	
5-Bm						DL-B	B1-A0	-34.24	Gamma
5-Bm						DL-DR	F#0-A0	4.38	Theta
6-E	1	Left	Soprano (S)	B3	246.94	S-A	G#3-B3	39.29	Gamma
6-E	2	Right	Alto (A)	G#3	207.65	S-B	E2-B3	164.53	
6-E	3	Left	Tenor (T)	E3	164.81	S-DR	F#0-B3	223.82	
6-E	4	Right	Bass (B)	E2	82.41	T-A	G#3-E3	-42.84	Gamma
6-E	5	Left	Drone-Left (DL)	A0	27.5	T-B	E2-E3	82.4	
6-E	6	Right	Drone-Right (DR)	F#0	23.12	T-DR	F#0-E3	141.69	
6-E						DL-A	G#3-A0	-180.15	
6-E						DL-B	E2-A0	-54.91	
6-E						DL-DR	F#0-A0	4.38	Theta
7-A	1	Left	Soprano (S)	C#4	277.18	S-A	A3-C#4	57.18	
7-A	2	Right	Alto (A)	A3	220	S-B	A1-C#4	222.18	
7-A	3	Left	Tenor (T)	E3	164.81	S-DR	F#0-C#4	254.06	
7-A	4	Right	Bass (B)	A1	55	T-A	A3-E3	-55.19	
7-A	5	Left	Drone-Left (DL)	A0	27.5	T-B	A1-E3	109.81	
7-A	6	Right	Drone-Right (DR)	F#0	23.12	T-DR	F#0-E3	141.69	
7-A						DL-A	A3-A0	-192.5	
7-A						DL-B	A1-A0	-27.5	Beta
7-A						DL-DR	F#0-A0	4.38	Theta

Electronic Brain Etude:
A Binaural Arpeggio Loop in Six Parts
MEASURE 6 BINAURAL MAPPING

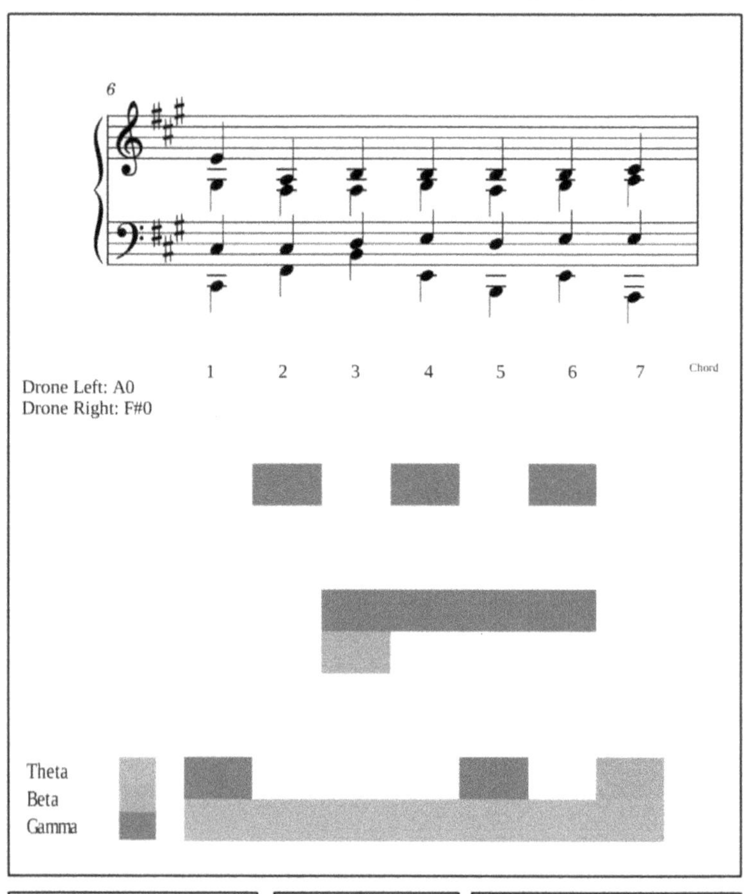

Chord Progression	Binaural Ranges	Intervals
C#m-F#m-Bm-E-Bm-E-A	Delta: 0.5-4Hz	S-A: Soprano/Alto
	Theta: 4-8Hz	S-B: Soprano/Bass
Parts	Alpha: 8-13Hz	S-DR: Soprano/Drone-Right
1-Soprano/High (L)	Beta: 13-30Hz	T-A: Tenor/Alto
2-Alto/MedHigh(R)	Gamma: 30-42Hz	T-B: Tenor/Bass
3-Tenor/MedLow(L)	(Absolute Values)	T-DR: Tenor/Drone-Right
4-Bass/Low(R)		DL-A: Drone-Left/Alto
5-Drone-Left(L)		DL-B: Drone-Left/Bass
6-Drone-Right(R)		DL-DR: Drone-Left/Drone-Right

Electronic Brain Etude:
A Binaural Arpeggio Loop in Six Parts
MEASURE 6 BINAURAL MAPPING

Chord	Part #	Side	Part Name	Note	Freq (Hz)	Interval Name	Interval Val	Freq Diff (Hz)	Binaural Type	
1-C#m	1	Left	Soprano (S)	E4	329.63	S-A	G#3-E4	121.98		
1-C#m	2	Right	Alto (A)	G#3	207.65	S-B	C#2-E4	260.33		
1-C#m	3	Left	Tenor (T)	C#3	138.59	S-DR	F#0-E4	306.51		
1-C#m	4	Right	Bass (B)	C#2	69.3	T-A	G#3-C#3	-69.06		
1-C#m	5	Left	Drone-Left (DL)	A0	27.5	T-B	C#2-C#3	69.29		
1-C#m	6	Right	Drone-Right (DR)	F#0	23.12	T-DR	F#0-C#3	115.47		
1-C#m						DL-A	G#3-A0	-180.15		
1-C#m						DL-B	C#2-A0	-41.8	Gamma	
1-C#m						DL-DR	F#0-A0	4.38	Theta	
2-F#m	1	Left	Soprano (S)	A3	220	S-A	F#3-A3	35	Gamma	
2-F#m	2	Right	Alto (A)	F#3	185	S-B	F#2-A3	127.5		
2-F#m	3	Left	Tenor (T)	C#3	138.59	S-DR	F#0-A3	196.88		
2-F#m	4	Right	Bass (B)	F#2	92.5	T-A	F#3-C#3	-46.41		
2-F#m	5	Left	Drone-Left (DL)	A0	27.5	T-B	F#2-C#3	46.09		
2-F#m	6	Right	Drone-Right (DR)	F#0	23.12	T-DR	F#0-C#3	115.47		
2-F#m						DL-A	F#3-A0	-157.5		
2-F#m						DL-B	F#2-A0	-65		
2-F#m						DL-DR	F#0-A0	4.38	Theta	
3-Bm	1	Left	Soprano (S)	B3	246.94	S-A	F#3-B3	61.94		
3-Bm	2	Right	Alto (A)	F#3	185	S-B	B2-B3	123.47		
3-Bm	3	Left	Tenor (T)	D3	146.83	S-DR	F#0-B3	223.82		
3-Bm	4	Right	Bass (B)	B2	123.47	T-A	F#3-D3	-38.17	Gamma	
3-Bm	5	Left	Drone-Left (DL)	A0	27.5	T-B	B2-D3	23.36	Beta	
3-Bm	6	Right	Drone-Right (DR)	F#0	23.12	T-DR	F#0-D3	123.71		
3-Bm						DL-A	F#3-A0	-157.5		
3-Bm						DL-B	B2-A0	-95.97		
3-Bm						DL-DR	F#0-A0	4.38	Theta	
4-E	1	Left	Soprano (S)	B3	246.94	S-A	G#3-B3	39.29	Gamma	
4-E	2	Right	Alto (A)	G#3	207.65	S-B	E2-B3	164.53		
4-E	3	Left	Tenor (T)	E3	164.81	S-DR	F#0-B3	223.82		
4-E	4	Right	Bass (B)	E2	82.41	T-A	G#3-E3	-42.84	Gamma	
4-E	5	Left	Drone-Left (DL)	A0	27.5	T-B	E2-E3	82.4		
4-E	6	Right	Drone-Right (DR)	F#0	23.12	T-DR	F#0-E3	141.69		
4-E						DL-A	G#3-A0	-180.15		
4-E						DL-B	E2-A0	-54.91		
4-E						DL-DR	F#0-A0	4.38	Theta	
5-Bm	1	Left	Soprano (S)	B3	246.94	S-A	F#3-B3	61.94		
5-Bm	2	Right	Alto (A)	F#3	185	S-B	B1-B3	185.2		
5-Bm	3	Left	Tenor (T)	D3	146.83	S-DR	F#0-B3	223.82		
5-Bm	4	Right	Bass (B)	B1	61.74	T-A	F#3-D3	-38.17	Gamma	
5-Bm	5	Left	Drone-Left (DL)	A0	27.5	T-B	B1-D3	85.09		
5-Bm	6	Right	Drone-Right (DR)	F#0	23.12	T-DR	F#0-D3	123.71		
5-Bm						DL-A	F#3-A0	-157.5		
5-Bm						DL-B	B1-A0	-34.24	Gamma	
5-Bm						DL-DR	F#0-A0	4.38	Theta	
6-E	1	Left	Soprano (S)	B3	246.94	S-A	G#3-B3	39.29	Gamma	
6-E	2	Right	Alto (A)	G#3	207.65	S-B	E2-B3	164.53		
6-E	3	Left	Tenor (T)	E3	164.81	S-DR	F#0-B3	223.82		
6-E	4	Right	Bass (B)	E2	82.41	T-A	G#3-E3	-42.84	Gamma	
6-E	5	Left	Drone-Left (DL)	A0	27.5	T-B	E2-E3	82.4		
6-E	6	Right	Drone-Right (DR)	F#0	23.12	T-DR	F#0-E3	141.69		
6-E						DL-A	G#3-A0	-180.15		
6-E						DL-B	E2-A0	-54.91		
6-E						DL-DR	F#0-A0	4.38	Theta	
7-A	1	Left	Soprano (S)	C#4	277.18	S-A	A3-C#4	57.18		
7-A	2	Right	Alto (A)	A3	220	S-B	A1-C#4	222.18		
7-A	3	Left	Tenor (T)	E3	164.81	S-DR	F#0-C#4	254.06		
7-A	4	Right	Bass (B)	A1	55	T-A	A3-E3	-55.19		
7-A	5	Left	Drone-Left (DL)	A0	27.5	T-B	A1-E3	109.81		
7-A	6	Right	Drone-Right (DR)	F#0	23.12	T-DR	F#0-E3	141.69		
7-A						DL-A	A3-A0	-192.5		
7-A						DL-B	A1-A0	-27.5	Beta	
7-A						DL-DR	F#0-A0	4.38	Theta	

Electronic Brain Etude:
A Binaural Arpeggio Loop in Six Parts
MEASURE 7 BINAURAL MAPPING

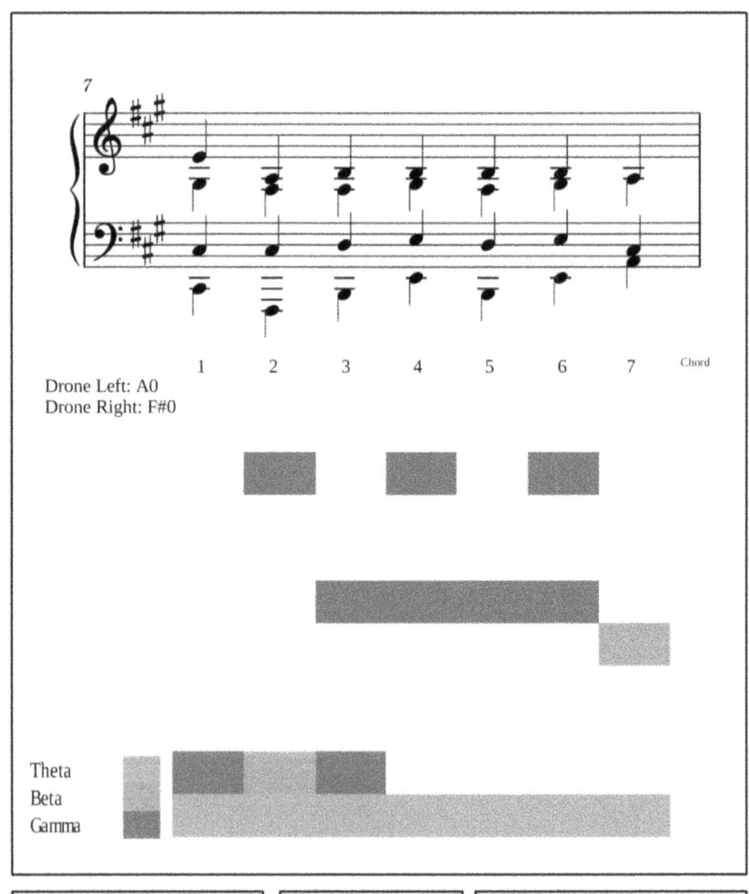

Chord Progression
C#m-F#m-Bm-E-Bm-E-A

Parts
1-Soprano/High (L)
2-Alto/MedHigh(R)
3-Tenor/MedLow(L)
4-Bass/Low(R)
5-Drone-Left(L)
6-Drone-Right(R)

Binaural Ranges
Delta: 0.5-4Hz
Theta: 4-8Hz
Alpha: 8-13Hz
Beta: 13-30Hz
Gamma: 30-42Hz
(Absolute Values)

Intervals
S-A: Soprano/Alto
S-B: Soprano/Bass
S-DR: Soprano/Drone-Right
T-A: Tenor/Alto
T-B: Tenor/Bass
T-DR: Tenor/Drone-Right
DL-A: Drone-Left/Alto
DL-B: Drone-Left/Bass
DL-DR: Drone-Left/Drone-Right

Electronic Brain Etude:
A Binaural Arpeggio Loop in Six Parts
MEASURE 7 BINAURAL MAPPING

Chord	Part #	Side	Part Name	Note	Freq (Hz)	Interval Name	Interval Val	Freq Diff (Hz)	Binaural Type	
1-C#m	1	Left	Soprano (S)	E4	329.63	S-A	G#3-E4	121.98		
1-C#m	2	Right	Alto (A)	G#3	207.65	S-B	C#2-E4	260.33		
1-C#m	3	Left	Tenor (T)	C#3	138.59	S-DR	F#0-E4	306.51		
1-C#m	4	Right	Bass (B)	C#2	69.3	T-A	G#3-C#3	-69.06		
1-C#m	5	Left	Drone-Left (DL)	A0	27.5	T-B	C#2-C#3	69.29		
1-C#m	6	Right	Drone-Right (DR)	F#0	23.12	T-DR	F#0-C#3	115.47		
1-C#m						DL-A	G#3-A0	-180.15		
1-C#m						DL-B	C#2-A0	-41.8	Gamma	
1-C#m						DL-DR	F#0-A0	4.38	Theta	
2-F#m	1	Left	Soprano (S)	A3	220	S-A	F#3-A3	35	Gamma	
2-F#m	2	Right	Alto (A)	F#3	185	S-B	F#1-A3	173.75		
2-F#m	3	Left	Tenor (T)	C#3	138.59	S-DR	F#0-A3	196.88		
2-F#m	4	Right	Bass (B)	F#1	46.25	T-A	F#3-C#3	-46.41		
2-F#m	5	Left	Drone-Left (DL)	A0	27.5	T-B	F#1-C#3	92.34		
2-F#m	6	Right	Drone-Right (DR)	F#0	23.12	T-DR	F#0-C#3	115.47		
2-F#m						DL-A	F#3-A0	-157.5		
2-F#m						DL-B	F#1-A0	-18.75	Beta	
2-F#m						DL-DR	F#0-A0	4.38	Theta	
3-Bm	1	Left	Soprano (S)	B3	246.94	S-A	F#3-B3	61.94		
3-Bm	2	Right	Alto (A)	F#3	185	S-B	B1-B3	185.2		
3-Bm	3	Left	Tenor (T)	D3	146.83	S-DR	F#0-B3	223.82		
3-Bm	4	Right	Bass (B)	B1	61.74	T-A	F#3-D3	-38.17	Gamma	
3-Bm	5	Left	Drone-Left (DL)	A0	27.5	T-B	B1-D3	85.09		
3-Bm	6	Right	Drone-Right (DR)	F#0	23.12	T-DR	F#0-D3	123.71		
3-Bm						DL-A	F#3-A0	-157.5		
3-Bm						DL-B	B1-A0	-34.24	Gamma	
3-Bm						DL-DR	F#0-A0	4.38	Theta	
4-E	1	Left	Soprano (S)	B3	246.94	S-A	G#3-B3	39.29	Gamma	
4-E	2	Right	Alto (A)	G#3	207.65	S-B	E2-B3	164.53		
4-E	3	Left	Tenor (T)	E3	164.81	S-DR	F#0-B3	223.82		
4-E	4	Right	Bass (B)	E2	82.41	T-A	G#3-E3	-42.84	Gamma	
4-E	5	Left	Drone-Left (DL)	A0	27.5	T-B	E2-E3	82.4		
4-E	6	Right	Drone-Right (DR)	F#0	23.12	T-DR	F#0-E3	141.69		
4-E						DL-A	G#3-A0	-180.15		
4-E						DL-B	E2-A0	-54.91		
4-E						DL-DR	F#0-A0	4.38	Theta	
5-Bm	1	Left	Soprano (S)	B3	246.94	S-A	F#3-B3	61.94		
5-Bm	2	Right	Alto (A)	F#3	185	S-B	B1-B3	185.2		
5-Bm	3	Left	Tenor (T)	D3	146.83	S-DR	F#0-B3	223.82		
5-Bm	4	Right	Bass (B)	B1	61.74	T-A	F#3-D3	-38.17	Gamma	
5-Bm	5	Left	Drone-Left (DL)	A0	27.5	T-B	B1-D3	85.09		
5-Bm	6	Right	Drone-Right (DR)	F#0	23.12	T-DR	F#0-D3	123.71		
5-Bm						DL-A	F#3-A0	-157.5		
5-Bm						DL-B	B1-A0	-34.24	Gamma	
5-Bm						DL-DR	F#0-A0	4.38	Theta	
6-E	1	Left	Soprano (S)	B3	246.94	S-A	G#3-B3	39.29	Gamma	
6-E	2	Right	Alto (A)	G#3	207.65	S-B	E2-B3	164.53		
6-E	3	Left	Tenor (T)	E3	164.81	S-DR	F#0-B3	223.82		
6-E	4	Right	Bass (B)	E2	82.41	T-A	G#3-E3	-42.84	Gamma	
6-E	5	Left	Drone-Left (DL)	A0	27.5	T-B	E2-E3	82.4		
6-E	6	Right	Drone-Right (DR)	F#0	23.12	T-DR	F#0-E3	141.69		
6-E						DL-A	G#3-A0	-180.15		
6-E						DL-B	E2-A0	-54.91		
6-E						DL-DR	F#0-A0	4.38	Theta	
7-A	1	Left	Soprano (S)	A3	220	S-A	A3-A3	0		
7-A	2	Right	Alto (A)	A3	220	S-B	A2-A3	110		
7-A	3	Left	Tenor (T)	C#3	138.59	S-DR	F#0-A3	196.88		
7-A	4	Right	Bass (B)	A2	110	T-A	A3-C#3	-81.41		
7-A	5	Left	Drone-Left (DL)	A0	27.5	T-B	A2-C#3	28.59	Beta	
7-A	6	Right	Drone-Right (DR)	F#0	23.12	T-DR	F#0-C#3	115.47		
7-A						DL-A	A3-A0	-192.5		
7-A						DL-B	A2-A0	-82.5		
7-A						DL-DR	F#0-A0	4.38	Theta	

Electronic Brain Etude:
A Binaural Arpeggio Loop in Six Parts
MEASURE 8 BINAURAL MAPPING

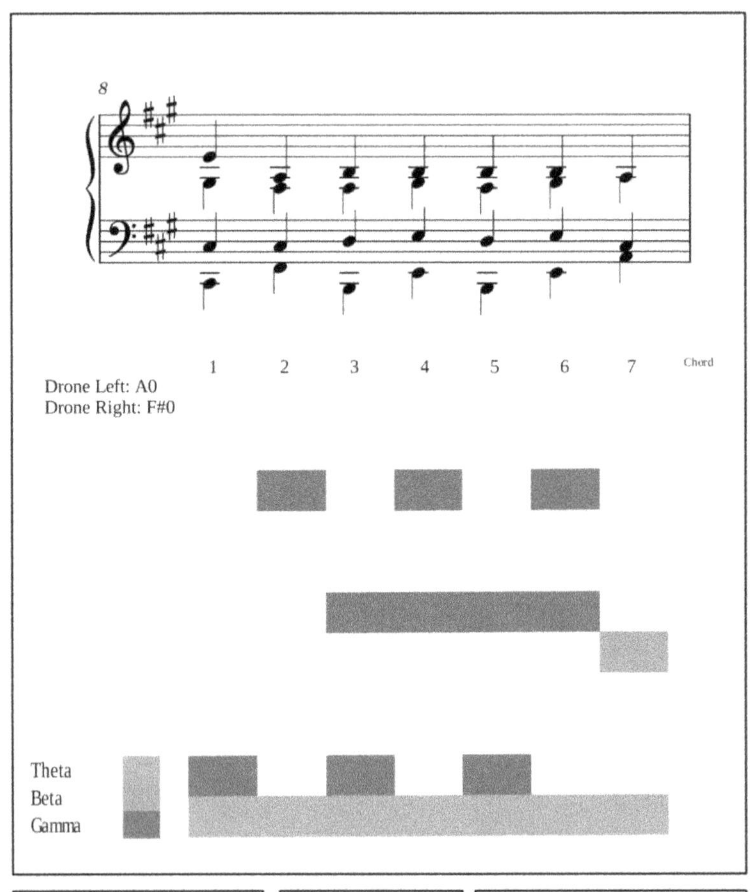

Chord Progression
C#m-F#m-Bm-E-Bm-E-A

Parts
1-Soprano/High (L)
2-Alto/MedHigh(R)
3-Tenor/MedLow(L)
4-Bass/Low(R)
5-Drone-Left(L)
6-Drone-Right(R)

Binaural Ranges
Delta: 0.5-4Hz
Theta: 4-8Hz
Alpha: 8-13Hz
Beta: 13-30Hz
Gamma: 30-42Hz
(Absolute Values)

Intervals
S-A: Soprano/Alto
S-B: Soprano/Bass
S-DR: Soprano/Drone-Right
T-A: Tenor/Alto
T-B: Tenor/Bass
T-DR: Tenor/Drone-Right
DL-A: Drone-Left/Alto
DL-B: Drone-Left/Bass
DL-DR: Drone-Left/Drone-Right

Electronic Brain Etude:
A Binaural Arpeggio Loop in Six Parts
MEASURE 8 BINAURAL MAPPING

Chord	Part #	Side	Part Name	Note	Freq (Hz)	Interval Name	Interval Val	Freq Diff (Hz)	Binaural Type
1-C#m	1	Left	Soprano (S)	E4	329.63	S-A	G#3-E4	121.98	
1-C#m	2	Right	Alto (A)	G#3	207.65	S-B	C#2-E4	260.33	
1-C#m	3	Left	Tenor (T)	C#3	138.59	S-DR	F#0-E4	306.51	
1-C#m	4	Right	Bass (B)	C#2	69.3	T-A	G#3-C#3	-69.06	
1-C#m	5	Left	Drone-Left (DL)	A0	27.5	T-B	C#2-C#3	69.29	
1-C#m	6	Right	Drone-Right (DR)	F#0	23.12	T-DR	F#0-C#3	115.47	
1-C#m						DL-A	G#3-A0	-180.15	
1-C#m						DL-B	C#2-A0	-41.8	Gamma
1-C#m						DL-DR	F#0-A0	4.38	Theta
2-F#m	1	Left	Soprano (S)	A3	220	S-A	F#3-A3	35	Gamma
2-F#m	2	Right	Alto (A)	F#3	185	S-B	F#2-A3	127.5	
2-F#m	3	Left	Tenor (T)	C#3	138.59	S-DR	F#0-A3	196.88	
2-F#m	4	Right	Bass (B)	F#2	92.5	T-A	F#3-C#3	-46.41	
2-F#m	5	Left	Drone-Left (DL)	A0	27.5	T-B	F#2-C#3	46.09	
2-F#m	6	Right	Drone-Right (DR)	F#0	23.12	T-DR	F#0-C#3	115.47	
2-F#m						DL-A	F#3-A0	-157.5	
2-F#m						DL-B	F#2-A0	-65	
2-F#m						DL-DR	F#0-A0	4.38	Theta
3-Bm	1	Left	Soprano (S)	B3	246.94	S-A	F#3-B3	61.94	
3-Bm	2	Right	Alto (A)	F#3	185	S-B	B1-B3	185.2	
3-Bm	3	Left	Tenor (T)	D3	146.83	S-DR	F#0-B3	223.82	
3-Bm	4	Right	Bass (B)	B1	61.74	T-A	F#3-D3	-38.17	Gamma
3-Bm	5	Left	Drone-Left (DL)	A0	27.5	T-B	B1-D3	85.09	
3-Bm	6	Right	Drone-Right (DR)	F#0	23.12	T-DR	F#0-D3	123.71	
3-Bm						DL-A	F#3-A0	-157.5	
3-Bm						DL-B	B1-A0	-34.24	Gamma
3-Bm						DL-DR	F#0-A0	4.38	Theta
4-E	1	Left	Soprano (S)	B3	246.94	S-A	G#3-B3	39.29	Gamma
4-E	2	Right	Alto (A)	G#3	207.65	S-B	E2-B3	164.53	
4-E	3	Left	Tenor (T)	E3	164.81	S-DR	F#0-B3	223.82	
4-E	4	Right	Bass (B)	E2	82.41	T-A	G#3-E3	-42.84	Gamma
4-E	5	Left	Drone-Left (DL)	A0	27.5	T-B	E2-E3	82.4	
4-E	6	Right	Drone-Right (DR)	F#0	23.12	T-DR	F#0-E3	141.69	
4-E						DL-A	G#3-A0	-180.15	
4-E						DL-B	E2-A0	-54.91	
4-E						DL-DR	F#0-A0	4.38	Theta
5-Bm	1	Left	Soprano (S)	B3	246.94	S-A	F#3-B3	61.94	
5-Bm	2	Right	Alto (A)	F#3	185	S-B	B1-B3	185.2	
5-Bm	3	Left	Tenor (T)	D3	146.83	S-DR	F#0-B3	223.82	
5-Bm	4	Right	Bass (B)	B1	61.74	T-A	F#3-D3	-38.17	Gamma
5-Bm	5	Left	Drone-Left (DL)	A0	27.5	T-B	B1-D3	85.09	
5-Bm	6	Right	Drone-Right (DR)	F#0	23.12	T-DR	F#0-D3	123.71	
5-Bm						DL-A	F#3-A0	-157.5	
5-Bm						DL-B	B1-A0	-34.24	Gamma
5-Bm						DL-DR	F#0-A0	4.38	Theta
6-E	1	Left	Soprano (S)	B3	246.94	S-A	G#3-B3	39.29	Gamma
6-E	2	Right	Alto (A)	G#3	207.65	S-B	E2-B3	164.53	
6-E	3	Left	Tenor (T)	E3	164.81	S-DR	F#0-B3	223.82	
6-E	4	Right	Bass (B)	E2	82.41	T-A	G#3-E3	-42.84	Gamma
6-E	5	Left	Drone-Left (DL)	A0	27.5	T-B	E2-E3	82.4	
6-E	6	Right	Drone-Right (DR)	F#0	23.12	T-DR	F#0-E3	141.69	
6-E						DL-A	G#3-A0	-180.15	
6-E						DL-B	E2-A0	-54.91	
6-E						DL-DR	F#0-A0	4.38	Theta
7-A	1	Left	Soprano (S)	A3	220	S-A	A3-A3	0	
7-A	2	Right	Alto (A)	A3	220	S-B	A2-A3	110	
7-A	3	Left	Tenor (T)	C#3	138.59	S-DR	F#0-A3	196.88	
7-A	4	Right	Bass (B)	A2	110	T-A	A3-C#3	-81.41	
7-A	5	Left	Drone-Left (DL)	A0	27.5	T-B	A2-C#3	28.59	Beta
7-A	6	Right	Drone-Right (DR)	F#0	23.12	T-DR	F#0-C#3	115.47	
7-A						DL-A	A3-A0	-192.5	
7-A						DL-B	A2-A0	-82.5	
7-A						DL-DR	F#0-A0	4.38	Theta

Electronic Brain Etude:
A Binaural Arpeggio Loop in Six Parts
MEASURE 9 BINAURAL MAPPING

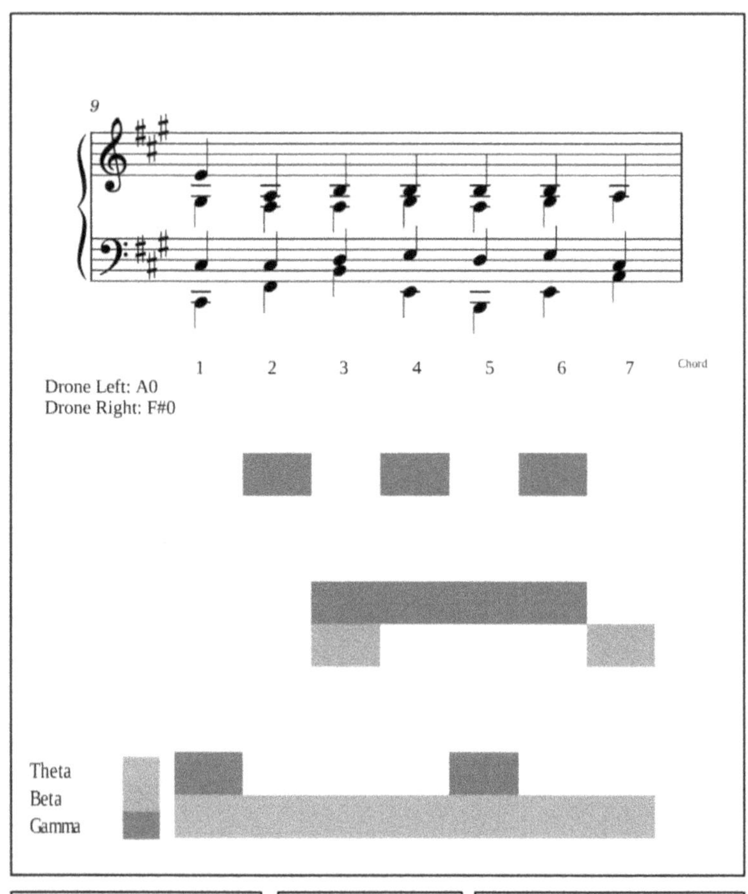

Chord Progression	Binaural Ranges	Intervals
C#m-F#m-Bm-E-Bm-E-A	Delta: 0.5-4Hz	S-A: Soprano/Alto
	Theta: 4-8Hz	S-B: Soprano/Bass
Parts	Alpha: 8-13Hz	S-DR: Soprano/Drone-Right
1-Soprano/High (L)	Beta: 13-30Hz	T-A: Tenor/Alto
2-Alto/MedHigh(R)	Gamma: 30-42Hz	T-B: Tenor/Bass
3-Tenor/MedLow(L)	(Absolute Values)	T-DR: Tenor/Drone-Right
4-Bass/Low(R)		DL-A: Drone-Left/Alto
5-Drone-Left(L)		DL-B: Drone-Left/Bass
6-Drone-Right(R)		DL-DR: Drone-Left/Drone-Right

Electronic Brain Etude:
A Binaural Arpeggio Loop in Six Parts
MEASURE 9 BINAURAL MAPPING

Chord	Part #	Side	Part Name	Note	Freq (Hz)	Interval Name	Interval Val	Freq Diff (Hz)	Binaural Type
1-C#m	1	Left	Soprano (S)	E4	329.63	S-A	G#3-E4	121.98	
1-C#m	2	Right	Alto (A)	G#3	207.65	S-B	C#2-E4	260.33	
1-C#m	3	Left	Tenor (T)	C#3	138.59	S-DR	F#0-E4	306.51	
1-C#m	4	Right	Bass (B)	C#2	69.3	T-A	G#3-C#3	-69.06	
1-C#m	5	Left	Drone-Left (DL)	A0	27.5	T-B	C#2-C#3	69.29	
1-C#m	6	Right	Drone-Right (DR)	F#0	23.12	T-DR	F#0-C#3	115.47	
1-C#m						DL-A	G#3-A0	-180.15	
1-C#m						DL-B	C#2-A0	-41.8	Gamma
1-C#m						DL-DR	F#0-A0	4.38	Theta
2-F#m	1	Left	Soprano (S)	A3	220	S-A	F#3-A3	35	Gamma
2-F#m	2	Right	Alto (A)	F#3	185	S-B	F#2-A3	127.5	
2-F#m	3	Left	Tenor (T)	C#3	138.59	S-DR	F#0-A3	196.88	
2-F#m	4	Right	Bass (B)	F#2	92.5	T-A	F#3-C#3	-46.41	
2-F#m	5	Left	Drone-Left (DL)	A0	27.5	T-B	F#2-C#3	46.09	
2-F#m	6	Right	Drone-Right (DR)	F#0	23.12	T-DR	F#0-C#3	115.47	
2-F#m						DL-A	F#3-A0	-157.5	
2-F#m						DL-B	F#2-A0	-65	
2-F#m						DL-DR	F#0-A0	4.38	Theta
3-Bm	1	Left	Soprano (S)	B3	246.94	S-A	F#3-B3	61.94	
3-Bm	2	Right	Alto (A)	F#3	185	S-B	B2-B3	123.47	
3-Bm	3	Left	Tenor (T)	D3	146.83	S-DR	F#0-B3	223.82	
3-Bm	4	Right	Bass (B)	B2	123.47	T-A	F#3-D3	-38.17	Gamma
3-Bm	5	Left	Drone-Left (DL)	A0	27.5	T-B	B2-D3	23.36	Beta
3-Bm	6	Right	Drone-Right (DR)	F#0	23.12	T-DR	F#0-D3	123.71	
3-Bm						DL-A	F#3-A0	-157.5	
3-Bm						DL-B	B2-A0	-95.97	
3-Bm						DL-DR	F#0-A0	4.38	Theta
4-E	1	Left	Soprano (S)	B3	246.94	S-A	G#3-B3	39.29	Gamma
4-E	2	Right	Alto (A)	G#3	207.65	S-B	E2-B3	164.53	
4-E	3	Left	Tenor (T)	E3	164.81	S-DR	F#0-B3	223.82	
4-E	4	Right	Bass (B)	E2	82.41	T-A	G#3-E3	-42.84	Gamma
4-E	5	Left	Drone-Left (DL)	A0	27.5	T-B	E2-E3	82.4	
4-E	6	Right	Drone-Right (DR)	F#0	23.12	T-DR	F#0-E3	141.69	
4-E						DL-A	G#3-A0	-180.15	
4-E						DL-B	E2-A0	-54.91	
4-E						DL-DR	F#0-A0	4.38	Theta
5-Bm	1	Left	Soprano (S)	B3	246.94	S-A	F#3-B3	61.94	
5-Bm	2	Right	Alto (A)	F#3	185	S-B	B1-B3	185.2	
5-Bm	3	Left	Tenor (T)	D3	146.83	S-DR	F#0-B3	223.82	
5-Bm	4	Right	Bass (B)	B1	61.74	T-A	F#3-D3	-38.17	Gamma
5-Bm	5	Left	Drone-Left (DL)	A0	27.5	T-B	B1-D3	85.09	
5-Bm	6	Right	Drone-Right (DR)	F#0	23.12	T-DR	F#0-D3	123.71	
5-Bm						DL-A	F#3-A0	-157.5	
5-Bm						DL-B	B1-A0	-34.24	Gamma
5-Bm						DL-DR	F#0-A0	4.38	Theta
6-E	1	Left	Soprano (S)	B3	246.94	S-A	G#3-B3	39.29	Gamma
6-E	2	Right	Alto (A)	G#3	207.65	S-B	E2-B3	164.53	
6-E	3	Left	Tenor (T)	E3	164.81	S-DR	F#0-B3	223.82	
6-E	4	Right	Bass (B)	E2	82.41	T-A	G#3-E3	-42.84	Gamma
6-E	5	Left	Drone-Left (DL)	A0	27.5	T-B	E2-E3	82.4	
6-E	6	Right	Drone-Right (DR)	F#0	23.12	T-DR	F#0-E3	141.69	
6-E						DL-A	G#3-A0	-180.15	
6-E						DL-B	E2-A0	-54.91	
6-E						DL-DR	F#0-A0	4.38	Theta
7-A	1	Left	Soprano (S)	A3	220	S-A	A3-A3	0	
7-A	2	Right	Alto (A)	A3	220	S-B	A2-A3	110	
7-A	3	Left	Tenor (T)	C#3	138.59	S-DR	F#0-A3	196.88	
7-A	4	Right	Bass (B)	A2	110	T-A	A3-C#3	-81.41	
7-A	5	Left	Drone-Left (DL)	A0	27.5	T-B	A2-C#3	28.59	Beta
7-A	6	Right	Drone-Right (DR)	F#0	23.12	T-DR	F#0-C#3	115.47	
7-A						DL-A	A3-A0	-192.5	
7-A						DL-B	A2-A0	-82.5	
7-A						DL-DR	F#0-A0	4.38	Theta

Electronic Brain Etude:
A Binaural Arpeggio Loop in Six Parts
MEASURE 10 BINAURAL MAPPING

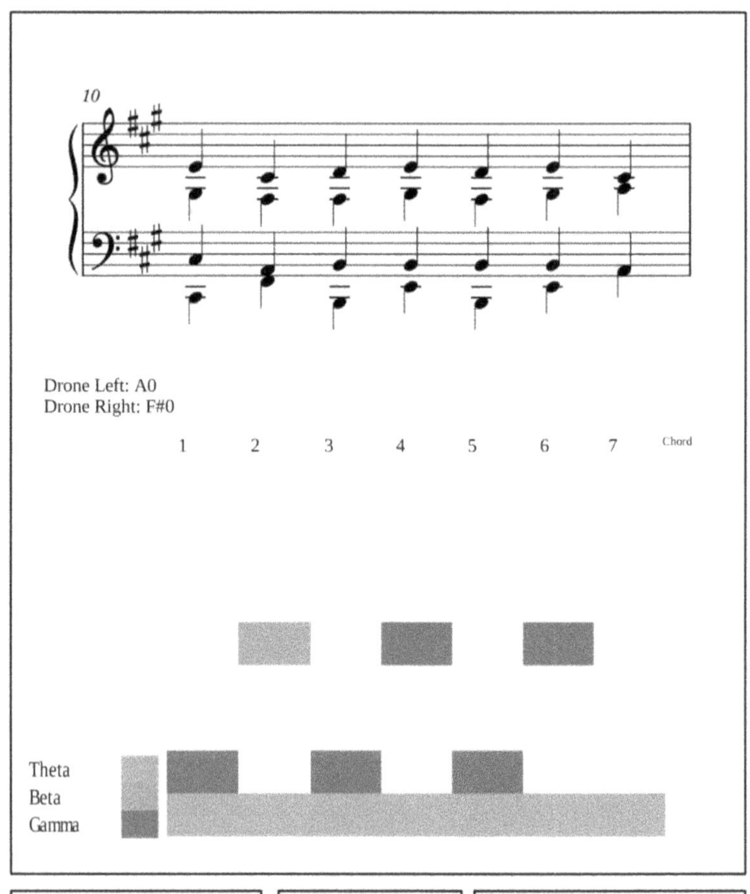

<table>
<tr><td>

<u>Chord Progression</u>
C#m-F#m-Bm-E-Bm-E-A

<u>Parts</u>
1-Soprano/High (L)
2-Alto/MedHigh(R)
3-Tenor/MedLow(L)
4-Bass/Low(R)
5-Drone-Left(L)
6-Drone-Right(R)

</td><td>

<u>Binaural Ranges</u>
Delta: 0.5-4Hz
Theta: 4-8Hz
Alpha: 8-13Hz
Beta: 13-30Hz
Gamma: 30-42Hz
(Absolute Values)

</td><td>

<u>Intervals</u>
S-A: Soprano/Alto
S-B: Soprano/Bass
S-DR: Soprano/Drone-Right
T-A: Tenor/Alto
T-B: Tenor/Bass
T-DR: Tenor/Drone-Right
DL-A: Drone-Left/Alto
DL-B: Drone-Left/Bass
DL-DR: Drone-Left/Drone-Right

</td></tr>
</table>

Electronic Brain Etude:
A Binaural Arpeggio Loop in Six Parts
MEASURE 10 BINAURAL MAPPING

Chord	Part #	Side	Part Name	Note	Freq (Hz)	Interval Name	Interval Val	Freq Diff (Hz)	Binaural Type	
1-C#m	1	Left	Soprano (S)	E4	329.63	S-A	G#3-E4	121.98		
1-C#m	2	Right	Alto (A)	G#3	207.65	S-B	C#2-E4	260.33		
1-C#m	3	Left	Tenor (T)	C#3	138.59	S-DR	F#0-E4	306.51		
1-C#m	4	Right	Bass (B)	C#2	69.3	T-A	G#3-C#3	-69.06		
1-C#m	5	Left	Drone-Left (DL)	A0	27.5	T-B	C#2-C#3	69.29		
1-C#m	6	Right	Drone-Right (DR)	F#0	23.12	T-DR	F#0-C#3	115.47		
1-C#m						DL-A	G#3-A0	-180.15		
1-C#m						DL-B	C#2-A0	-41.8	Gamma	
1-C#m						DL-DR	F#0-A0	4.38	Theta	
2-F#m	1	Left	Soprano (S)	C#4	277.18	S-A	F#3-C#4	92.18		
2-F#m	2	Right	Alto (A)	F#3	185	S-B	F#2-C#4	184.68		
2-F#m	3	Left	Tenor (T)	A2	110	S-DR	F#0-C#4	254.06		
2-F#m	4	Right	Bass (B)	F#2	92.5	T-A	F#3-A2	-75		
2-F#m	5	Left	Drone-Left (DL)	A0	27.5	T-B	F#2-A2	17.5	Beta	
2-F#m	6	Right	Drone-Right (DR)	F#0	23.12	T-DR	F#0-A2	86.88		
2-F#m						DL-A	F#3-A0	-157.5		
2-F#m						DL-B	F#2-A0	-65		
2-F#m						DL-DR	F#0-A0	4.38	Theta	
3-Bm	1	Left	Soprano (S)	D4	293.66	S-A	F#3-D4	108.66		
3-Bm	2	Right	Alto (A)	F#3	185	S-B	B1-D4	231.92		
3-Bm	3	Left	Tenor (T)	B2	123.47	S-DR	F#0-D4	270.54		
3-Bm	4	Right	Bass (B)	B1	61.74	T-A	F#3-B2	-61.53		
3-Bm	5	Left	Drone-Left (DL)	A0	27.5	T-B	B1-B2	61.73		
3-Bm	6	Right	Drone-Right (DR)	F#0	23.12	T-DR	F#0-B2	100.35		
3-Bm						DL-A	F#3-A0	-157.5		
3-Bm						DL-B	B1-A0	-34.24	Gamma	
3-Bm						DL-DR	F#0-A0	4.38	Theta	
4-E	1	Left	Soprano (S)	E4	329.63	S-A	G#3-E4	121.98		
4-E	2	Right	Alto (A)	G#3	207.65	S-B	E2-E4	247.22		
4-E	3	Left	Tenor (T)	B2	123.47	S-DR	F#0-E4	306.51		
4-E	4	Right	Bass (B)	E2	82.41	T-A	G#3-B2	-84.18		
4-E	5	Left	Drone-Left (DL)	A0	27.5	T-B	E2-B2	41.06	Gamma	
4-E	6	Right	Drone-Right (DR)	F#0	23.12	T-DR	F#0-B2	100.35		
4-E						DL-A	G#3-A0	-180.15		
4-E						DL-B	E2-A0	-54.91		
4-E						DL-DR	F#0-A0	4.38	Theta	
5-Bm	1	Left	Soprano (S)	D4	293.66	S-A	F#3-D4	108.66		
5-Bm	2	Right	Alto (A)	F#3	185	S-B	B1-D4	231.92		
5-Bm	3	Left	Tenor (T)	B2	123.47	S-DR	F#0-D4	270.54		
5-Bm	4	Right	Bass (B)	B1	61.74	T-A	F#3-B2	-61.53		
5-Bm	5	Left	Drone-Left (DL)	A0	27.5	T-B	B1-B2	61.73		
5-Bm	6	Right	Drone-Right (DR)	F#0	23.12	T-DR	F#0-B2	100.35		
5-Bm						DL-A	F#3-A0	-157.5		
5-Bm						DL-B	B1-A0	-34.24	Gamma	
5-Bm						DL-DR	F#0-A0	4.38	Theta	
6-E	1	Left	Soprano (S)	E4	329.63	S-A	G#3-E4	121.98		
6-E	2	Right	Alto (A)	G#3	207.65	S-B	E2-E4	247.22		
6-E	3	Left	Tenor (T)	B2	123.47	S-DR	F#0-E4	306.51		
6-E	4	Right	Bass (B)	E2	82.41	T-A	G#3-B2	-84.18		
6-E	5	Left	Drone-Left (DL)	A0	27.5	T-B	E2-B2	41.06	Gamma	
6-E	6	Right	Drone-Right (DR)	F#0	23.12	T-DR	F#0-B2	100.35		
6-E						DL-A	G#3-A0	-180.15		
6-E						DL-B	E2-A0	-54.91		
6-E						DL-DR	F#0-A0	4.38	Theta	
7-A	1	Left	Soprano (S)	C#4	277.18	S-A	A3-C#4	57.18		
7-A	2	Right	Alto (A)	A3	220	S-B	A2-C#4	167.18		
7-A	3	Left	Tenor (T)	A2	110	S-DR	F#0-C#4	254.06		
7-A	4	Right	Bass (B)	A2	110	T-A	A3-A2	-110		
7-A	5	Left	Drone-Left (DL)	A0	27.5	T-B	A2-A2	0		
7-A	6	Right	Drone-Right (DR)	F#0	23.12	T-DR	F#0-A2	86.88		
7-A						DL-A	A3-A0	-192.5		
7-A						DL-B	A2-A0	-82.5		
7-A						DL-DR	F#0-A0	4.38	Theta	

Electronic Brain Etude:
A Binaural Arpeggio Loop in Six Parts
MEASURE 11 BINAURAL MAPPING

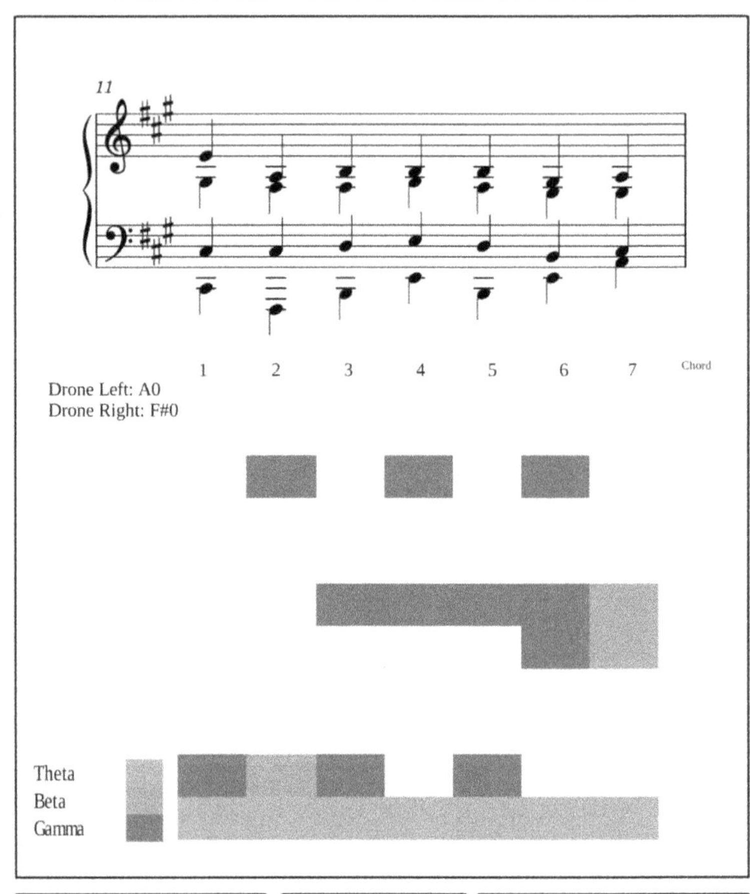

<table>
<tr><td>

Chord Progression
C#m-F#m-Bm-E-Bm-E-A

Parts
1-Soprano/High (L)
2-Alto/MedHigh(R)
3-Tenor/MedLow(L)
4-Bass/Low(R)
5-Drone-Left(L)
6-Drone-Right(R)

</td><td>

Binaural Ranges
Delta: 0.5-4Hz
Theta: 4-8Hz
Alpha: 8-13Hz
Beta: 13-30Hz
Gamma: 30-42Hz
(Absolute Values)

</td><td>

Intervals
S-A: Soprano/Alto
S-B: Soprano/Bass
S-DR: Soprano/Drone-Right
T-A: Tenor/Alto
T-B: Tenor/Bass
T-DR: Tenor/Drone-Right
DL-A: Drone-Left/Alto
DL-B: Drone-Left/Bass
DL-DR: Drone-Left/Drone-Right

</td></tr>
</table>

Electronic Brain Etude:
A Binaural Arpeggio Loop in Six Parts
MEASURE 11 BINAURAL MAPPING

Chord	Part #	Side	Part Name	Note	Freq (Hz)	Interval Name	Interval Val	Freq Diff (Hz)	Binaural Type
1-C#m	1	Left	Soprano (S)	E4	329.63	S-A	G#3-E4	121.98	
1-C#m	2	Right	Alto (A)	G#3	207.65	S-B	C#2-E4	260.33	
1-C#m	3	Left	Tenor (T)	C#3	138.59	S-DR	F#0-E4	306.51	
1-C#m	4	Right	Bass (B)	C#2	69.3	T-A	G#3-C#3	-69.06	
1-C#m	5	Left	Drone-Left (DL)	A0	27.5	T-B	C#2-C#3	69.29	
1-C#m	6	Right	Drone-Right (DR)	F#0	23.12	T-DR	F#0-C#3	115.47	
1-C#m						DL-A	G#3-A0	-180.15	
1-C#m						DL-B	C#2-A0	-41.8	Gamma
1-C#m						DL-DR	F#0-A0	4.38	Theta
2-F#m	1	Left	Soprano (S)	A3	220	S-A	F#3-A3	35	Gamma
2-F#m	2	Right	Alto (A)	F#3	185	S-B	F#1-A3	173.75	
2-F#m	3	Left	Tenor (T)	C#3	138.59	S-DR	F#0-A3	196.88	
2-F#m	4	Right	Bass (B)	F#1	46.25	T-A	F#3-C#3	-46.41	
2-F#m	5	Left	Drone-Left (DL)	A0	27.5	T-B	F#1-C#3	92.34	
2-F#m	6	Right	Drone-Right (DR)	F#0	23.12	T-DR	F#0-C#3	115.47	
2-F#m						DL-A	F#3-A0	-157.5	
2-F#m						DL-B	F#1-A0	-18.75	Beta
2-F#m						DL-DR	F#0-A0	4.38	Theta
3-Bm	1	Left	Soprano (S)	B3	246.94	S-A	F#3-B3	61.94	
3-Bm	2	Right	Alto (A)	F#3	185	S-B	B1-B3	185.2	
3-Bm	3	Left	Tenor (T)	D3	146.83	S-DR	F#0-B3	223.82	
3-Bm	4	Right	Bass (B)	B1	61.74	T-A	F#3-D3	-38.17	Gamma
3-Bm	5	Left	Drone-Left (DL)	A0	27.5	T-B	B1-D3	85.09	
3-Bm	6	Right	Drone-Right (DR)	F#0	23.12	T-DR	F#0-D3	123.71	
3-Bm						DL-A	F#3-A0	-157.5	
3-Bm						DL-B	B1-A0	-34.24	Gamma
3-Bm						DL-DR	F#0-A0	4.38	Theta
4-E	1	Left	Soprano (S)	B3	246.94	S-A	G#3-B3	39.29	Gamma
4-E	2	Right	Alto (A)	G#3	207.65	S-B	E2-B3	164.53	
4-E	3	Left	Tenor (T)	E3	164.81	S-DR	F#0-B3	223.82	
4-E	4	Right	Bass (B)	E2	82.41	T-A	G#3-E3	-42.84	Gamma
4-E	5	Left	Drone-Left (DL)	A0	27.5	T-B	E2-E3	82.4	
4-E	6	Right	Drone-Right (DR)	F#0	23.12	T-DR	F#0-E3	141.69	
4-E						DL-A	G#3-A0	-180.15	
4-E						DL-B	E2-A0	-54.91	
4-E						DL-DR	F#0-A0	4.38	Theta
5-Bm	1	Left	Soprano (S)	B3	246.94	S-A	F#3-B3	61.94	
5-Bm	2	Right	Alto (A)	F#3	185	S-B	B1-B3	185.2	
5-Bm	3	Left	Tenor (T)	D3	146.83	S-DR	F#0-B3	223.82	
5-Bm	4	Right	Bass (B)	B1	61.74	T-A	F#3-D3	-38.17	Gamma
5-Bm	5	Left	Drone-Left (DL)	A0	27.5	T-B	B1-D3	85.09	
5-Bm	6	Right	Drone-Right (DR)	F#0	23.12	T-DR	F#0-D3	123.71	
5-Bm						DL-A	F#3-A0	-157.5	
5-Bm						DL-B	B1-A0	-34.24	Gamma
5-Bm						DL-DR	F#0-A0	4.38	Theta
6-E	1	Left	Soprano (S)	G#3	207.65	S-A	E3-G#3	42.84	Gamma
6-E	2	Right	Alto (A)	E3	164.81	S-B	E2-G#3	125.24	
6-E	3	Left	Tenor (T)	B2	123.47	S-DR	F#0-G#3	184.53	
6-E	4	Right	Bass (B)	E2	82.41	T-A	E3-B2	-41.34	Gamma
6-E	5	Left	Drone-Left (DL)	A0	27.5	T-B	E2-B2	41.06	Gamma
6-E	6	Right	Drone-Right (DR)	F#0	23.12	T-DR	F#0-B2	100.35	
6-E						DL-A	E3-A0	-137.31	
6-E						DL-B	E2-A0	-54.91	
6-E						DL-DR	F#0-A0	4.38	Theta
7-A	1	Left	Soprano (S)	A3	220	S-A	E3-A3	55.19	
7-A	2	Right	Alto (A)	E3	164.81	S-B	A2-A3	110	
7-A	3	Left	Tenor (T)	C#3	138.59	S-DR	F#0-A3	196.88	
7-A	4	Right	Bass (B)	A2	110	T-A	E3-C#3	-26.22	Beta
7-A	5	Left	Drone-Left (DL)	A0	27.5	T-B	A2-C#3	28.59	Beta
7-A	6	Right	Drone-Right (DR)	F#0	23.12	T-DR	F#0-C#3	115.47	
7-A						DL-A	E3-A0	-137.31	
7-A						DL-B	A2-A0	-82.5	
7-A						DL-DR	F#0-A0	4.38	Theta

Electronic Brain Etude:
A Binaural Arpeggio Loop in Six Parts
MEASURE 12 BINAURAL MAPPING

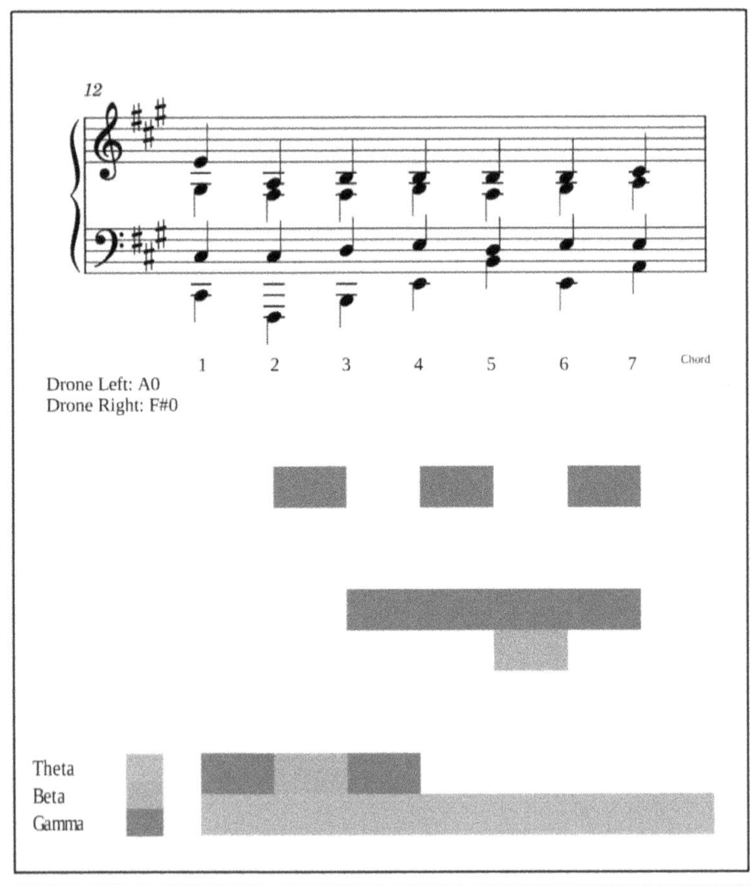

Chord Progression
C#m-F#m-Bm-E-Bm-E-A

Parts
1-Soprano/High (L)
2-Alto/MedHigh(R)
3-Tenor/MedLow(L)
4-Bass/Low(R)
5-Drone-Left(L)
6-Drone-Right(R)

Binaural Ranges
Delta: 0.5-4Hz
Theta: 4-8Hz
Alpha: 8-13Hz
Beta: 13-30Hz
Gamma: 30-42Hz
(Absolute Values)

Intervals
S-A: Soprano/Alto
S-B: Soprano/Bass
S-DR: Soprano/Drone-Right
T-A: Tenor/Alto
T-B: Tenor/Bass
T-DR: Tenor/Drone-Right
DL-A: Drone-Left/Alto
DL-B: Drone-Left/Bass
DL-DR: Drone-Left/Drone-Right

Electronic Brain Etude:
A Binaural Arpeggio Loop in Six Parts
MEASURE 12 BINAURAL MAPPING

Chord	Part #	Side	Part Name	Note	Freq (Hz)	Interval Name	Interval Val	Freq Diff (Hz)	Binaural Type
1-C#m	1	Left	Soprano (S)	E4	329.63	S-A	G#3-E4	121.98	
1-C#m	2	Right	Alto (A)	G#3	207.65	S-B	C#2-E4	260.33	
1-C#m	3	Left	Tenor (T)	C#3	138.59	S-DR	F#0-E4	306.51	
1-C#m	4	Right	Bass (B)	C#2	69.3	T-A	G#3-C#3	-69.06	
1-C#m	5	Left	Drone-Left (DL)	A0	27.5	T-B	C#2-C#3	69.29	
1-C#m	6	Right	Drone-Right (DR)	F#0	23.12	T-DR	F#0-C#3	115.47	
1-C#m						DL-A	G#3-A0	-180.15	
1-C#m						DL-B	C#2-A0	-41.8	Gamma
1-C#m						DL-DR	F#0-A0	4.38	Theta
2-F#m	1	Left	Soprano (S)	A3	220	S-A	F#3-A3	35	Gamma
2-F#m	2	Right	Alto (A)	F#3	185	S-B	F#1-A3	173.75	
2-F#m	3	Left	Tenor (T)	C#3	138.59	S-DR	F#0-A3	196.88	
2-F#m	4	Right	Bass (B)	F#1	46.25	T-A	F#3-C#3	-46.41	
2-F#m	5	Left	Drone-Left (DL)	A0	27.5	T-B	F#1-C#3	92.34	
2-F#m	6	Right	Drone-Right (DR)	F#0	23.12	T-DR	F#0-C#3	115.47	
2-F#m						DL-A	F#3-A0	-157.5	
2-F#m						DL-B	F#1-A0	-18.75	Beta
2-F#m						DL-DR	F#0-A0	4.38	Theta
3-Bm	1	Left	Soprano (S)	B3	246.94	S-A	F#3-B3	61.94	
3-Bm	2	Right	Alto (A)	F#3	185	S-B	B1-B3	185.2	
3-Bm	3	Left	Tenor (T)	D3	146.83	S-DR	F#0-B3	223.82	
3-Bm	4	Right	Bass (B)	B1	61.74	T-A	F#3-D3	-38.17	Gamma
3-Bm	5	Left	Drone-Left (DL)	A0	27.5	T-B	B1-D3	85.09	
3-Bm	6	Right	Drone-Right (DR)	F#0	23.12	T-DR	F#0-D3	123.71	
3-Bm						DL-A	F#3-A0	-157.5	
3-Bm						DL-B	B1-A0	-34.24	Gamma
3-Bm						DL-DR	F#0-A0	4.38	Theta
4-E	1	Left	Soprano (S)	B3	246.94	S-A	G#3-B3	39.29	Gamma
4-E	2	Right	Alto (A)	G#3	207.65	S-B	E2-B3	164.53	
4-E	3	Left	Tenor (T)	E3	164.81	S-DR	F#0-B3	223.82	
4-E	4	Right	Bass (B)	E2	82.41	T-A	G#3-E3	-42.84	Gamma
4-E	5	Left	Drone-Left (DL)	A0	27.5	T-B	E2-E3	82.4	
4-E	6	Right	Drone-Right (DR)	F#0	23.12	T-DR	F#0-E3	141.69	
4-E						DL-A	G#3-A0	-180.15	
4-E						DL-B	E2-A0	-54.91	
4-E						DL-DR	F#0-A0	4.38	Theta
5-Bm	1	Left	Soprano (S)	B3	246.94	S-A	F#3-B3	61.94	
5-Bm	2	Right	Alto (A)	F#3	185	S-B	B2-B3	123.47	
5-Bm	3	Left	Tenor (T)	D3	146.83	S-DR	F#0-B3	223.82	
5-Bm	4	Right	Bass (B)	B2	123.47	T-A	F#3-D3	-38.17	Gamma
5-Bm	5	Left	Drone-Left (DL)	A0	27.5	T-B	B2-D3	23.36	Beta
5-Bm	6	Right	Drone-Right (DR)	F#0	23.12	T-DR	F#0-D3	123.71	
5-Bm						DL-A	F#3-A0	-157.5	
5-Bm						DL-B	B2-A0	-95.97	
5-Bm						DL-DR	F#0-A0	4.38	Theta
6-E	1	Left	Soprano (S)	B3	246.94	S-A	G#3-B3	39.29	Gamma
6-E	2	Right	Alto (A)	G#3	207.65	S-B	E2-B3	164.53	
6-E	3	Left	Tenor (T)	E3	164.81	S-DR	F#0-B3	223.82	
6-E	4	Right	Bass (B)	E2	82.41	T-A	G#3-E3	-42.84	Gamma
6-E	5	Left	Drone-Left (DL)	A0	27.5	T-B	E2-E3	82.4	
6-E	6	Right	Drone-Right (DR)	F#0	23.12	T-DR	F#0-E3	141.69	
6-E						DL-A	G#3-A0	-180.15	
6-E						DL-B	E2-A0	-54.91	
6-E						DL-DR	F#0-A0	4.38	Theta
7-A	1	Left	Soprano (S)	C#4	277.18	S-A	A3-C#4	57.18	
7-A	2	Right	Alto (A)	A3	220	S-B	A2-C#4	167.18	
7-A	3	Left	Tenor (T)	E3	164.81	S-DR	F#0-C#4	254.06	
7-A	4	Right	Bass (B)	A2	110	T-A	A3-E3	-55.19	
7-A	5	Left	Drone-Left (DL)	A0	27.5	T-B	A2-E3	54.81	
7-A	6	Right	Drone-Right (DR)	F#0	23.12	T-DR	F#0-E3	141.69	
7-A						DL-A	A3-A0	-192.5	
7-A						DL-B	A2-A0	-82.5	
7-A						DL-DR	F#0-A0	4.38	Theta

Electronic Brain Etude:
A Binaural Arpeggio Loop in Six Parts
MEASURE 13 BINAURAL MAPPING

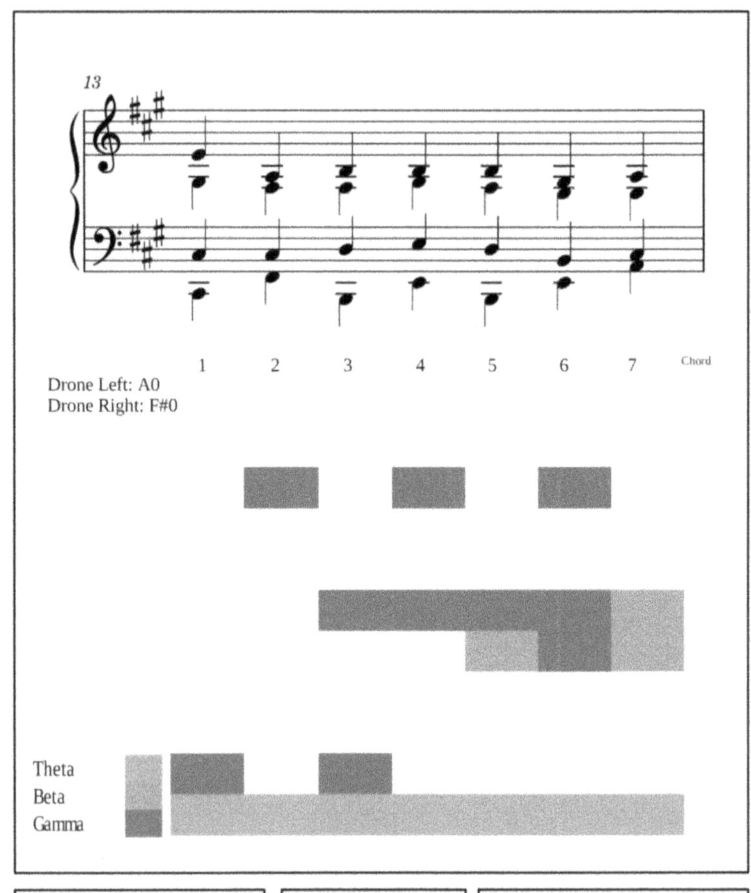

<u>Chord Progression</u>
C#m-F#m-Bm-E-Bm-E-A

<u>Parts</u>
1-Soprano/High (L)
2-Alto/MedHigh(R)
3-Tenor/MedLow(L)
4-Bass/Low(R)
5-Drone-Left(L)
6-Drone-Right(R)

<u>Binaural Ranges</u>
Delta: 0.5-4Hz
Theta: 4-8Hz
Alpha: 8-13Hz
Beta: 13-30Hz
Gamma: 30-42Hz
(Absolute Values)

<u>Intervals</u>
S-A: Soprano/Alto
S-B: Soprano/Bass
S-DR: Soprano/Drone-Right
T-A: Tenor/Alto
T-B: Tenor/Bass
T-DR: Tenor/Drone-Right
DL-A: Drone-Left/Alto
DL-B: Drone-Left/Bass
DL-DR: Drone-Left/Drone-Right

Electronic Brain Etude:
A Binaural Arpeggio Loop in Six Parts
MEASURE 13 BINAURAL MAPPING

Chord	Part #	Side	Part Name	Note	Freq (Hz)	Interval Name	Interval Val	Freq Diff (Hz)	Binaural Type	
1-C#m	1	Left	Soprano (S)	E4	329.63	S-A	G#3-E4	121.98		
1-C#m	2	Right	Alto (A)	G#3	207.65	S-B	C#2-E4	260.33		
1-C#m	3	Left	Tenor (T)	C#3	138.59	S-DR	F#0-E4	306.51		
1-C#m	4	Right	Bass (B)	C#2	69.3	T-A	G#3-C#3	-69.06		
1-C#m	5	Left	Drone-Left (DL)	A0	27.5	T-B	C#2-C#3	69.29		
1-C#m	6	Right	Drone-Right (DR)	F#0	23.12	T-DR	F#0-C#3	115.47		
1-C#m						DL-A	G#3-A0	-180.15		
1-C#m						DL-B	C#2-A0	-41.8	Gamma	
1-C#m						DL-DR	F#0-A0	4.38	Theta	
2-F#m	1	Left	Soprano (S)	A3	220	S-A	F#3-A3	35	Gamma	
2-F#m	2	Right	Alto (A)	F#3	185	S-B	F#2-A3	127.5		
2-F#m	3	Left	Tenor (T)	C#3	138.59	S-DR	F#0-A3	196.88		
2-F#m	4	Right	Bass (B)	F#2	92.5	T-A	F#3-C#3	-46.41		
2-F#m	5	Left	Drone-Left (DL)	A0	27.5	T-B	F#2-C#3	46.09		
2-F#m	6	Right	Drone-Right (DR)	F#0	23.12	T-DR	F#0-C#3	115.47		
2-F#m						DL-A	F#3-A0	-157.5		
2-F#m						DL-B	F#2-A0	-65		
2-F#m						DL-DR	F#0-A0	4.38	Theta	
3-Bm	1	Left	Soprano (S)	B3	246.94	S-A	F#3-B3	61.94		
3-Bm	2	Right	Alto (A)	F#3	185	S-B	B1-B3	185.2		
3-Bm	3	Left	Tenor (T)	D3	146.83	S-DR	F#0-B3	223.82		
3-Bm	4	Right	Bass (B)	B1	61.74	T-A	F#3-D3	-38.17	Gamma	
3-Bm	5	Left	Drone-Left (DL)	A0	27.5	T-B	B1-D3	85.09		
3-Bm	6	Right	Drone-Right (DR)	F#0	23.12	T-DR	F#0-D3	123.71		
3-Bm						DL-A	F#3-A0	-157.5		
3-Bm						DL-B	B1-A0	-34.24	Gamma	
3-Bm						DL-DR	F#0-A0	4.38	Theta	
4-E	1	Left	Soprano (S)	B3	246.94	S-A	G#3-B3	39.29	Gamma	
4-E	2	Right	Alto (A)	G#3	207.65	S-B	E2-B3	164.53		
4-E	3	Left	Tenor (T)	E3	164.81	S-DR	F#0-B3	223.82		
4-E	4	Right	Bass (B)	E2	82.41	T-A	G#3-E3	-42.84	Gamma	
4-E	5	Left	Drone-Left (DL)	A0	27.5	T-B	E2-E3	82.4		
4-E	6	Right	Drone-Right (DR)	F#0	23.12	T-DR	F#0-E3	141.69		
4-E						DL-A	G#3-A0	-180.15		
4-E						DL-B	E2-A0	-54.91		
4-E						DL-DR	F#0-A0	4.38	Theta	
5-Bm	1	Left	Soprano (S)	B3	246.94	S-A	F#3-B3	61.94		
5-Bm	2	Right	Alto (A)	F#3	185	S-B	B2-B3	123.47		
5-Bm	3	Left	Tenor (T)	D3	146.83	S-DR	F#0-B3	223.82		
5-Bm	4	Right	Bass (B)	B2	123.47	T-A	F#3-D3	-38.17	Gamma	
5-Bm	5	Left	Drone-Left (DL)	A0	27.5	T-B	B2-D3	23.36	Beta	
5-Bm	6	Right	Drone-Right (DR)	F#0	23.12	T-DR	F#0-D3	123.71		
5-Bm						DL-A	F#3-A0	-157.5		
5-Bm						DL-B	B2-A0	-95.97		
5-Bm						DL-DR	F#0-A0	4.38	Theta	
6-E	1	Left	Soprano (S)	G#3	207.65	S-A	E3-G#3	42.84	Gamma	
6-E	2	Right	Alto (A)	E3	164.81	S-B	E2-G#3	125.24		
6-E	3	Left	Tenor (T)	B2	123.47	S-DR	F#0-G#3	184.53		
6-E	4	Right	Bass (B)	E2	82.41	T-A	E3-B2	-41.34	Gamma	
6-E	5	Left	Drone-Left (DL)	A0	27.5	T-B	E2-B2	41.06	Gamma	
6-E	6	Right	Drone-Right (DR)	F#0	23.12	T-DR	F#0-B2	100.35		
6-E						DL-A	E3-A0	-137.31		
6-E						DL-B	E2-A0	-54.91		
6-E						DL-DR	F#0-A0	4.38	Theta	
7-A	1	Left	Soprano (S)	A3	220	S-A	E3-A3	55.19		
7-A	2	Right	Alto (A)	E3	164.81	S-B	A2-A3	110		
7-A	3	Left	Tenor (T)	C#3	138.59	S-DR	F#0-A3	196.88		
7-A	4	Right	Bass (B)	A2	110	T-A	E3-C#3	-26.22	Beta	
7-A	5	Left	Drone-Left (DL)	A0	27.5	T-B	A2-C#3	28.59	Beta	
7-A	6	Right	Drone-Right (DR)	F#0	23.12	T-DR	F#0-C#3	115.47		
7-A						DL-A	E3-A0	-137.31		
7-A						DL-B	A2-A0	-82.5		
7-A						DL-DR	F#0-A0	4.38	Theta	

Electronic Brain Etude:
A Binaural Arpeggio Loop in Six Parts
MEASURE 14 BINAURAL MAPPING

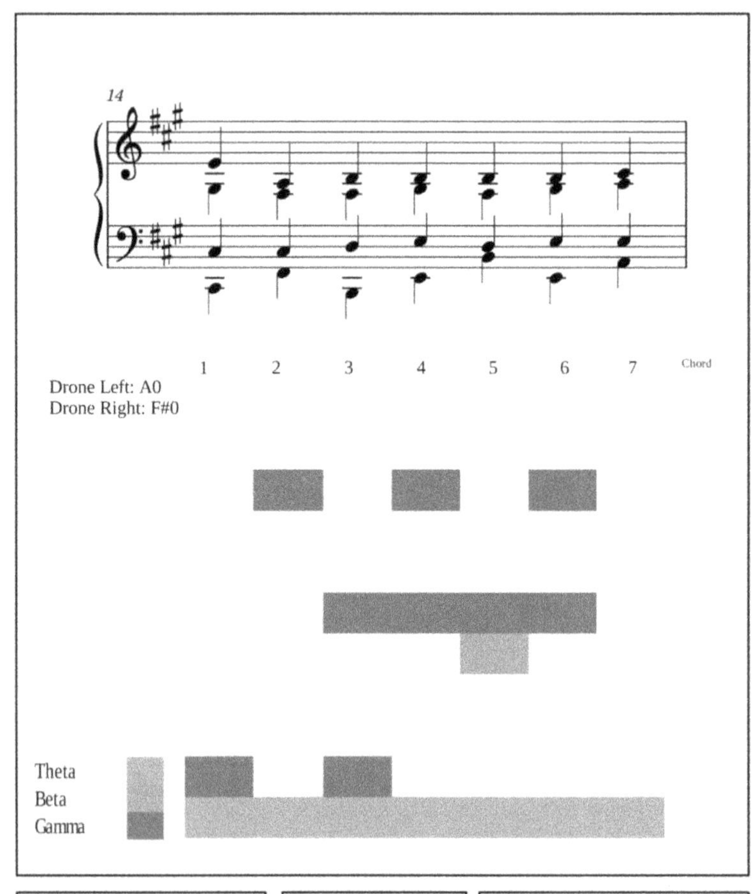

Chord Progression	Binaural Ranges	Intervals
C#m-F#m-Bm-E-Bm-E-A	Delta: 0.5-4Hz	S-A: Soprano/Alto
	Theta: 4-8Hz	S-B: Soprano/Bass
Parts	Alpha: 8-13Hz	S-DR: Soprano/Drone-Right
1-Soprano/High (L)	Beta: 13-30Hz	T-A: Tenor/Alto
2-Alto/MedHigh(R)	Gamma: 30-42Hz	T-B: Tenor/Bass
3-Tenor/MedLow(L)	(Absolute Values)	T-DR: Tenor/Drone-Right
4-Bass/Low(R)		DL-A: Drone-Left/Alto
5-Drone-Left(L)		DL-B: Drone-Left/Bass
6-Drone-Right(R)		DL-DR: Drone-Left/Drone-Right

Electronic Brain Etude: A Binaural Arpeggio Loop in Six Parts
MEASURE 14 BINAURAL MAPPING

Chord	Part #	Side	Part Name	Note	Freq (Hz)	Interval Name	Interval Val	Freq Diff (Hz)	Binaural Type
1-C#m	1	Left	Soprano (S)	E4	329.63	S-A	G#3-E4	121.98	
1-C#m	2	Right	Alto (A)	G#3	207.65	S-B	C#2-E4	260.33	
1-C#m	3	Left	Tenor (T)	C#3	138.59	S-DR	F#0-E4	306.51	
1-C#m	4	Right	Bass (B)	C#2	69.3	T-A	G#3-C#3	-69.06	
1-C#m	5	Left	Drone-Left (DL)	A0	27.5	T-B	C#2-C#3	69.29	
1-C#m	6	Right	Drone-Right (DR)	F#0	23.12	T-DR	F#0-C#3	115.47	
1-C#m						DL-A	G#3-A0	-180.15	
1-C#m						DL-B	C#2-A0	-41.8	Gamma
1-C#m						DL-DR	F#0-A0	4.38	Theta
2-F#m	1	Left	Soprano (S)	A3	220	S-A	F#3-A3	35	Gamma
2-F#m	2	Right	Alto (A)	F#3	185	S-B	F#2-A3	127.5	
2-F#m	3	Left	Tenor (T)	C#3	138.59	S-DR	F#0-A3	196.88	
2-F#m	4	Right	Bass (B)	F#2	92.5	T-A	F#3-C#3	-46.41	
2-F#m	5	Left	Drone-Left (DL)	A0	27.5	T-B	F#2-C#3	46.09	
2-F#m	6	Right	Drone-Right (DR)	F#0	23.12	T-DR	F#0-C#3	115.47	
2-F#m						DL-A	F#3-A0	-157.5	
2-F#m						DL-B	F#2-A0	-65	
2-F#m						DL-DR	F#0-A0	4.38	Theta
3-Bm	1	Left	Soprano (S)	B3	246.94	S-A	F#3-B3	61.94	
3-Bm	2	Right	Alto (A)	F#3	185	S-B	B1-B3	185.2	
3-Bm	3	Left	Tenor (T)	D3	146.83	S-DR	F#0-B3	223.82	
3-Bm	4	Right	Bass (B)	B1	61.74	T-A	F#3-D3	-38.17	Gamma
3-Bm	5	Left	Drone-Left (DL)	A0	27.5	T-B	B1-D3	85.09	
3-Bm	6	Right	Drone-Right (DR)	F#0	23.12	T-DR	F#0-D3	123.71	
3-Bm						DL-A	F#3-A0	-157.5	
3-Bm						DL-B	B1-A0	-34.24	Gamma
3-Bm						DL-DR	F#0-A0	4.38	Theta
4-E	1	Left	Soprano (S)	B3	246.94	S-A	G#3-B3	39.29	Gamma
4-E	2	Right	Alto (A)	G#3	207.65	S-B	E2-B3	164.53	
4-E	3	Left	Tenor (T)	E3	164.81	S-DR	F#0-B3	223.82	
4-E	4	Right	Bass (B)	E2	82.41	T-A	G#3-E3	-42.84	Gamma
4-E	5	Left	Drone-Left (DL)	A0	27.5	T-B	E2-E3	82.4	
4-E	6	Right	Drone-Right (DR)	F#0	23.12	T-DR	F#0-E3	141.69	
4-E						DL-A	G#3-A0	-180.15	
4-E						DL-B	E2-A0	-54.91	
4-E						DL-DR	F#0-A0	4.38	Theta
5-Bm	1	Left	Soprano (S)	B3	246.94	S-A	F#3-B3	61.94	
5-Bm	2	Right	Alto (A)	F#3	185	S-B	B2-B3	123.47	
5-Bm	3	Left	Tenor (T)	D3	146.83	S-DR	F#0-B3	223.82	
5-Bm	4	Right	Bass (B)	B2	123.47	T-A	F#3-D3	-38.17	Gamma
5-Bm	5	Left	Drone-Left (DL)	A0	27.5	T-B	B2-D3	23.36	Beta
5-Bm	6	Right	Drone-Right (DR)	F#0	23.12	T-DR	F#0-D3	123.71	
5-Bm						DL-A	F#3-A0	-157.5	
5-Bm						DL-B	B2-A0	-95.97	
5-Bm						DL-DR	F#0-A0	4.38	Theta
6-E	1	Left	Soprano (S)	B3	246.94	S-A	G#3-B3	39.29	Gamma
6-E	2	Right	Alto (A)	G#3	207.65	S-B	E2-B3	164.53	
6-E	3	Left	Tenor (T)	E3	164.81	S-DR	F#0-B3	223.82	
6-E	4	Right	Bass (B)	E2	82.41	T-A	G#3-E3	-42.84	Gamma
6-E	5	Left	Drone-Left (DL)	A0	27.5	T-B	E2-E3	82.4	
6-E	6	Right	Drone-Right (DR)	F#0	23.12	T-DR	F#0-E3	141.69	
6-E						DL-A	G#3-A0	-180.15	
6-E						DL-B	E2-A0	-54.91	
6-E						DL-DR	F#0-A0	4.38	Theta
7-A	1	Left	Soprano (S)	C#4	277.18	S-A	A3-C#4	57.18	
7-A	2	Right	Alto (A)	A3	220	S-B	A2-C#4	167.18	
7-A	3	Left	Tenor (T)	E3	164.81	S-DR	F#0-C#4	254.06	
7-A	4	Right	Bass (B)	A2	110	T-A	A3-E3	-55.19	
7-A	5	Left	Drone-Left (DL)	A0	27.5	T-B	A2-E3	54.81	
7-A	6	Right	Drone-Right (DR)	F#0	23.12	T-DR	F#0-E3	141.69	
7-A						DL-A	A3-A0	-192.5	
7-A						DL-B	A2-A0	-82.5	
7-A						DL-DR	F#0-A0	4.38	Theta

Electronic Brain Etude:
A Binaural Arpeggio Loop in Six Parts
MEASURE 15 BINAURAL MAPPING

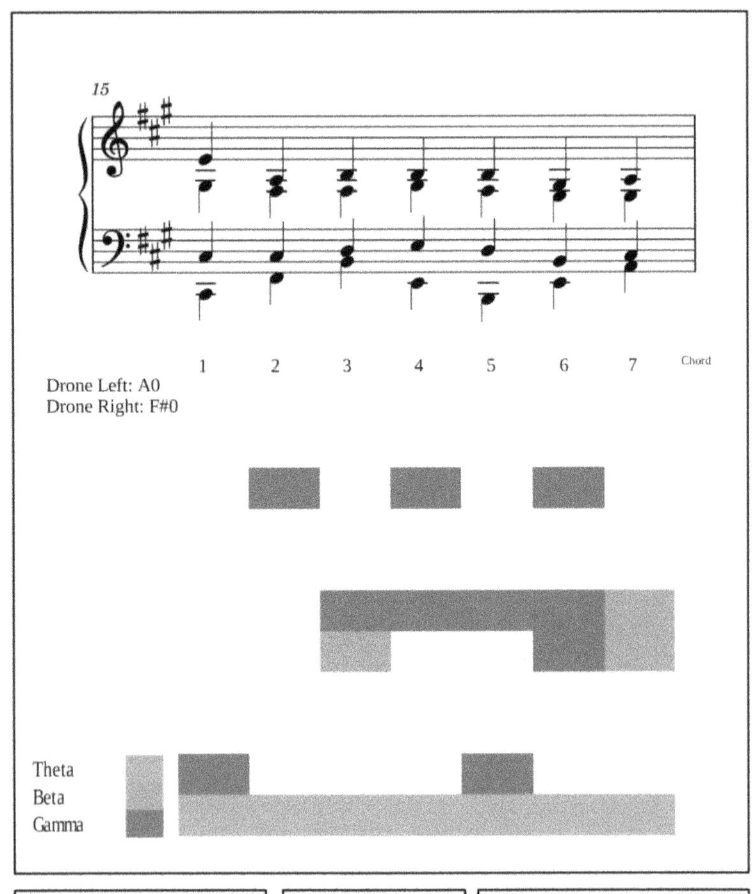

<table>
<tr><td>

Chord Progression
C#m-F#m-Bm-E-Bm-E-A

Parts
1-Soprano/High (L)
2-Alto/MedHigh(R)
3-Tenor/MedLow(L)
4-Bass/Low(R)
5-Drone-Left(L)
6-Drone-Right(R)

</td><td>

Binaural Ranges
Delta: 0.5-4Hz
Theta: 4-8Hz
Alpha: 8-13Hz
Beta: 13-30Hz
Gamma: 30-42Hz
(Absolute Values)

</td><td>

Intervals
S-A: Soprano/Alto
S-B: Soprano/Bass
S-DR: Soprano/Drone-Right
T-A: Tenor/Alto
T-B: Tenor/Bass
T-DR: Tenor/Drone-Right
DL-A: Drone-Left/Alto
DL-B: Drone-Left/Bass
DL-DR: Drone-Left/Drone-Right

</td></tr>
</table>

Electronic Brain Etude:
A Binaural Arpeggio Loop in Six Parts
MEASURE 15 BINAURAL MAPPING

Chord	Part #	Side	Part Name	Note	Freq (Hz)	Interval Name	Interval Val	Freq Diff (Hz)	Binaural Type
1-C#m	1	Left	Soprano (S)	E4	329.63	S-A	G#3-E4	121.98	
1-C#m	2	Right	Alto (A)	G#3	207.65	S-B	C#2-E4	260.33	
1-C#m	3	Left	Tenor (T)	C#3	138.59	S-DR	F#0-E4	306.51	
1-C#m	4	Right	Bass (B)	C#2	69.3	T-A	G#3-C#3	-69.06	
1-C#m	5	Left	Drone-Left (DL)	A0	27.5	T-B	C#2-C#3	69.29	
1-C#m	6	Right	Drone-Right (DR)	F#0	23.12	T-DR	F#0-C#3	115.47	
1-C#m						DL-A	G#3-A0	-180.15	
1-C#m						DL-B	C#2-A0	-41.8	Gamma
1-C#m						DL-DR	F#0-A0	4.38	Theta
2-F#m	1	Left	Soprano (S)	A3	220	S-A	F#3-A3	35	Gamma
2-F#m	2	Right	Alto (A)	F#3	185	S-B	F#2-A3	127.5	
2-F#m	3	Left	Tenor (T)	C#3	138.59	S-DR	F#0-A3	196.88	
2-F#m	4	Right	Bass (B)	F#2	92.5	T-A	F#3-C#3	-46.41	
2-F#m	5	Left	Drone-Left (DL)	A0	27.5	T-B	F#2-C#3	46.09	
2-F#m	6	Right	Drone-Right (DR)	F#0	23.12	T-DR	F#0-C#3	115.47	
2-F#m						DL-A	F#3-A0	-157.5	
2-F#m						DL-B	F#2-A0	-65	
2-F#m						DL-DR	F#0-A0	4.38	Theta
3-Bm	1	Left	Soprano (S)	B3	246.94	S-A	F#3-B3	61.94	
3-Bm	2	Right	Alto (A)	F#3	185	S-B	B2-B3	123.47	
3-Bm	3	Left	Tenor (T)	D3	146.83	S-DR	F#0-B3	223.82	
3-Bm	4	Right	Bass (B)	B2	123.47	T-A	F#3-D3	-38.17	Gamma
3-Bm	5	Left	Drone-Left (DL)	A0	27.5	T-B	B2-D3	23.36	Beta
3-Bm	6	Right	Drone-Right (DR)	F#0	23.12	T-DR	F#0-D3	123.71	
3-Bm						DL-A	F#3-A0	-157.5	
3-Bm						DL-B	B2-A0	-95.97	
3-Bm						DL-DR	F#0-A0	4.38	Theta
4-E	1	Left	Soprano (S)	B3	246.94	S-A	G#3-B3	39.29	Gamma
4-E	2	Right	Alto (A)	G#3	207.65	S-B	E2-B3	164.53	
4-E	3	Left	Tenor (T)	E3	164.81	S-DR	F#0-B3	223.82	
4-E	4	Right	Bass (B)	E2	82.41	T-A	G#3-E3	-42.84	Gamma
4-E	5	Left	Drone-Left (DL)	A0	27.5	T-B	E2-E3	82.4	
4-E	6	Right	Drone-Right (DR)	F#0	23.12	T-DR	F#0-E3	141.69	
4-E						DL-A	G#3-A0	-180.15	
4-E						DL-B	E2-A0	-54.91	
4-E						DL-DR	F#0-A0	4.38	Theta
5-Bm	1	Left	Soprano (S)	B3	246.94	S-A	F#3-B3	61.94	
5-Bm	2	Right	Alto (A)	F#3	185	S-B	B1-B3	185.2	
5-Bm	3	Left	Tenor (T)	D3	146.83	S-DR	F#0-B3	223.82	
5-Bm	4	Right	Bass (B)	B1	61.74	T-A	F#3-D3	-38.17	Gamma
5-Bm	5	Left	Drone-Left (DL)	A0	27.5	T-B	B1-D3	85.09	
5-Bm	6	Right	Drone-Right (DR)	F#0	23.12	T-DR	F#0-D3	123.71	
5-Bm						DL-A	F#3-A0	-157.5	
5-Bm						DL-B	B1-A0	-34.24	Gamma
5-Bm						DL-DR	F#0-A0	4.38	Theta
6-E	1	Left	Soprano (S)	G#3	207.65	S-A	E3-G#3	42.84	Gamma
6-E	2	Right	Alto (A)	E3	164.81	S-B	E2-G#3	125.24	
6-E	3	Left	Tenor (T)	B2	123.47	S-DR	F#0-G#3	184.53	
6-E	4	Right	Bass (B)	E2	82.41	T-A	E3-B2	-41.34	Gamma
6-E	5	Left	Drone-Left (DL)	A0	27.5	T-B	E2-B2	41.06	Gamma
6-E	6	Right	Drone-Right (DR)	F#0	23.12	T-DR	F#0-B2	100.35	
6-E						DL-A	E3-A0	-137.31	
6-E						DL-B	E2-A0	-54.91	
6-E						DL-DR	F#0-A0	4.38	Theta
7-A	1	Left	Soprano (S)	A3	220	S-A	E3-A3	55.19	
7-A	2	Right	Alto (A)	E3	164.81	S-B	A2-A3	110	
7-A	3	Left	Tenor (T)	C#3	138.59	S-DR	F#0-A3	196.88	
7-A	4	Right	Bass (B)	A2	110	T-A	E3-C#3	-26.22	Beta
7-A	5	Left	Drone-Left (DL)	A0	27.5	T-B	A2-C#3	28.59	Beta
7-A	6	Right	Drone-Right (DR)	F#0	23.12	T-DR	F#0-C#3	115.47	
7-A						DL-A	E3-A0	-137.31	
7-A						DL-B	A2-A0	-82.5	
7-A						DL-DR	F#0-A0	4.38	Theta

A CASE STUDY OF FLATLINE PROMISES

By Michael Gallowglas

This present is a horrific un-horrorshow future.
click—scroll—click—scroll;
scrooooooooooolllll—click…
Pixels stream in ten thousand colors
and almost hypnotize me enough to forget
lies made by the media of my adolescence
about the neon chrome future I'd be living in.
Saint Gibson deliver me from this frakkin drek.
Where's my mailorder midnight lady
anime goddess I incubate in my spare bathtub?
I'm supposed to be having too much artificial sex
to worry about not having unintelligible
generative grammar checks offering
suggestions perilously close to plagiarism.
Will you accept these cookies was supposed
to have an entirely different meaning.
I'm supposed to surf the net directly
against my retinas instead of staring dumbly
at this tiny lump of circuits, plastic, and glass
I can't seem to put down. Whatever happened
to the credo of our unrealized future?
I'm supposed to live fast, die young.
I'm supposed to exist in style over substance.
I was supposed to burn out before this fading away.
Everything is fading to monochrome and grayscale
despite the overstimulation of colors.
Style—click through. Substance—scroll down.
click—scroll—click—scroll;
scrooooooooooolllll—click—click—click…
I was supposed to be more horrorshow than this.

After Franny Choi

THE LOSER
By Jardine Libaire

An actor spits up clam bisque
Kneeling at the toilet, he's good at this

Closeup on the star, her eyes dart

They drag JUNKIE #2 to the interrogation room
He babbles, faints two minutes in
Whatta waste a humanity, the cop says

Nightclub sidewalk, hot girl calls dealer
But the actress is healthy, happy,
sober & vegan in life
desperate to seem desperate
under the location's lavender neonlight

Slinking down a motel hallway, strangers cross paths
His hand steals into a handbag; no blinking

The lawyer in recovery, lead role, lonely & penitent,
Humorless, but by god he'll change the world
Eventually

Closeup on:
Airplane bottles in suitjacket pockets.
Silverfish in church basement carpets.

The suburban teenage runaway
always has a backpack
Hello Kitty or something that spells
F-O-R-F-E-I-T-E-D C-H-I-L-D-H-O-O-D

Main character stands
Reluctant
at the meeting,
head hangs low
Then
makes everyone cry
Drops mic

Snow falls, but she sees powder

Angle on: addict scratching his nose

She confesses
The judge says: *Speak louder*

The woman playing the mother
says sternly but with kindness
but with disdain but also awareness
and despair, to her husband,
on their yacht (they're millionaires!)
about their on-screen stepdaughter:
It's time to let go, we've finally lost her

But I'm seven years lucid and
Just walking my dog
Down a suddenly discovered alley
In my own neighborhood
Masses of magenta flowers
Gold coins of sunshine
Rainbow graffiti on the wall
We're lost in the sweet hush
of shadows inside shadows

from
BOOTLESS GRIPS
By A∴ A∴ Ron Sheppard
samplings from *Chapter the Eighth* and *Chapter the Ninth* and *Chapter the Twenty-fourth*

Pitch graduated into ever-increasing light, warm by sight of flickering flame which did dance away shadowed gargoyle partners, them tiptoeing across cathedral walls into curved corners of ever-expanding vaulted heights. Occasional drops and moments of spilt buds blossomed into petals of wounds fresh, into yonder skeletal splinters as curdled thorn masses confounding powdered wigs. As he continued along, opulent jackets and war-decorated coats appeared bunched and inflated due to contents of meat. Supple walls of peach around him eventually extended into expanded grandiosity of arc to expose cold cavern of disheveled ballroom; its contents, remnants of brio held in time as if punctured by pins leaving mid-beat anticipation to hang and drip with echoing red *drop … drop … drop …* It was there, in that vast room, Notierra had interrupted remaining scurry, within dark blankets of viscidity, opulent sirens oft still mid-plunder. Under the grand organ even. Upon marble cold, gurglings gathered thick, popping last words from severed throat, he witnessed one such beaut writhing her many finned snakes to open feasting teeth and sink upon a noble's remaining body whole.

Blood of variation, both dark and vibrant, clouded the silk-lined interior of The Rose beyond central nave. Extending in many directions, sounds of slaughter persisted. This ruin, Her Lady Loundre's school of deflowered conchubinas had been loosed as murder of sprite, them each spattering – bloodletting by way of exposed tracts of seed, bowel and reed. Among them, amongst layered howls of masochistic device, Notierra remained unsuccessful in pinpointing the Debutante's whereabouts. Breathing interstitial fluid beyond mere crimson and bile pale, emptied contents of bladders, scrotal sacks, mucus-lined sinuses and watering eyes, such vital herbs pursed Notierra to experience a vampyre's hair-of-the-dog wafting D-aspartic and N-methyl: a fisherman's sail of oyster, mussel and zinc-shucking. Puppies of the sea gnawed at libidos' aphrodisiac across harpsichord instruments having been played in new fashion. White worn by men had been reduced to fillets grinning with stares upward at chandeliers quaking. White coats had absorbed waterfalls of colors creamy – cabernet christening. Primordial urge pounded throughout Notierra's own loin until he found himself mounting ribbons of gnawing upon his own lobster shell appetizer. Pass lemon and crackers, please.

Cast and catch, with and without release; is it not in wont of throwing thy net for bountiful feast? The place is here as is the host who cannot forget the wine, for the smorgasbord is divine if one is to dine on the feasters and not the beast. Flowers for graving into another under The Rose; is it to be of the utmost grave to indulge upon the host-of-hosts' traveling amongst the droves whom might herself be wined? Split open thy coats! Split apart thy seams! For it be dinnertime! Silken glove may be removed to rebuff pork ribs unsavory or within crispiness par; the bark, likewise, not tender. Tear and smear upon the wall all that is ripe, all that is fowl. For the night could not get younger than we. Tonight ends the day whose coming out will treat in finding that orbs are not round – under and through with blunt knives will be found the treasures we seek as sweetbreads retain their sweetness but meatheads pass ultimately sweeter. Indulge! Indulge! And find the night fighting to keep its hobbledehoy satisfactory, complete with natural sauces, juices, gravy and other condiments for the beautiful ones who upon them now dine!

It was the *tap tap* upon his shoulder that moved him 'round, his own personal succubus having taken flight before such cause and touch.... There she was, his treasure last found!

"Madam, Loundre, I chill with warmth upon remembering never having known, only now to be again."

"Lord Notierra, your presence was let known upon me 2 leagues out. The port welcomes promises as they return, and for that I as well welcome thee. Hush now and let this moment live its longevity…. Hither!"

She grabbed hold of Notierra's arm tightly and thrust him into secret compartments alongside. The first of which was a hidden door not far away. A brisk turn brought them into a long service corridor functionally equipped with sconces sculpted into elongated tentacles with ever longer testicles holding flares of golden resonance. Through a door and down another holey trail, a third place even lower beneath macabre massacre, she led him until there finally came a time when his hidden flesh was able to confront that of Her Excellency's own.

She groped at his arms exuding excited longing, looking unto him with soft eyes of off-color satin surrounding fluttering curtains of deep black velvety feather. There was also a twist of not-so-obscured, tantalizing lip…. "Landry and folly quit me not. To see you with attention requiring such hubbub leaves me speechless and, alas, to have us alone. My dear Madam Loundre, I've wished for nothing more than to experience you. Touch my hands as you tantalize my arms and tell me of your situation. My listening is open as are my hearts."

She replied…. "My Lord had changed! Yet I still knew it to be thee although the images brought before me were quite different! We are safe for now but tell me, art thou foul or fair situated otherwise? Please. Breathe into me." Loundre reached with cascading fingers to mildly touch and run along his head's closest cornucopia.

> Dark matter … antimatter … more so, it is having knowledge as to the replication of nonmatter that propels The Collective Agency. Antiparticles do assist The Agency naturally by annihilating physical matter, or otherwise throwing it into other oblivion, away from current realms of reality – yet the formulation and

knowhow for the production of nonmatter remains sole focus.

It has been said, through information handed down in attempts to be transcribed, that their mission is to create that which cannot be created, yet still exists without volume or mass of any kind, that beyond time itself. If such insight can be trusted, larger enigmas remain....

Hair now blushed with rising senses of coral.... "Surely, Lord Notierra, whether from land, sea or dark matter, such words are only to be understood as blasphemy. Sex is one thing, death upon some quays, quite another. My mother, Eva, was surely immortalized by the double-edged sword flailed by my own Lord and Father; thrown from his heart and into his courts for her wrongdoings and such accusatory 'mishandling' ... breadcrumbs ... mere specks of a trail, regardless of her trial, fin to tail I shall quell follow!"

Lady Loundre, because she much anticipated Notierra's arrival, and, if for this anticipation alone, she would not have denied them their own slice of shared sushi within any one of her many halls – of The Rose, of which she was readily well acquainted – yet due to such expectation, she planned to take him someplace unique beyond the bustle of burgeoning bustles exposing erotic rows of teeth not her own, to any one of many a section on this, her special night.

She pressed the near wall's buzzer as they breathed into one another's mouths, gripping tongues, shaking upon the deal. Yes, any of The Rose's four inner pedals (the fifth wing currently used simply for pomp and entourage excluded) would have been more than suitable for this romancing of states, as well, the more intimate inner pedals should have provided an environment for administering such pleasure. She had slated their escape from debauchery into that of their own atop the centermost tier of six.

Ding – the lift timidly announced its arrival as the two fell into the space upon one another. His and her foreplay had evolved its course leaving them noodling each in wanton bawd. Residue from the night remained with her.... Digging around inside as a quick floss of vagina dentate, pinky nonchalant, Loundre removed bones of flesh that had stripped through ingestion with a giddy upturned eye and only slightly embarrassed chagrin.

"O' PULL DOWN THE SCREEN, SCRAWNY FAWN UTMOST FOUL!..."

One of each of the three stars of brilliance shines beyond shining and falls upon all in the space repugnant, redundant, repugnant, redundant, redundant, ant, ant, ant, t, t, t....

Proxima this and Proxima that, t, t, t ... – explanations of origins begin to sound redundant, repugnant ... et al. death has already cum. And after it came I left. Genitals are flesh filled with cancer applied to the face and arms already disproportionate in any way of understanding aesthetics. Eat.

For how many times can facsimiles be effective? My funny valentine isn't me ... is not mine ... is not a day, and yet each day is, inevitably, Valentine's Day.

In winter's song, I'll look below and remember you, my darling. From Autumn to Spring, you will owe each to me. You will own, and owe, each to me your soul not to be surrected from the ice below, the stomping pompous asses asking unanswerable questions about love and loving you that only I know as black pours from my sack, my mouth, my plaque.... Ice can only embrace you. Ice is your loving louse without malice, without callous, without counts upon your head until they own it down to your legs. Embraced, preserved and contained within transparent love of nature, even from your doughty legs, your mighty midsection, your determined breasts your heart and mind, encapsulate your unlovable sex until the thawing of Spring. Until that March begins, we skate upon

<blockquote>
your brow without full doubt or regret. At which point you thaw and mold before us in exhale although pore-ous.
</blockquote>

Hypocrisy is a fur coat made lead-laden. Enter stage left, the shpizzletizor.

It would not be mistakenly understated to say that, although Loundre had shied away from his first advance towards her to take her rouse of a kempt soul and body into his own, their cumingling upon reaching the 6th tier's peak outdoors on thin balcony was a fierce weaving together of existences fated to be matched, unattainable by the most emblazoned of lovers for which exotic ballads are composed, hoping to someday within one's fleeting life to partake, did then immediately occur between these two at hand. Notierra's body, as a fish with manufacturing another galaxy away by a species without need for procreation, found itself transforming into an instrument to be used for the sake of experiencing sincere passion alone. A flare stirred and roared deep from within. Such fire further darkened the charcoal hue of scales and flesh overall so that an outline of fireworks was the only contrastingly visible phenomenon to delineate silhouetted features. It was the Lady's presence, with all attention now his own, that advanced Notierra to such a state. It was her pearlescent plumpness of heightened flesh atop her own scales below, sparkling as rows of multifaceted gems, her scratching claws as loving red razors exploring pressure points otherwise remaining dormant inside him, her strands of strategically-piled bouffant now unfurling to fly freely in warm currents all encompassing, her bosom ripe and buoyant, waves of flowing femininity being thrust against him that awakened his consciousness beyond any he could ever have fathomed.

Against each of these, her vulnerable gifts given willingly, with copasetic violence, it was then that Notierra noticed additional metamorphosis in his own physicality begin to take shape. Such as his bodily contrasts had become even more indistinguishable as disappeared transparency against exuding explosions of heliotrope all along his Jacob's Ladder otherwise to sing, it complimented that of Lady Loundre's being as she escalated in becoming, instead, opaque tones increasingly more solid. Such Yin-Yang of foreplay swirled to unfold breaths with beatings of hearts, back and forth, in and out.

He felt he might cease to exist at that moment, prematurely leaving his body completely under her absolute possession. Instead, the burning Phoenix between them blossomed into unconscionable bewilderment of copasetic partaking.

Loundre's lower caudal did unfold as ripened peach split into two halves to ingest his own abaft stinger beneath dentate rows of biting.

Notierra's unprogrammed, unknown, as-of-late ignorant, yet currently ravenous sexual gadget, had emerged from within to become external. This such arm that pulled itself from his scaly tail was meant to be held tight by each of her Laden incisors. Fluid that flowed through him located punctures made upon the fully-grown phallus inside her torn-open mouth below. With devastation and surprise, pain ebbed quickly into heightened exaltation, a somehow out-of-body soothing. The sensations elevated him to another plane of awareness and although Loundre felt each emotion simultaneously herself, she greeted her own exulted level of rapture without surprise for she was quite aware of what his kind was capable of, if he himself was not.

Fables of The Edrik had been hushed, especially such stories as their current consummation, of which she had longed to uncover. The Oracle of The Great Abyss had laughed in her face, pulling on each of her earlobes aft anglerfish had chased her as she broke free from St. Lawrence's dome in a bursting of shards moving forward to consult her. Lord Leviathan himself had ineffectually swallowed Loundre in attempts to detain her from gaining such of any awareness of The Edrik. Her own making of myths was another story entirely, from which she obtained additional layers of pleasure as flashing pictures in mind – fluctuations between her many fantasies imagined of such act were now overlaid by what

her mind's eye saw currently looking down upon them together –
to cause a lashing of screams in justified ecstasy speckled with
terror. Physical and psychological touch scooped out in her what
she had long awaited in a lover. It was now, in turn, her own time
to experiment with knowledge she had dug up from redacted
history. Thus, from the depths of Loundre's loin, so it began that
shunned folklore became primordial truth.

She could feel the organ within her stir to awaken and slither
alive. The organ, all her own, uncoiled so that Loundre felt its
movements underneath sternum bright letting out another level of
screaming laugher in delight, in defiance, and in lust of the
moment so that Notierra himself expelled his own reaction of
extended black eye and mouth. He let go of his tight grip upon
Loundre's curves as her lengthy hunger-stricken blindworm
burrowed inside Notierra's new found geoduck he had only just
began to become acquainted with.

The Oracle was right!... an image of the old toothless urchin
pulled Loundre's head into her own as she relived the past.
"HAAAAAAA! Do not underestimate it, my dear flounder!" she
had said, "The shpizzletizor is strong within you!"

And so, her snake organ gained in girth and dove further inside
and down through the tip of Notierra's phallus tearing flesh hole
further apart. He let go of her completely, that is, of his external
grips yet unable to manage his own member's pulsating growth to
violate and simultaneously become violated by her own
penetration. Additionally, unable to pull from Loundre's dentata
as teeth angled back allowed for entry yet disallowed escape, he
relinquished any and all control. Each loosened grip that Notierra
lacked energy for due to the escalation of energetic blood pumping
harder into his member, Loundre more than made up for by pulling
him inch-by-inch closer to her, into her, into him. Siren sounds of
desperation from each continued until shpizzletizor had climbed
completely inside Notierra's bladder. And there it stayed and there
it wriggled for an incalculable amount of time as a serpent
ferociously cleaning out the den of its dinner. Friction lessened by

the ever increasing flowing of liquids, reaming of fresh-bored holes overwhelming – piercings along his shaft oozed until bulbous attributes were letted.

Bodies conjoined below, marinated in liquid thicker than the dark water surrounding them, as convulsions expelled wisps as cobweb floating above exhaled action. Essence of each, Loundre and Notierra, had by this time completely abandoned shells to find flowing currents in a multitude of orgasmic release ever climbing to new heights above. That is when death of a sort manifested, to blame French baguette with escargot sopped in melted butter.

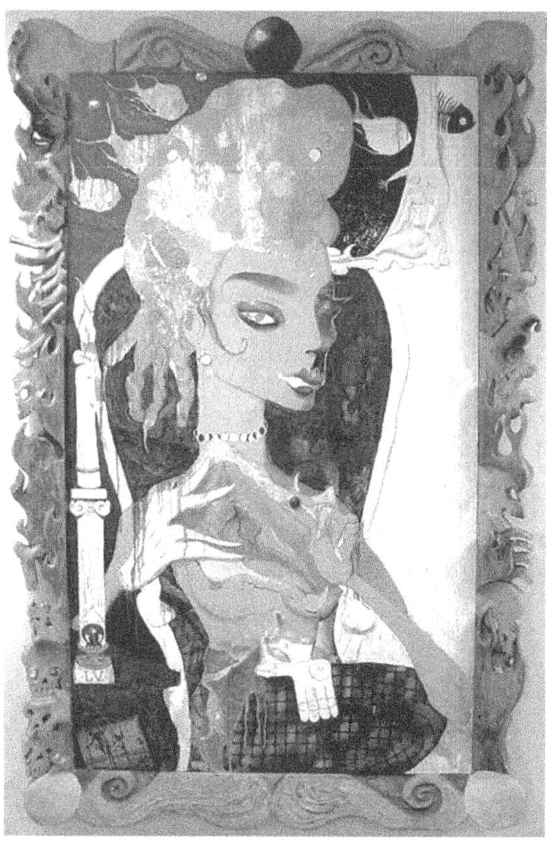

A Debutante's Eclipse by A∴A∴ Ron Sheppard

LITERARY AROUSAL –
AN INTERVIEW WITH PETER SCHUTES

Peter Schutes is a publisher of gay pornography and erotica literature. Pornography – *literature of the harlots* – is today thought of as a strictly visual format, but it has long textual history and today continues to thrive with publishers that are willing to take the risk, such as Mr. Schutes. Many books that are today considered classics were once banned as being obscene and pornographic. What does this say about our ever-shifting sense of morality and what is socially acceptable? And why is something as individual as private sexual arousal something that the powers-that-be would have the desire to control? With the current attacks on the LGBT+ community, such as the removal of the Pride flag from the Stonewall Monument, being out and proud is more important ever, and *Electronic Brain* applauds the work that Peter is doing for freedom of expression and pushing the boundaries of literary arousal.

Jean-Paul L. Garnier

JPG: *What was your introduction into pornography in its written form?*

PS: When I was a teen, I didn't know the first thing about sex. There was no Internet. My slightly older friend and I went to the Combat Zone in Boston, a neighborhood full of smut and sleaze. He popped into a dirty bookstore for me and bought me a pulp called "Bunkhouse Hunks." It was the first description of gay sex that I had ever read. It was a bit unrealistic, of course, but it was gold for me! I bought several dozen of those books over the years before they disappeared off the shelf. Now they're incredibly rare.

JPG: *What made you decide to start writing and publishing porn?*

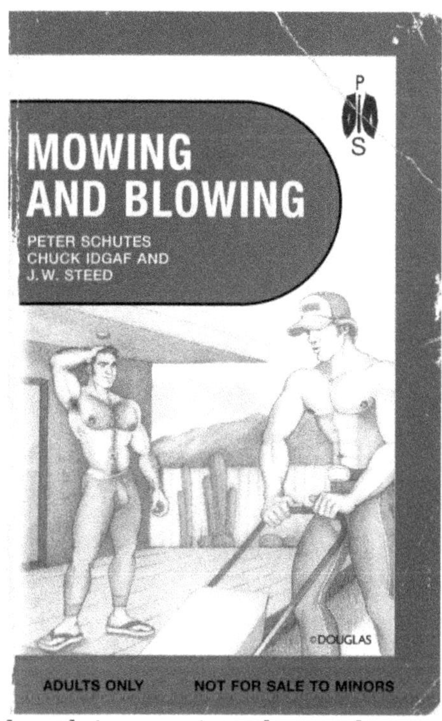

PS: Frankly, I missed those books that had disappeared from the shelves, and the shelves themselves disappearing as gay bookstores fell one by one. I made it my mission to recreate them, even if there were very few bookstores that would carry them. When I first started out, I was a bit ashamed of my predilection for smut, and I created Peter Schutes – a character who was born in 1896 and died in 1981. He was the author I had imagined creating "Bunkhouse Hunks." I wrote his autobiography – a novel-length journey into the tawdry sex life of an imaginary author.

Now I own my passions and my writing. I still write as Peter, but I'm not hiding behind him. I'm out about it to most of my friends and family. It's interesting how many closets we build or are built for us!

And pulp! Ah, pulp. When the Amazon AI got extremely fussy and started banning my stuff, I decided to jump ship and go with IngramSpark. They were hesitant to print my books, too, but I made an impassioned plea about the importance of First Amendment rights, and they saw my point. They didn't ban anything! I reached out to you and got the lowdown on IngramSpark. It was far more complicated than Amazon, but so rewarding. I was able to print the books on groundwood paper in pocket size. They look like the real deal!

JPG: *With book bans on the rise, specifically targeting LGBT+ books, what fears do you have for your press and how do you plan on fighting back?*

PS: As I mentioned, I've had several books banned on Amazon. Mostly ebooks, but even one paperback. Almost every one of my books has been banished to the "dungeon," which means it won't appear in searches of any kind unless the specific author or title is called out. The ban is real. When I tried to find out why, I got a cryptic answer. "You should know."

Several of the books I wrote were on taboo subjects that totally passed the censors with heterosexual authors. I don't know for sure, but I think they have a "strike" system, and just by being queer, a book is already one strike down from its heterosexual counterpart.

As for real fears: Project 2025 had a long, seemingly far-fetched section about the importance of jailing pornographers. Their position on trans folk seemed far-fetched to me, too, but it turned out to be as real as it gets. If they follow through, I may have to close up shop, and, who knows, spend a few years in jail for writing and publishing this stuff. I hope not.

JPG: *Pornography is largely considered to be a visual medium (despite the meaning of the word), what is special and titillating about text-based porn?*

PS: I recall a study that identified three forms of erotic arousal – visual, aural, and sensual (touch). It left out the erotic response to the written word, which is a fourth form of arousal. I don't think it's as rare as I once believed. It's the only one not tied directly to a sense, but rather, the imagination. I get off on all four, but I'd say literary arousal is my favorite. By allowing the reader to conjure up their own imagery and sounds, it has a limitless quality. If I write that someone is "well-endowed" it can have a myriad of meanings to the reader. One reader might imagine an elephant trunk while another imagines a modest, slightly above-average dick. It's an art to balance between the definite and the indefinite in description and story. I'm forever perfecting that art.

JPG: *What challenges have you faced with distribution for your press and what has been the response from bookstores about the nature of the books?*

PS: Aside from the aforementioned bans and dungeons, I haven't seen a lot of other challenges. I've emailed and called up bookstores and asked if they would take my books. The queer bookstores were mostly very receptive. They know that smut sells, and it's a nice complement to their other offerings.

  Some "hipster" bookstores were sort of insulting. One of my cover illustrators lives in Dallas, and she recommended a store there that she said was cool and the perfect fit for my erotica. They weren't. They said, "We don't have a shelf for that sort of stuff." Now, that was Texas, which already says quite a bit. But even the two main independent bookstores in the gay mecca of Palm Springs were pretty chilly when I stopped by. Q Trading, the dirty bookstore, was overjoyed, though, and they carry my stuff. It's right next to the Tool Shed, so be sure to stop by and support them. Space Cowboy in Joshua Tree is another one I can't recommend enough!

JPG: *Apparently, women make up the majority of erotica readers, why do you think this is the case?*

PS: Women make up the majority of readers, period. Or so I'm told. I cannot pretend to know why so many of them are drawn to gay porn. If I had to guess, I think it might create some sort of safe space for them to explore their sexuality outside of the context of a grabby straight guy who wants to ravish them as he sees fit. That's just a shot in the dark, though. I should ask some of my women readers to weigh in. Although I truly think my writing is so brutal and hypermasculine, it couldn't possibly appeal to a female reader. But I might be wrong about that.

I noticed that the majority of my one-star reviews came from female readers, while the majority of my five-star reviews came from people identifying as men.

JPG: *Where would you mark the distinction between porn / erotica / smut etc.?*

PS: I could go the dictionary route and talk about the Greek origin of the word pornography, but it's a bit too simple. Porn, to me, is what you see on "Pornhub" and other portals. In the days of my imaginary author Peter, porn was a film you saw at a theater and, later, a video you watched for 25 cents in a booth, often with a stranger on the other side of the wall and a glory hole between you. It is a visual medium, although literature can be labeled "pornographic."

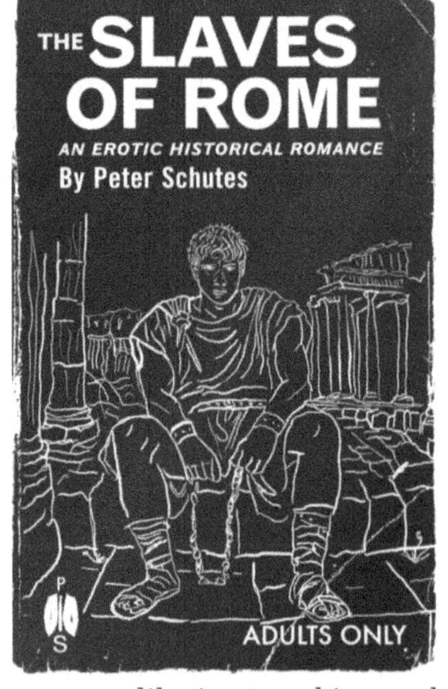

Erotica is written and recorded fiction focused on sex and sexuality. It can have a visual component, like in a graphic novel, but it is primarily based on the written or spoken word. It can be anywhere on the spectrum from sweet, romantic and tender to rough and rude. Again, that's my take on it, not necessarily from the dictionary.

Smut is a subset of erotica, with a large overlap into pornography. Smut is prurient – designed primarily to arouse the reader, and it is much more focused on the nitty-gritty of sex. It's an old-fashioned word, meant to be pejorative. I have embraced it, much like I now own the word "queer." I'm a smut-monger. A purveyor of tawdry tales. And proud of it!

JPG: *You also work as a volunteer librarian at the Tom of Finland Foundation. What has working with erotica of the past taught you about the nature of sexuality, and where do you think porn is headed in the future?*

PS: I have seen SO much variety in the library. We work only with books and magazines, and the collection doesn't include films or videos. There are things that may be too taboo to mention, but they are such an important glimpse into the variety of sexual experiences and the permission to tell them over the decades. There are muscle mags, nudist periodicals, coffee table books, fetish zines…you name it, they probably have it. They have a massive pulp collection, too. The graphic novels alone take up two shelves.

What I learned from cataloging so many of these books and magazines is that people can get turned on by just about anything. I'll bet there are people who have an orgasm thinking about the color blue. Certainly yellow and brown.

I saw a book there that I believe was one possible future of porn in book form. It was a series of sexual collages with QR codes. When you scan the code, the images appear as gifs on your phone, gyrating in kaleidoscopic swirls of dicks and butts. It blew my mind.

I have yet to experience VR porn. I think I might have aged out of that demographic. It feels icky when I think about it. AI porn is getting to the point that it's not quite uncanny anymore. By uncanny I mean you could tell something was off. Now, you have to just say, "I think this guy is fake, but I can't really be sure."

I look so much to the past with my pulp paperbacks. I'm not sure if some Gen-Xers are nostalgic for the slow downloads, when a picture took a minute to download from the BBS on a 9600 baud modem. I remember it, but it doesn't live in my heart in the same way that pulps do. I guess you always remember your first love, and mine was before I had a computer.

Do millennials miss Yahoo Groups? Will that be nostalgia for them? It's hard to say.

I see the future of erotic art at the Tom of Finland Foundation. The young artists in residence have such fresh new perspectives on the possibilities of erotic expression. I've seen rubber bondage scenes depicted in classical oil chiaroscuro. I've seen a video of Miss Piggy snorting cocaine off of Big Bird's cock. Those artists are pushing boundaries and exploring sexuality in ways I could have never imagined.

JPG: *While obscenity laws are currently changing, and are generally in flux, what do you think are the socially redeeming, and defensible, aspects of erotic literature?*

PS: What makes erotic literature defensible would be if it fits the criteria for any work of art or fiction – does it cause harm? Does it encourage and cause dangerous, harmful activity?

The example of harmful art from film school was Leni Riefenstahl's film *Triumph of the Will*. While a beautiful work of art, it was also highly irresponsible. It was so well-executed that it propelled Hitler into power.

From the point of view of erotica, we want to avoid prurient literature that encourages or causes cruelty, crime, or violence. There are laws that state that prurience itself is harmful, and I don't believe that. Prurience means that it causes the reader to get off. But literature that encourages its readers to get off to a child being tortured or used sexually crosses a line. I'd argue that the cutoff consent and therefore legal literary age of eighteen years in our country (twenty-one in some states) is a bit much. Sex was very dangerous and still is, but it usually happens shortly after puberty, whether parents like it or not.

I had sexual desires and fantasies before I reached eighteen. Most of us did. I am allowed to describe them (barely) in the context of a work of non-erotic fiction. As soon as such literature primarily sparks arousal, it becomes damnable. I would like to think that merely describing a consensual and arousing queer sex act between minors should be permissible, but it will get an author banned and condemned. Even suggesting that one of the partners appeared to be a bit underage got me permanently banned on one platform. So I have to

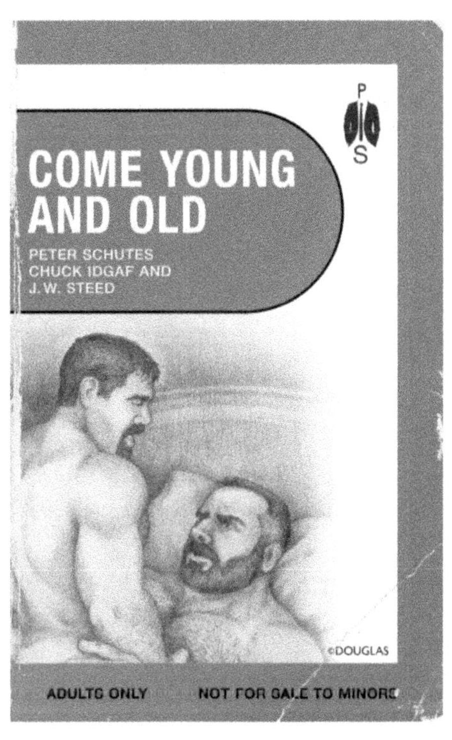

stay away from it. It is frustrating, however, that such an age difference or the appearance thereof is completely fine if the erotic scene is heterosexual and one of the partners is or appears to be young. That was why I wrote it – I'd seen hundreds of stories like that on that very same platform, but they were all heterosexual stories. Again, it is the "one strike if you're gay" rule that seems to be in play.

JPG: *In researching bookstores across the United States, I found that the vast majority are porn shops and Christian bookstores and reading rooms. What does this dichotomy say to you about American "values"?*

PS: This is a strange take on it, but here goes. I've met hundreds of Christians who are supportive of me as a gay man. Most of them would have no problem with me as a writer, and the few who do know were wildly supportive. One friend said, "I heartily support you to create smut!" I do hang out in some pretty rare circles, so I don't think my experience is the norm.

I visited a few Christian bookstores and found that a couple were a little more progressive than we'd think. But not all of them.

The dichotomy seems to illustrate the Puritan hypocrisy that began when our nation was founded. It's a poison that creeps into our daily lives, creating assumptions that are so ingrained, you would be considered a heretic for challenging them. Children should not be exposed to any kind of sexuality. Adults should not talk about or engage in sex. Sex is bad, evil, and shameful. And everybody wants it, including holy rollers and born agains. It is a national case of dissociative identity disorder.

JPG: *Porn is obviously a form of fantasy, where do you think this places it within the realm of speculative fiction, if at all?*

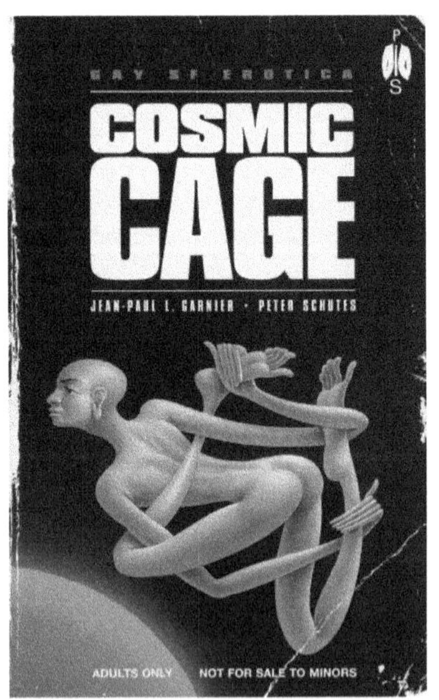

PS: As you probably know, since you carry the books, Peter Schutes Publishing has two queer erotic SF pulps with a third one on the way. Those stories are 100% speculative, of course.

I believe that the entire premise of Peter Schutes' autobiography was a smut-filled exploration of what it would be like to live with an appendage so enormous that it is a major handicap. In that sense, it was speculative, too. A majority of his stories focus on that theme.

The erotic subgenre called MPREG (male pregnancy) is also entirely speculative. What if men could carry a baby to term? My pulp trilogy *Tales of Two Daddies* explores three types of (barely) plausible male pregnancy and the drama surrounding the dads.

JPG: *Despite the popularity of romance fiction, why do you think porn is rarely discussed in regards to genre fiction?*

PS: Erotica is a recognized genre with its own shelf at the bookstore. I was in Georgia at a feminist bookshop and I was delighted to see that they carried *Bobbing Buoys and Salty Seamen*, one of my best pulps. So it exists, but you are correct that it is not discussed in polite circles.

Why not? We're a nation of prudes, and much of the world follows suit. You can go to prison or be sentenced to death for writing pornographic fiction in some places. It's on the vanguard of freedom of speech and expression. But all the religious and social hangups about sex label it a taboo subject.

I love bringing up Peter Schutes at a dinner party, to see people's reactions. Some folks lean in, fascinated, while others silently judge, blushing. When confronted, I call it my "Fifth Amendment fiction."

JPG: *Have you faced censorship in the work that you do, if so, what kinds, and how can writers and publishers protect themselves against the attempts to silence us?*

PS: Yes, I have faced corporate censorship and suppression from Amazon and a few eBook platforms. I have never had the courage to register my books with the Library of Congress. I'd read the pornography section of Project 2025 back in Summer 2024, so I knew what was coming down the pike.

How do we protect ourselves? What a sad question to have to ask in a country founded, in part, on the fundamental right of speech! I was born in the 1960s, and witnessed a nation that shed the shackles of sexual conformism and blossomed into a freer society.

I'm watching all that get taken away from us now. The right to an abortion and transgender protections were whisked away in an instant. Gay marriage and free speech are on the chopping block. The saddest part of the question is my final answer: we can only hope, vote, and try to fight back.

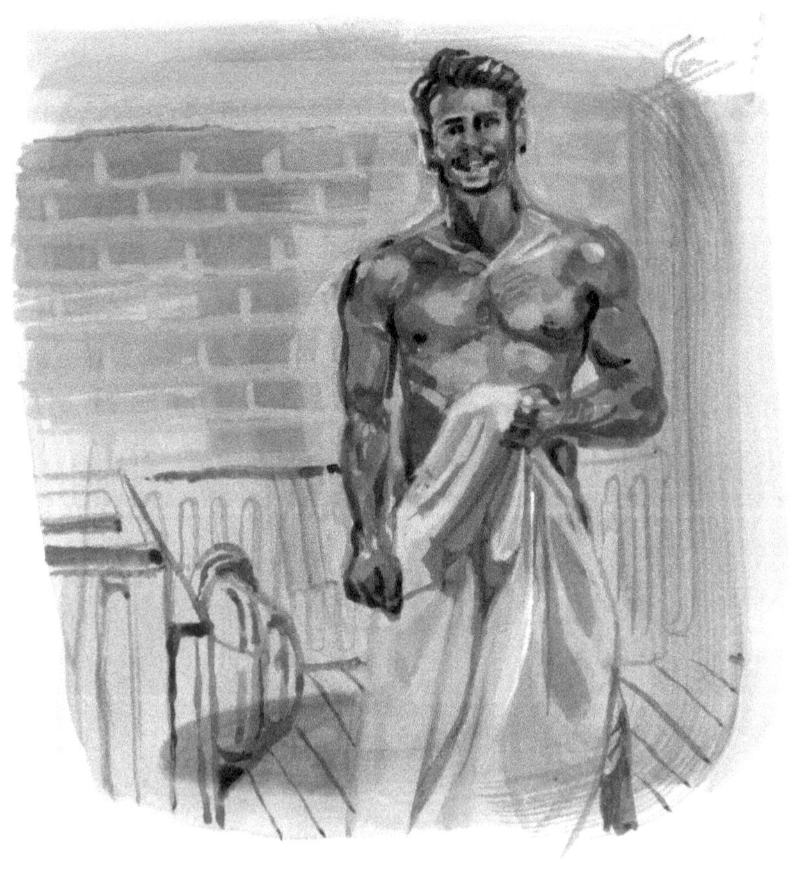

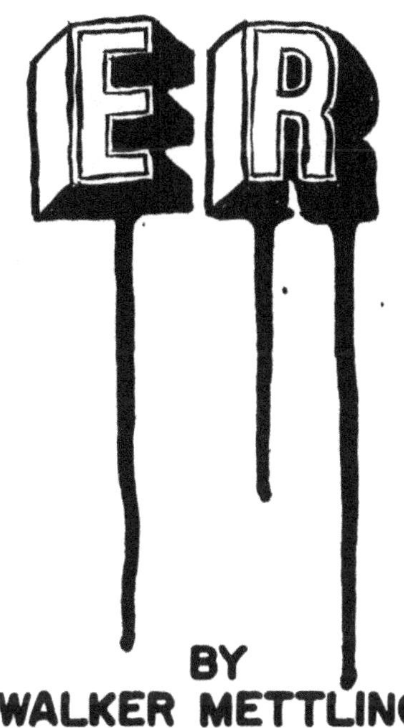

BY
WALKER METTLING

WARNING
DO NOT READ THIS STRAIGHT
THROUGH LIKE A NORMAL COMIC.
SIMILAR TO CHOOSE YR OWN
ADVENTUR OR FIGHTIN' FANTAZY YOU
GET TO DETERMINE WHICH WAY THE
STORY GOES.

AT THE BOTTOM OF EACH PANEL IT
WILL GIVE YOU AN OPTION OR
INSTRUCTION TO FLIP TO ANOTHER
PANEL. PRETTY SIMPLE.

HINT: WHAT I DO WITH THESE THINGS IS PLAY IT
THROUGH ALL THE WAY TO ONE ENDING, THEN I GO BACK
AND USE ALL FIVE FINGERS AS BOOK MARKS TO LOOK AT
ALL THE OTHER ROUTES. IF YOU'RE VARSITY YOU WRITE
DOWN THE OPTIONS AND MAKE YOUR OWN MAP! ENJOY!

YOU ARE IN THE EMERGENCY ROOM WITH YOUR ELDERLY MOM.

SHE WAS HOME ALONE WITH THE DOG. AND HE GOT TANGLED UP IN HER LEGS AND HER FACE HIT THE PAVEMENT. SHE IS CURRENTLY FEELING A SHARP AND CRUNCHY PAIN IN HER MOUTH...

IT'S A PLEASANT ENOUGH WAITING ROOM DESPITE SOME DISTANT YELLING AND A DEAD FISH FLOATING IN THE AQUARIUM.

THE NEWS IS PLAYING SILENTLY ON THE OVER HEAD MONITOR.

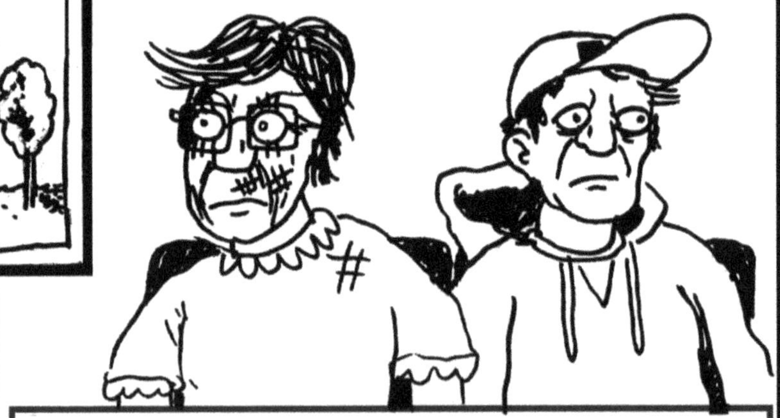

DO YOU SIT SILENTLY? FLIP TO 56

DO YOU WANT TO TALK TO THE OTHER PEOPLE WAITING? FLIP TO 12

DO YOU WANT TO WATCH THE NEWS? FLIP TO 55

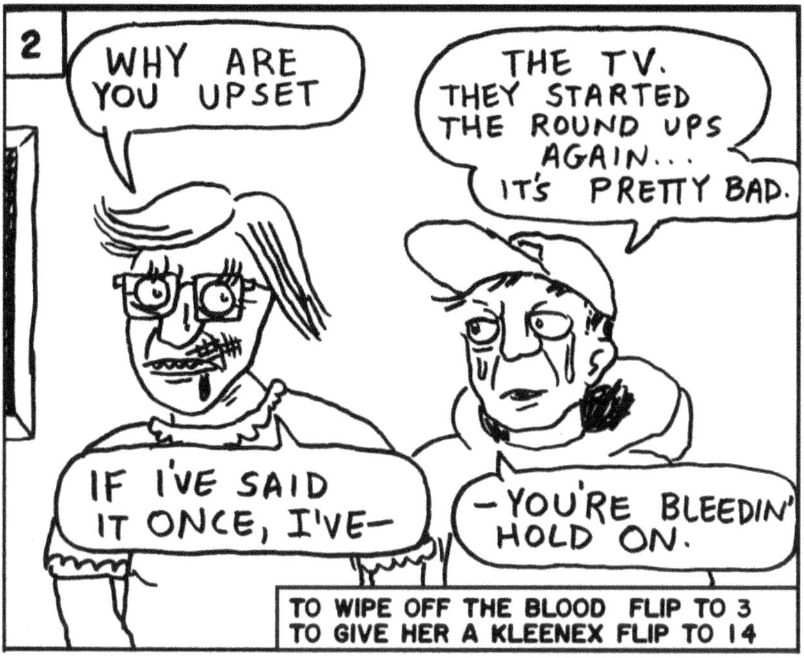

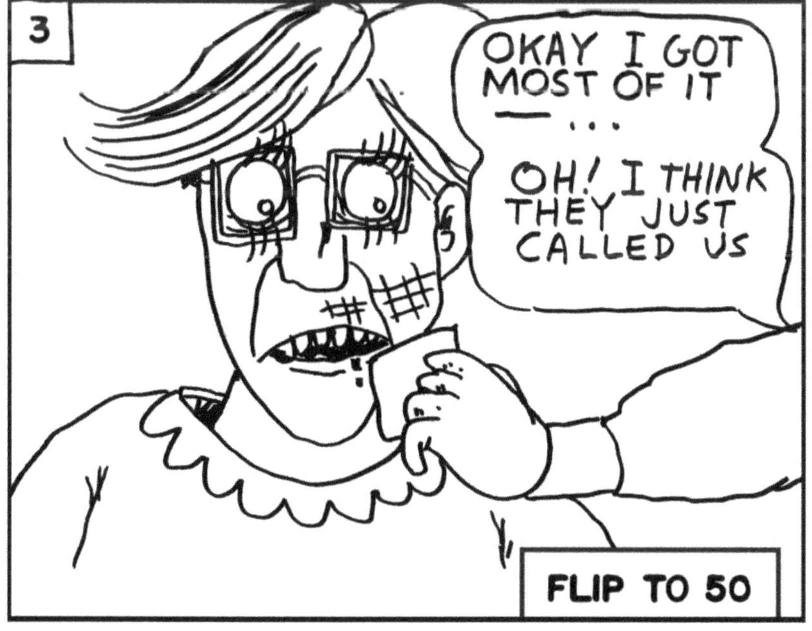

2
WHY ARE YOU UPSET
THE TV. THEY STARTED THE ROUND UPS AGAIN... IT'S PRETTY BAD.
IF I'VE SAID IT ONCE, I'VE—
—YOU'RE BLEEDIN' HOLD ON.
TO WIPE OFF THE BLOOD FLIP TO 3
TO GIVE HER A KLEENEX FLIP TO 14
3
OKAY I GOT MOST OF IT — ...
OH! I THINK THEY JUST CALLED US
FLIP TO 50

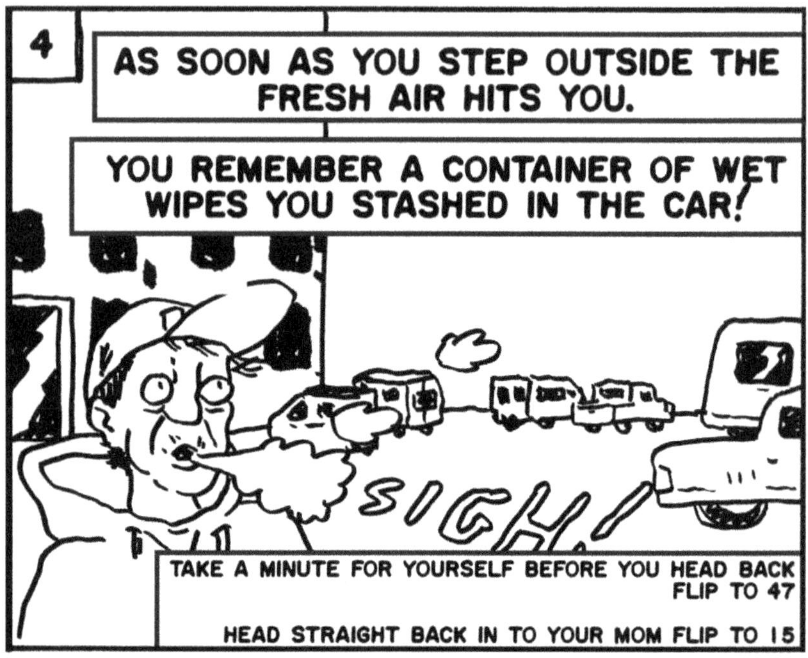

4
AS SOON AS YOU STEP OUTSIDE THE FRESH AIR HITS YOU.
YOU REMEMBER A CONTAINER OF WET WIPES YOU STASHED IN THE CAR!
SIGH!
TAKE A MINUTE FOR YOURSELF BEFORE YOU HEAD BACK FLIP TO 47
HEAD STRAIGHT BACK IN TO YOUR MOM FLIP TO 15

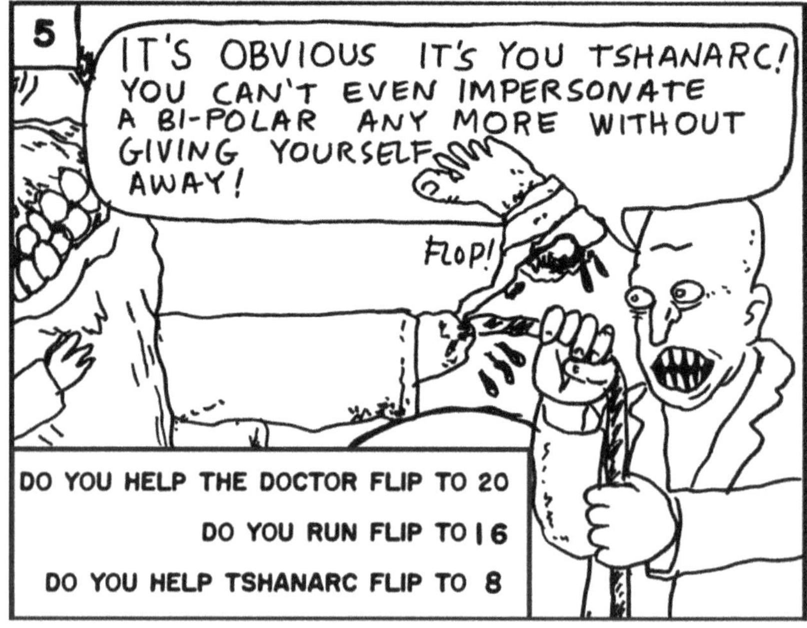

5
IT'S OBVIOUS IT'S YOU TSHANARC! YOU CAN'T EVEN IMPERSONATE A BI-POLAR ANY MORE WITHOUT GIVING YOURSELF AWAY!
FLOP!
DO YOU HELP THE DOCTOR FLIP TO 20
DO YOU RUN FLIP TO 16
DO YOU HELP TSHANARC FLIP TO 8

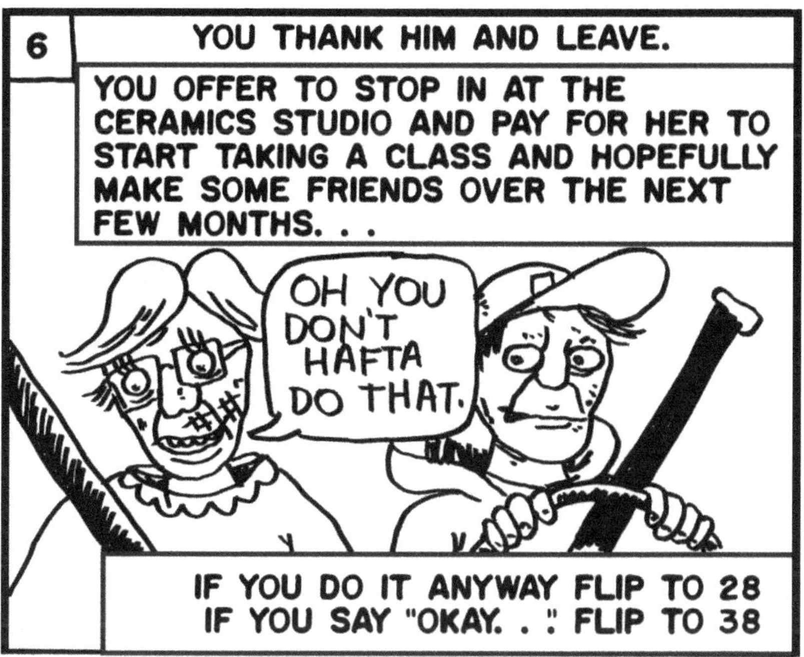
6
YOU THANK HIM AND LEAVE.
YOU OFFER TO STOP IN AT THE CERAMICS STUDIO AND PAY FOR HER TO START TAKING A CLASS AND HOPEFULLY MAKE SOME FRIENDS OVER THE NEXT FEW MONTHS. . .
OH YOU DON'T HAFTA DO THAT.
IF YOU DO IT ANYWAY FLIP TO 28
IF YOU SAY "OKAY. . ." FLIP TO 38

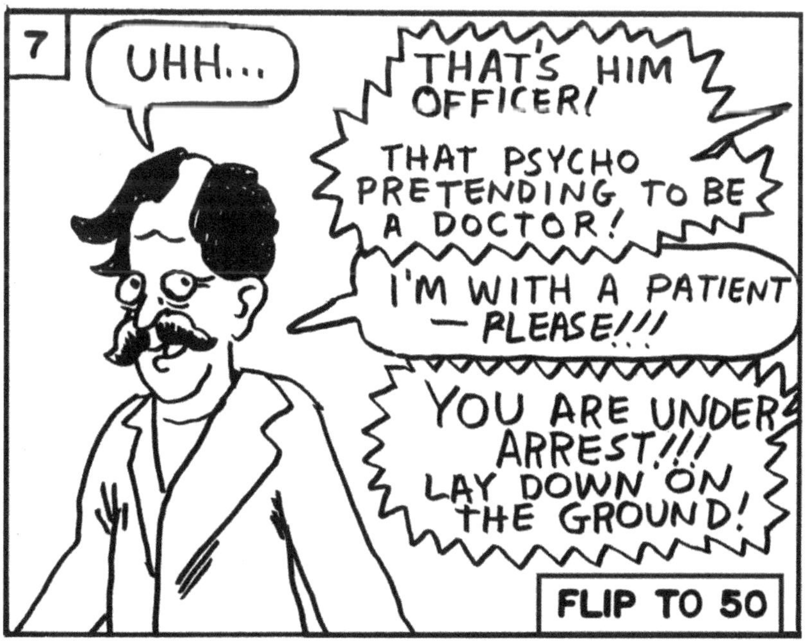
7
UHH...
THAT'S HIM OFFICER!
THAT PSYCHO PRETENDING TO BE A DOCTOR!
I'M WITH A PATIENT — PLEASE!!!
YOU ARE UNDER ARREST!!! LAY DOWN ON THE GROUND!
FLIP TO 50

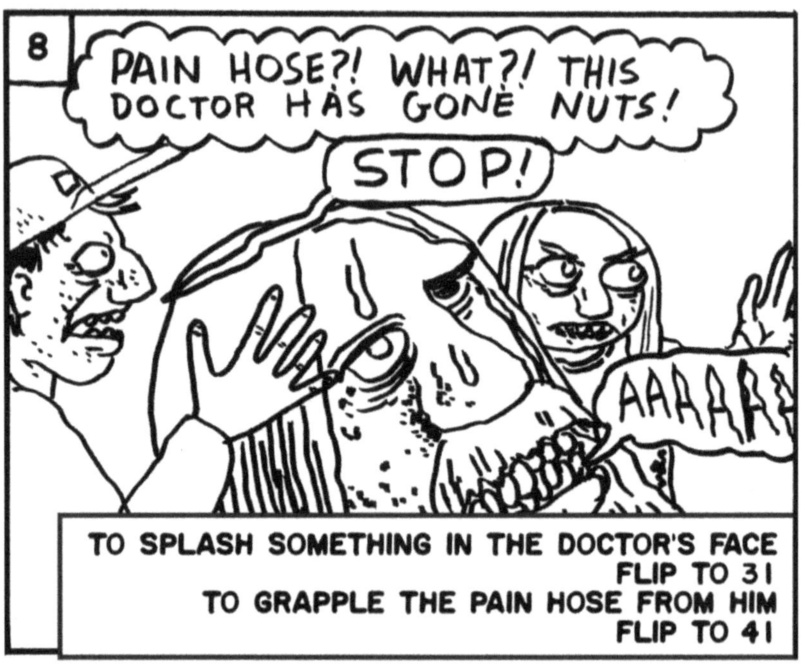
8
PAIN HOSE?! WHAT?! THIS DOCTOR HAS GONE NUTS!
STOP!
AAAAAA
TO SPLASH SOMETHING IN THE DOCTOR'S FACE
FLIP TO 31
TO GRAPPLE THE PAIN HOSE FROM HIM
FLIP TO 41

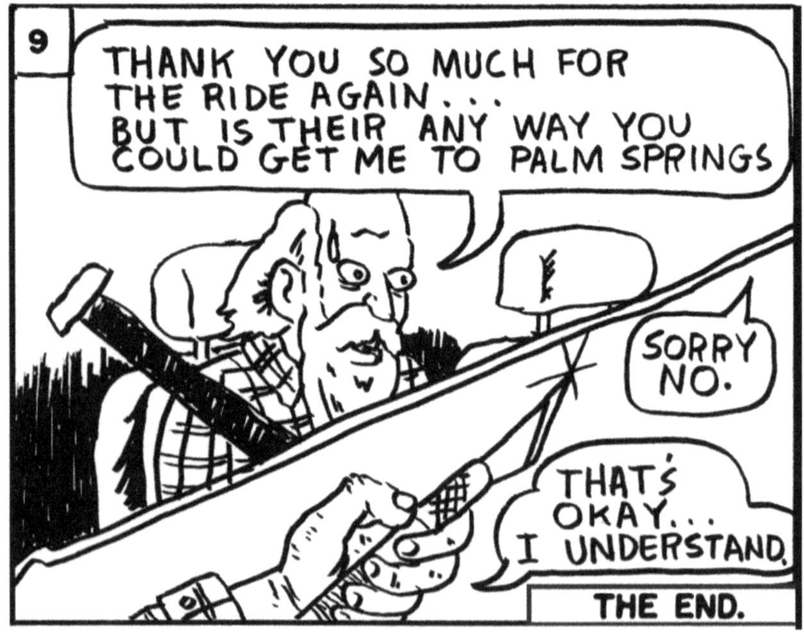
9
THANK YOU SO MUCH FOR THE RIDE AGAIN...
BUT IS THEIR ANY WAY YOU COULD GET ME TO PALM SPRINGS
SORRY NO.
THAT'S OKAY... I UNDERSTAND.
THE END.

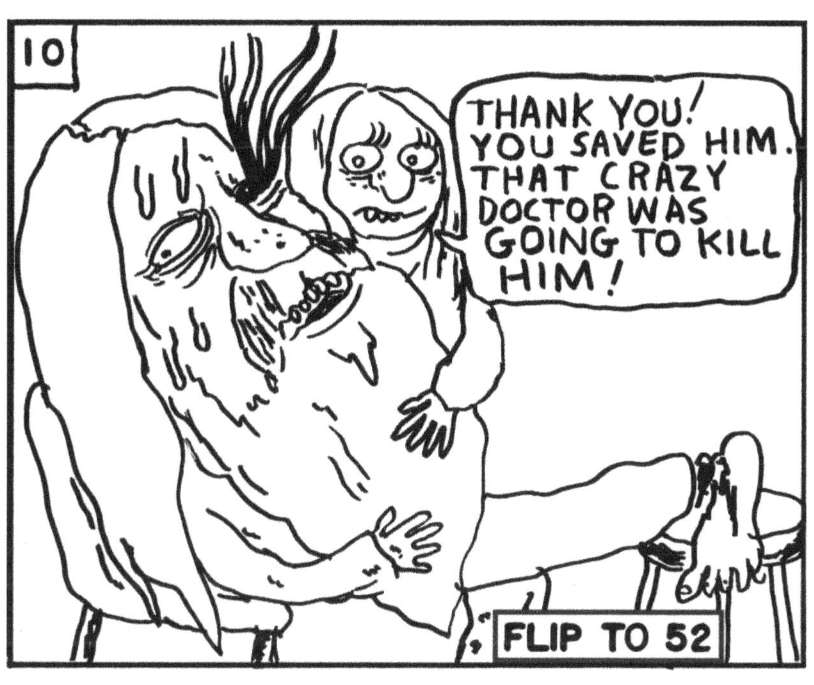
10
THANK YOU! YOU SAVED HIM. THAT CRAZY DOCTOR WAS GOING TO KILL HIM!
FLIP TO 52

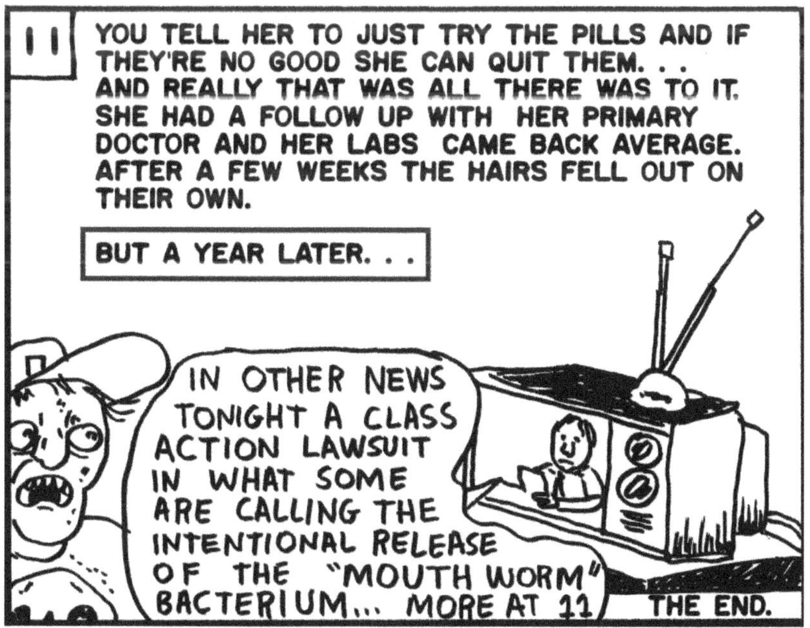
11
YOU TELL HER TO JUST TRY THE PILLS AND IF THEY'RE NO GOOD SHE CAN QUIT THEM. . . AND REALLY THAT WAS ALL THERE WAS TO IT. SHE HAD A FOLLOW UP WITH HER PRIMARY DOCTOR AND HER LABS CAME BACK AVERAGE. AFTER A FEW WEEKS THE HAIRS FELL OUT ON THEIR OWN.
BUT A YEAR LATER. . . .
IN OTHER NEWS TONIGHT A CLASS ACTION LAWSUIT IN WHAT SOME ARE CALLING THE INTENTIONAL RELEASE OF THE "MOUTH WORM" BACTERIUM... MORE AT 11
THE END.

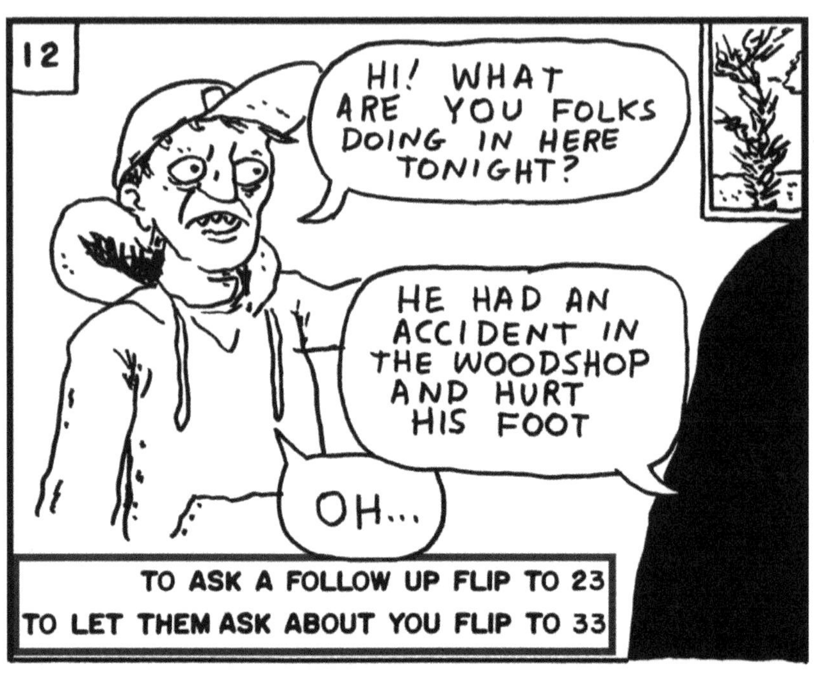

12
HI! WHAT ARE YOU FOLKS DOING IN HERE TONIGHT?
HE HAD AN ACCIDENT IN THE WOODSHOP AND HURT HIS FOOT
OH...
TO ASK A FOLLOW UP FLIP TO 23
TO LET THEM ASK ABOUT YOU FLIP TO 33

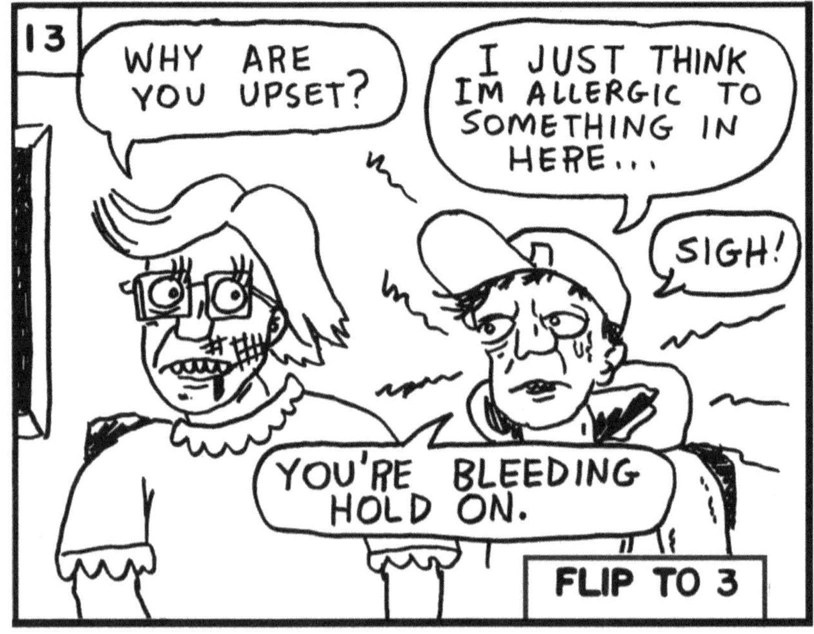

13
WHY ARE YOU UPSET?
I JUST THINK IM ALLERGIC TO SOMETHING IN HERE...
SIGH!
YOU'RE BLEEDING HOLD ON.
FLIP TO 3

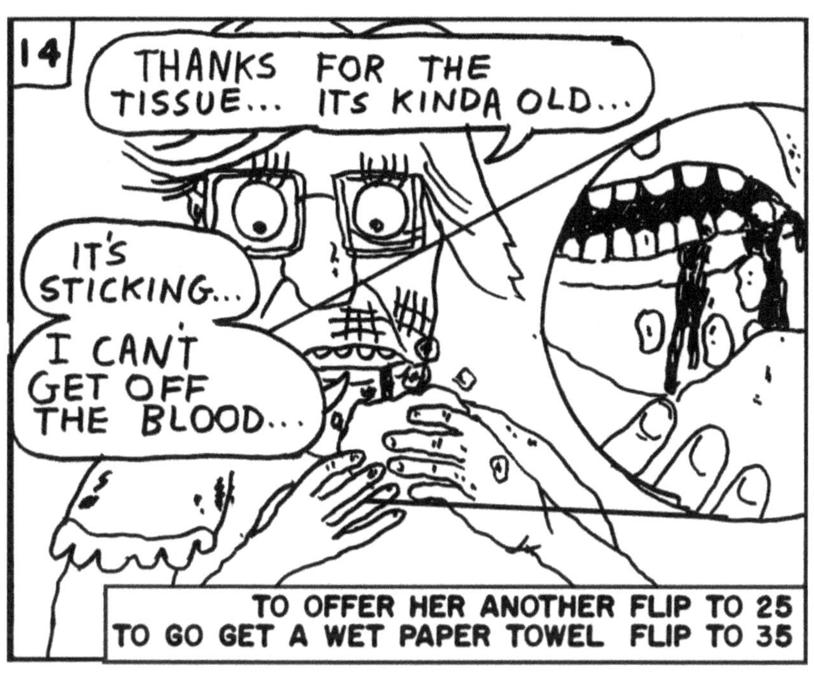

14
THANKS FOR THE TISSUE... IT'S KINDA OLD...
IT'S STICKING...
I CAN'T GET OFF THE BLOOD...
TO OFFER HER ANOTHER FLIP TO 25
TO GO GET A WET PAPER TOWEL FLIP TO 35

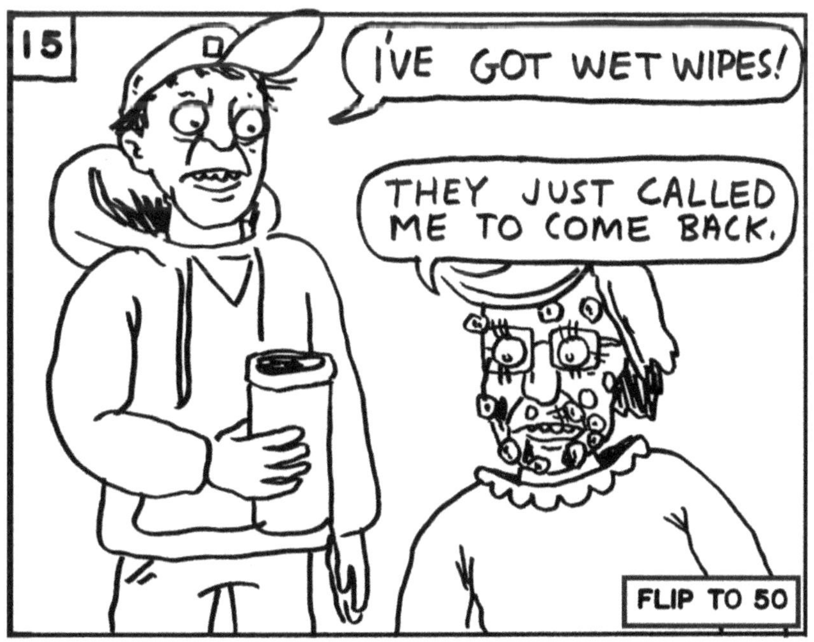

15
I'VE GOT WET WIPES!
THEY JUST CALLED ME TO COME BACK.
FLIP TO 50

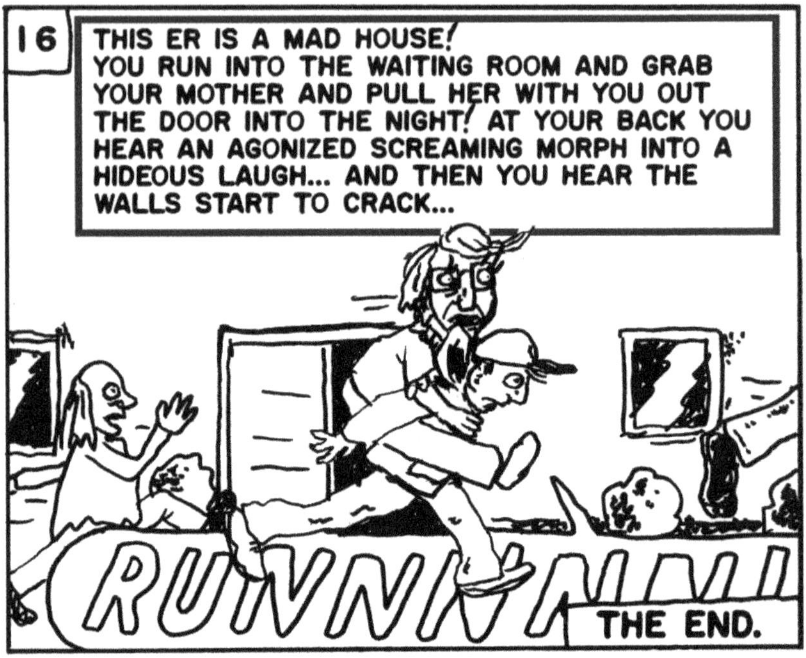

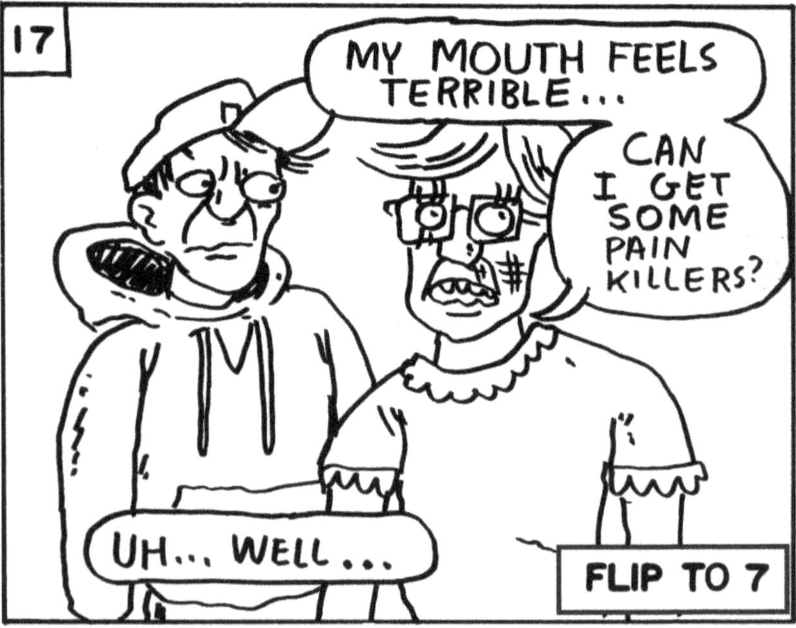
16
THIS ER IS A MAD HOUSE!
YOU RUN INTO THE WAITING ROOM AND GRAB
YOUR MOTHER AND PULL HER WITH YOU OUT
THE DOOR INTO THE NIGHT! AT YOUR BACK YOU
HEAR AN AGONIZED SCREAMING MORPH INTO A
HIDEOUS LAUGH... AND THEN YOU HEAR THE
WALLS START TO CRACK...
RUVNN...!
THE END.
17
MY MOUTH FEELS TERRIBLE...
CAN I GET SOME PAIN KILLERS?
UH... WELL...
FLIP TO 7

18 THE NEXT MORNING YOU GET UP EARLY GO FOR A RUN AND PUT THE EMERGENCY ROOM OUT OF YOUR MIND.

YOU ENROLL HER IN THE CERAMICS CLASS

AND THOUGH SHE STILL CLAIMS TO 'NOT BE AN ARTIST'. . . OVER 2 MONTHS SHE MAKES THREE DOZEN CUPS THAT LOOK LIKE THESE:

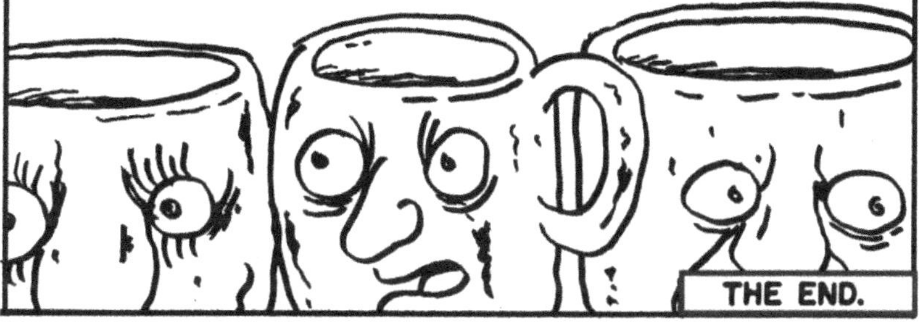

THE END.

19 YOU SCREAM AND YOU SCREAM AND YOU CAN'T STOP SCREAMING. . .

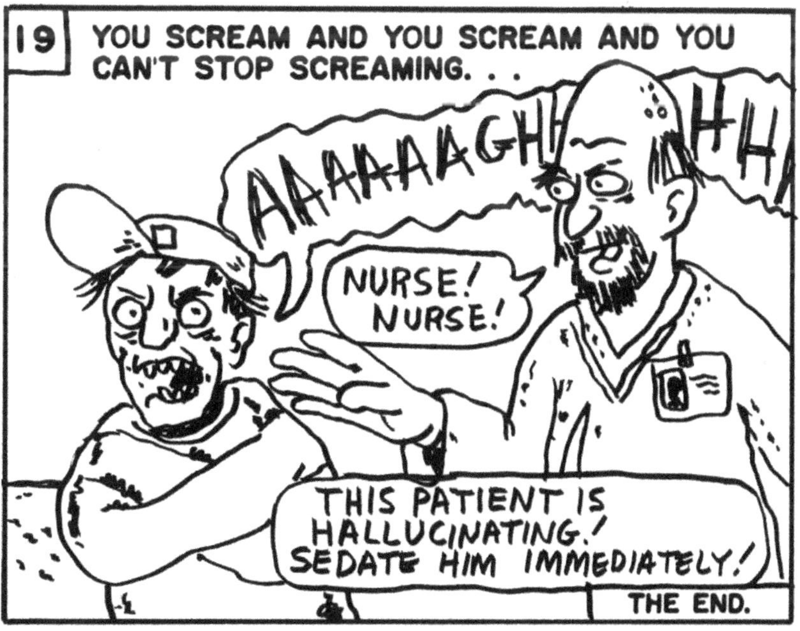

THE END.

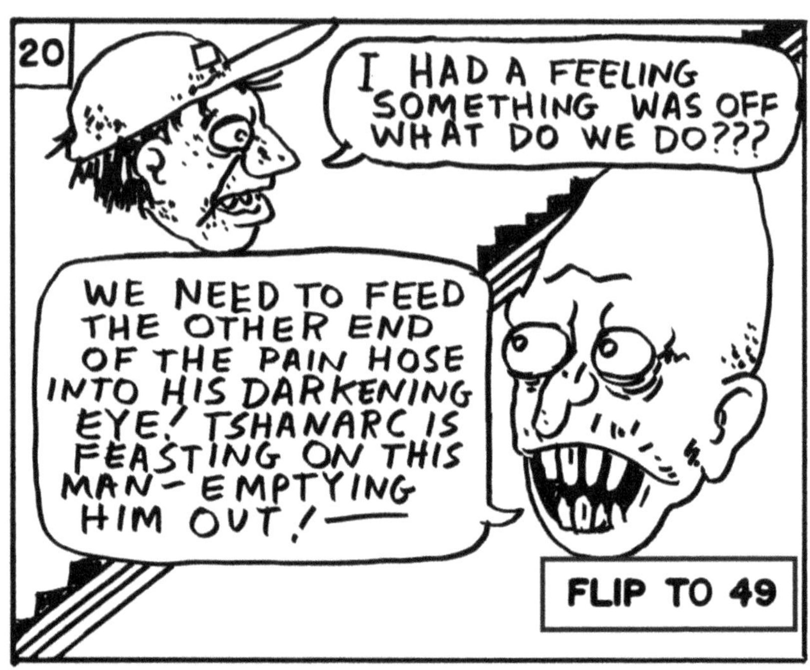

20
I HAD A FEELING SOMETHING WAS OFF WHAT DO WE DO???
WE NEED TO FEED THE OTHER END OF THE PAIN HOSE INTO HIS DARKENING EYE! TSHANARC IS FEASTING ON THIS MAN — EMPTYING HIM OUT!——
FLIP TO 49

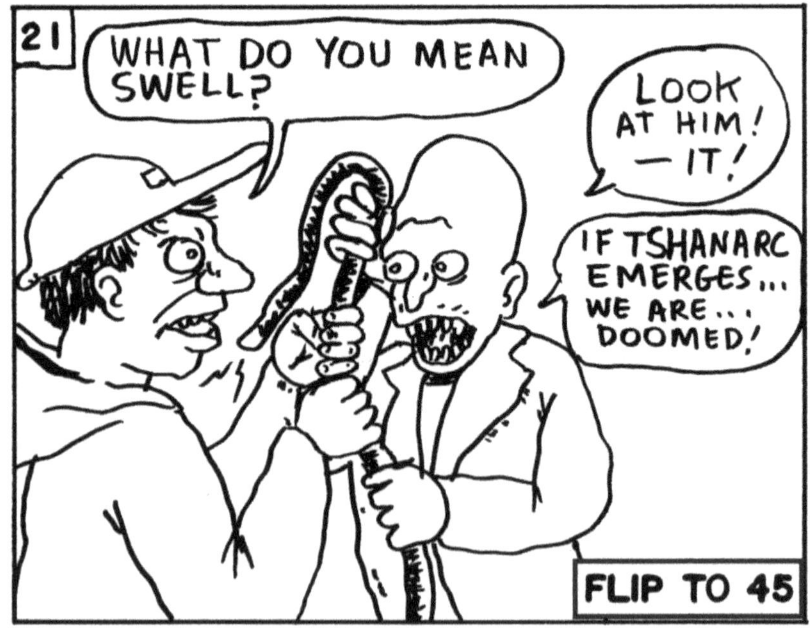

21
WHAT DO YOU MEAN SWELL?
LOOK AT HIM! — IT!
IF TSHANARC EMERGES... WE ARE... DOOMED!
FLIP TO 45

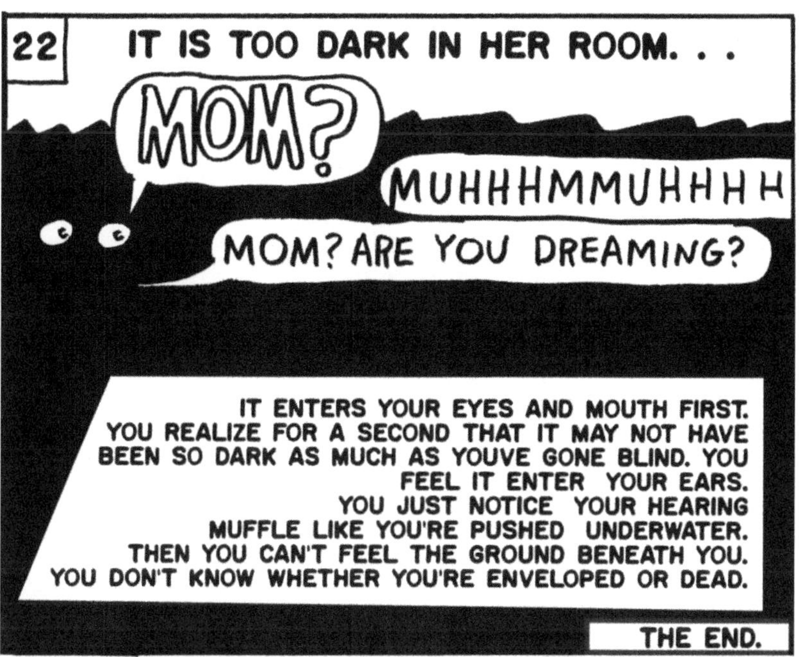

22
IT IS TOO DARK IN HER ROOM. . .
MOM?
MUHHHMMUHHHH
MOM? ARE YOU DREAMING?
IT ENTERS YOUR EYES AND MOUTH FIRST.
YOU REALIZE FOR A SECOND THAT IT MAY NOT HAVE
BEEN SO DARK AS MUCH AS YOUVE GONE BLIND. YOU
FEEL IT ENTER YOUR EARS.
YOU JUST NOTICE YOUR HEARING
MUFFLE LIKE YOU'RE PUSHED UNDERWATER.
THEN YOU CAN'T FEEL THE GROUND BENEATH YOU.
YOU DON'T KNOW WHETHER YOU'RE ENVELOPED OR DEAD.
THE END.

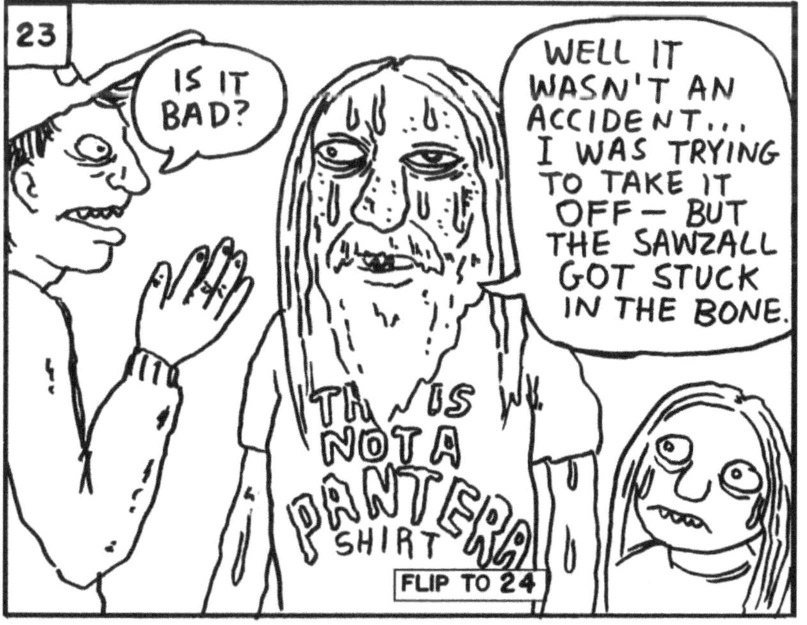

23
IS IT BAD?
WELL IT WASN'T AN ACCIDENT... I WAS TRYING TO TAKE IT OFF — BUT THE SAWZALL GOT STUCK IN THE BONE.
THIS IS NOT A PANTERA SHIRT
FLIP TO 24

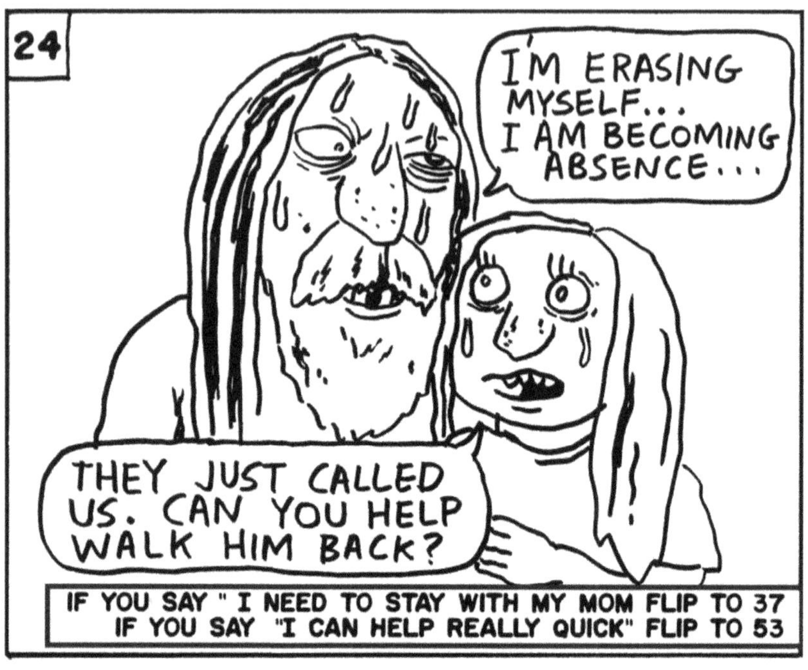

24
I'M ERASING MYSELF... I AM BECOMING ABSENCE...
THEY JUST CALLED US. CAN YOU HELP WALK HIM BACK?
IF YOU SAY " I NEED TO STAY WITH MY MOM FLIP TO 37
IF YOU SAY "I CAN HELP REALLY QUICK" FLIP TO 53

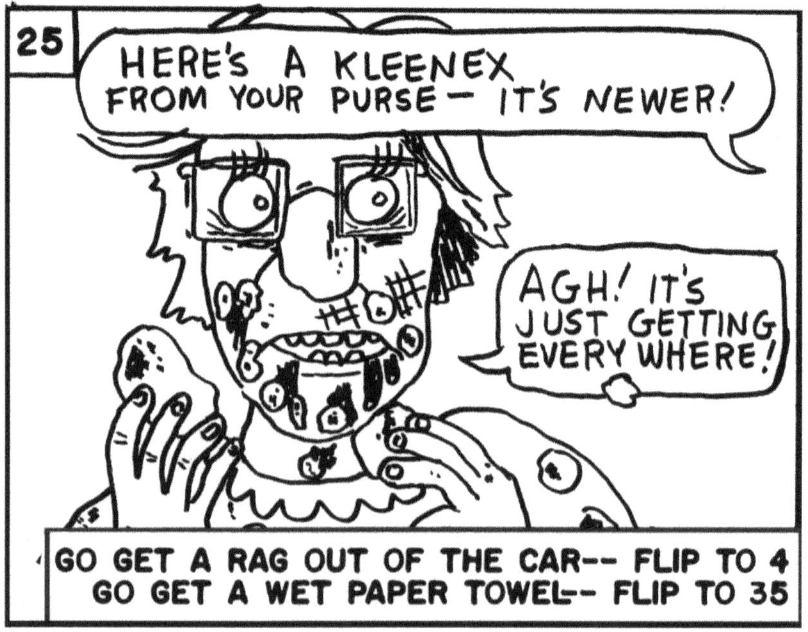

25
HERE'S A KLEENEX FROM YOUR PURSE— IT'S NEWER!
AGH! IT'S JUST GETTING EVERYWHERE!
GO GET A RAG OUT OF THE CAR-- FLIP TO 4
GO GET A WET PAPER TOWEL-- FLIP TO 35

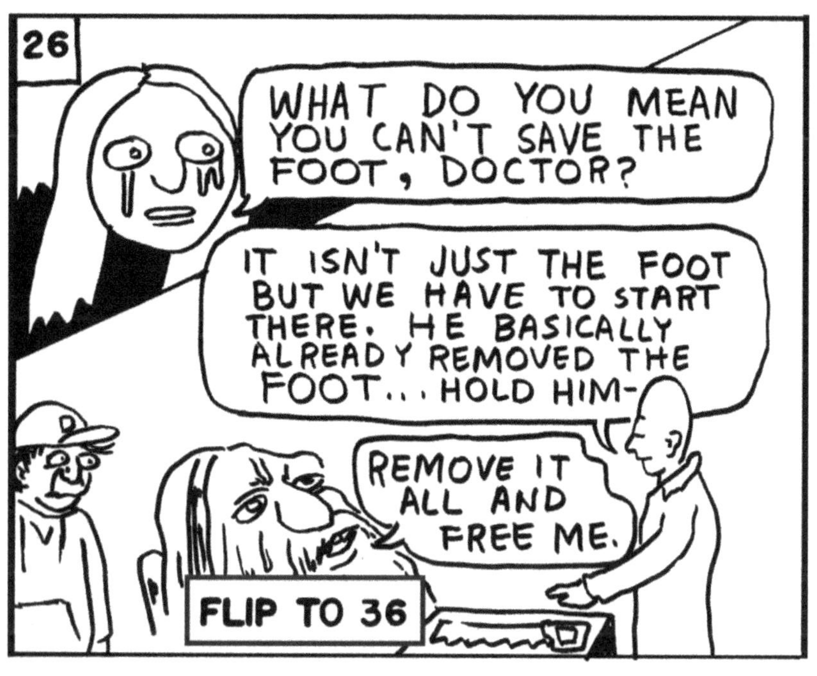

26
WHAT DO YOU MEAN YOU CAN'T SAVE THE FOOT, DOCTOR?
IT ISN'T JUST THE FOOT BUT WE HAVE TO START THERE. HE BASICALLY ALREADY REMOVED THE FOOT... HOLD HIM—
REMOVE IT ALL AND FREE ME.
FLIP TO 36

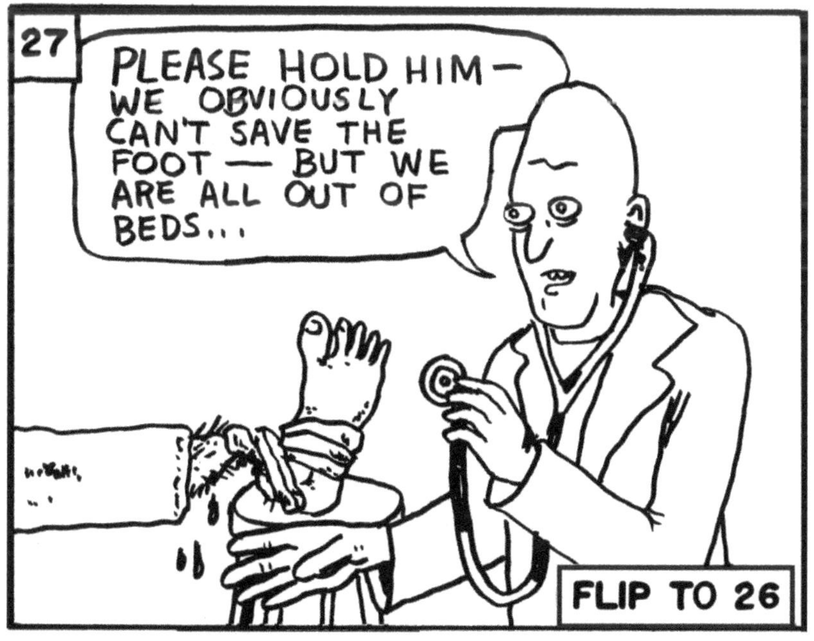

27
PLEASE HOLD HIM— WE OBVIOUSLY CAN'T SAVE THE FOOT — BUT WE ARE ALL OUT OF BEDS...
FLIP TO 26

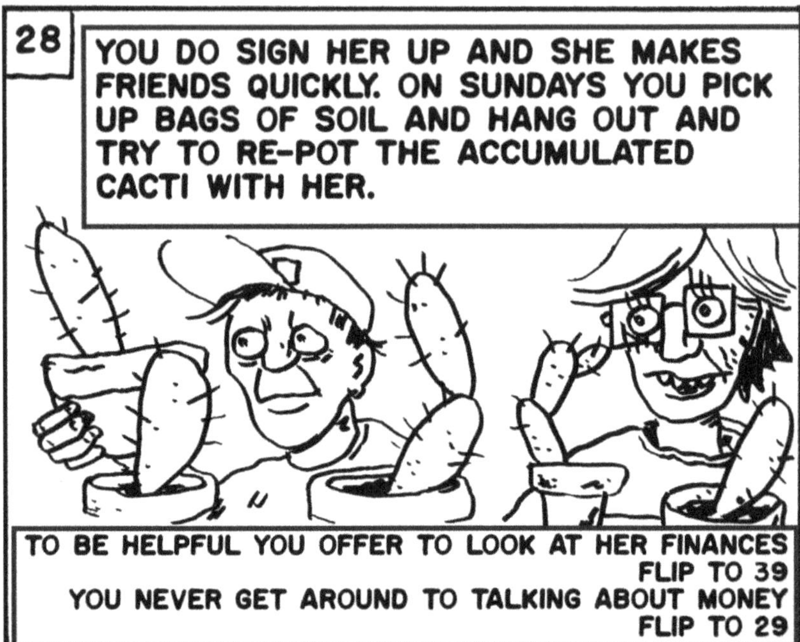
28
YOU DO SIGN HER UP AND SHE MAKES FRIENDS QUICKLY. ON SUNDAYS YOU PICK UP BAGS OF SOIL AND HANG OUT AND TRY TO RE-POT THE ACCUMULATED CACTI WITH HER.

TO BE HELPFUL YOU OFFER TO LOOK AT HER FINANCES
FLIP TO 39
YOU NEVER GET AROUND TO TALKING ABOUT MONEY
FLIP TO 29

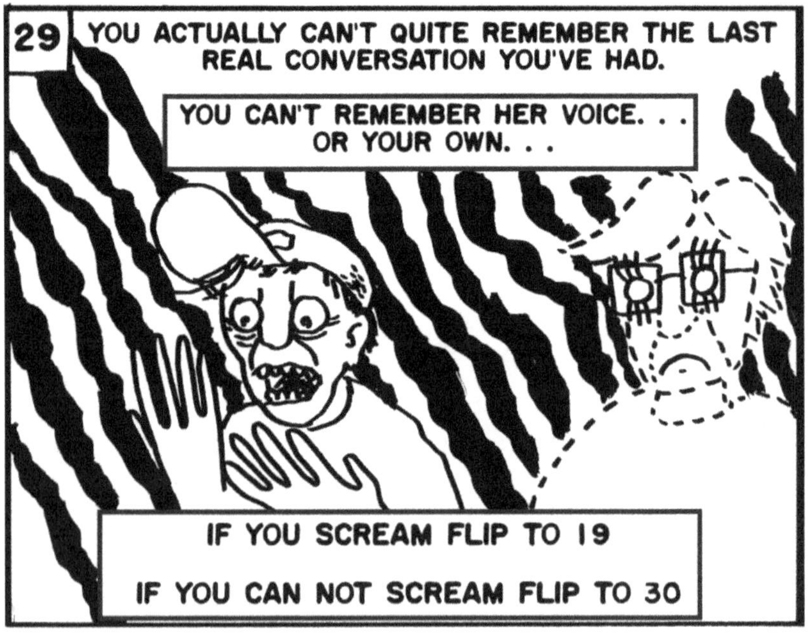
29
YOU ACTUALLY CAN'T QUITE REMEMBER THE LAST REAL CONVERSATION YOU'VE HAD.

YOU CAN'T REMEMBER HER VOICE. . .
OR YOUR OWN. . .

IF YOU SCREAM FLIP TO 19

IF YOU CAN NOT SCREAM FLIP TO 30

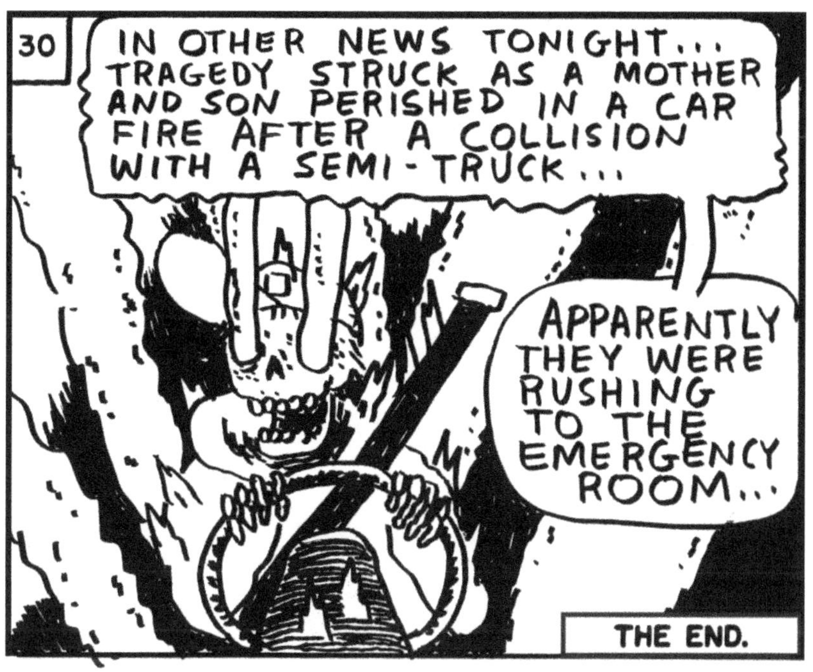

30
IN OTHER NEWS TONIGHT... TRAGEDY STRUCK AS A MOTHER AND SON PERISHED IN A CAR FIRE AFTER A COLLISION WITH A SEMI-TRUCK...
APPARENTLY THEY WERE RUSHING TO THE EMERGENCY ROOM...
THE END.

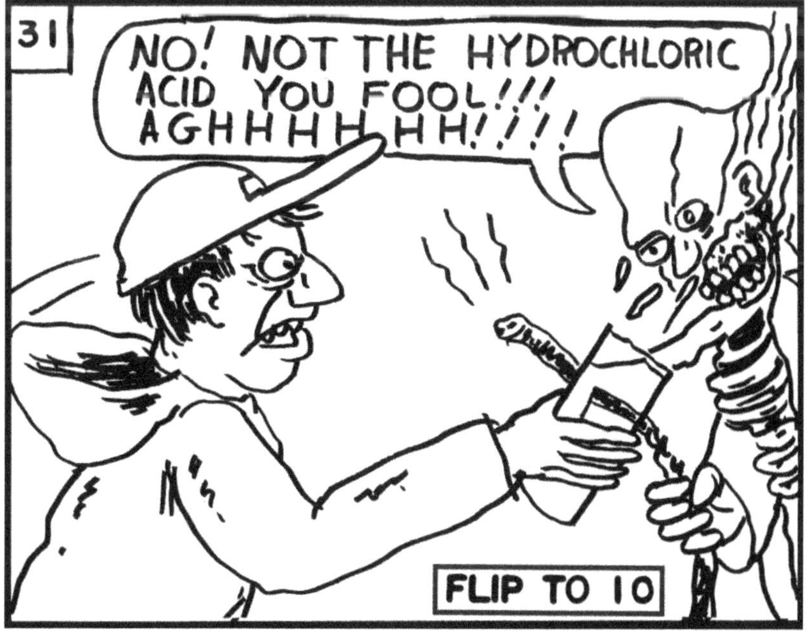

31
NO! NOT THE HYDROCHLORIC ACID YOU FOOL!!!! AGHHHHHHH!!!!!
FLIP TO 10

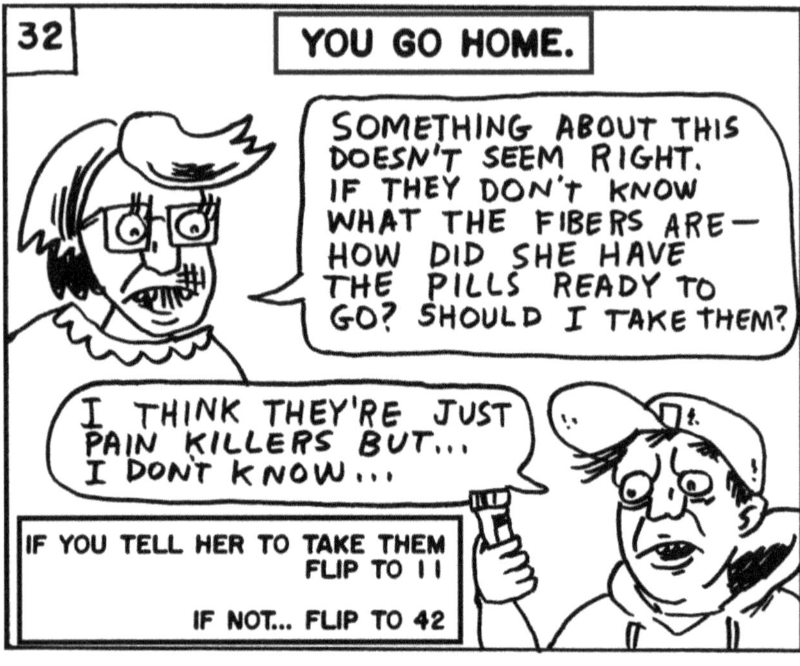

32
YOU GO HOME.
SOMETHING ABOUT THIS DOESN'T SEEM RIGHT. IF THEY DON'T KNOW WHAT THE FIBERS ARE— HOW DID SHE HAVE THE PILLS READY TO GO? SHOULD I TAKE THEM?
I THINK THEY'RE JUST PAIN KILLERS BUT... I DON'T KNOW...
IF YOU TELL HER TO TAKE THEM FLIP TO 11
IF NOT... FLIP TO 42

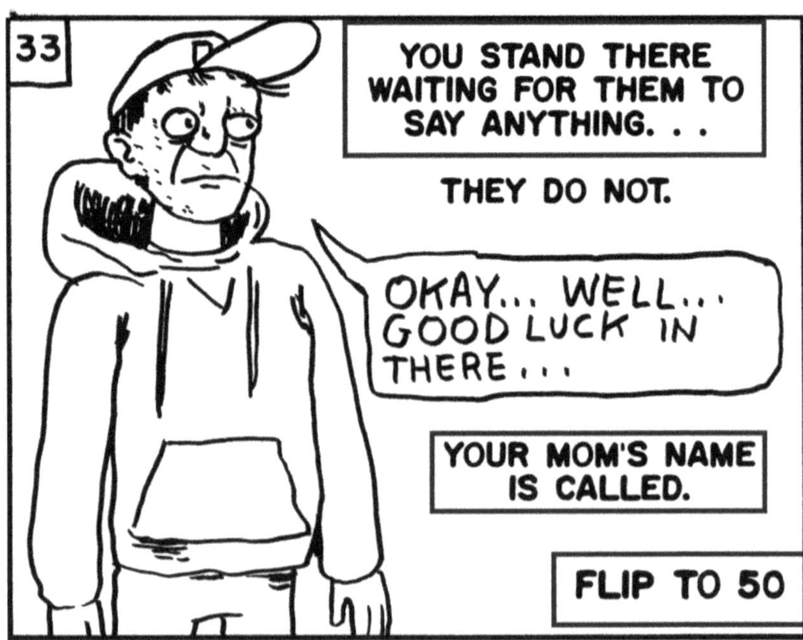

33
YOU STAND THERE WAITING FOR THEM TO SAY ANYTHING. . .
THEY DO NOT.
OKAY... WELL... GOOD LUCK IN THERE...
YOUR MOM'S NAME IS CALLED.
FLIP TO 50

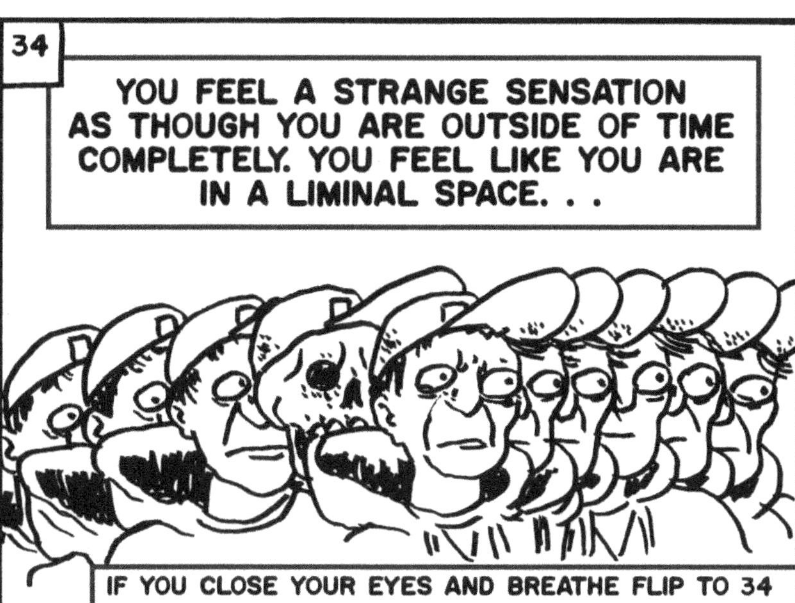
34
YOU FEEL A STRANGE SENSATION
AS THOUGH YOU ARE OUTSIDE OF TIME
COMPLETELY. YOU FEEL LIKE YOU ARE
IN A LIMINAL SPACE. . .
IF YOU CLOSE YOUR EYES AND BREATHE FLIP TO 34
IF YOU FEEL DEJA VU FLIP TO 34

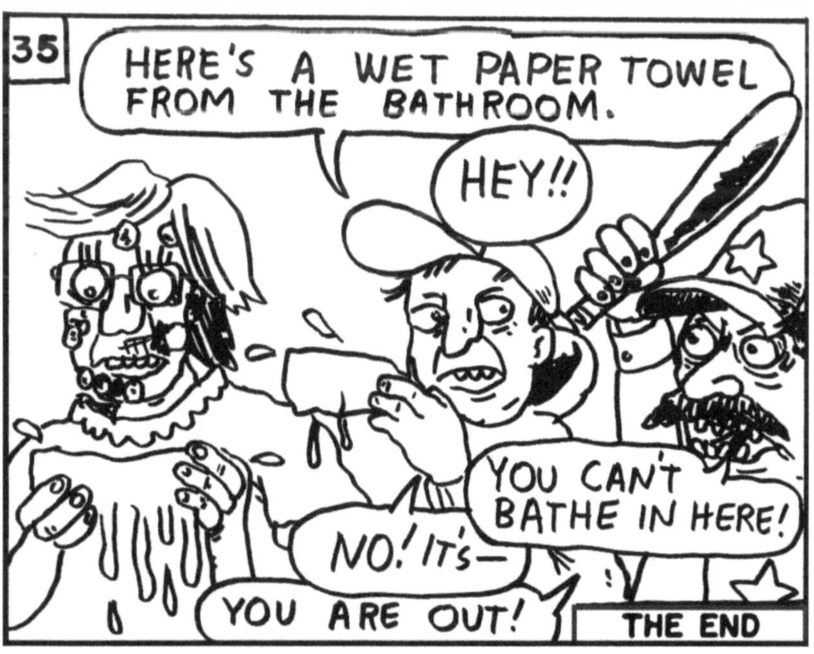
35
HERE'S A WET PAPER TOWEL FROM THE BATHROOM.
HEY!!
YOU CAN'T BATHE IN HERE!
NO! IT'S—
YOU ARE OUT!
THE END

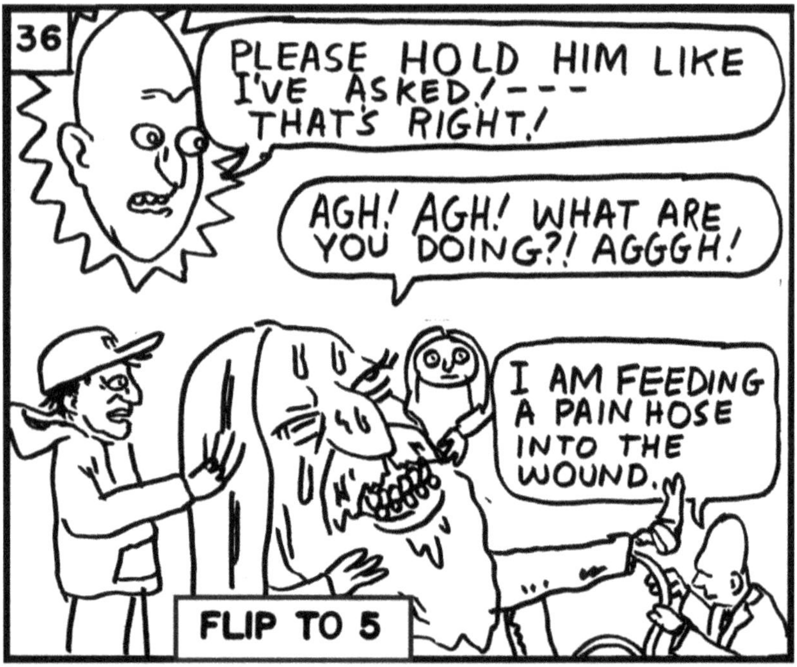

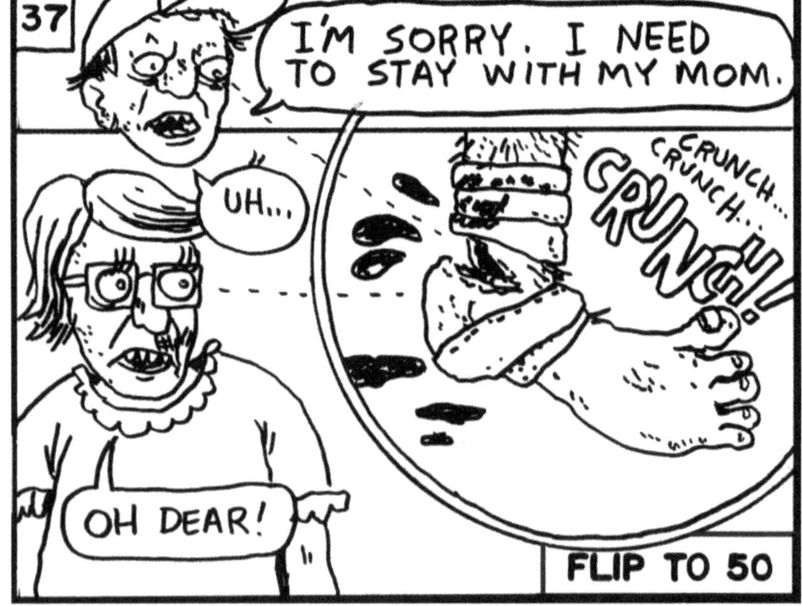

36
PLEASE HOLD HIM LIKE I'VE ASKED! --- THAT'S RIGHT!
AGH! AGH! WHAT ARE YOU DOING?! AGGGH!
I AM FEEDING A PAIN HOSE INTO THE WOUND.
FLIP TO 5
37
I'M SORRY. I NEED TO STAY WITH MY MOM.
UH...
OH DEAR!
CRUNCH...
CRUNCH...
CRUNCH!
FLIP TO 50

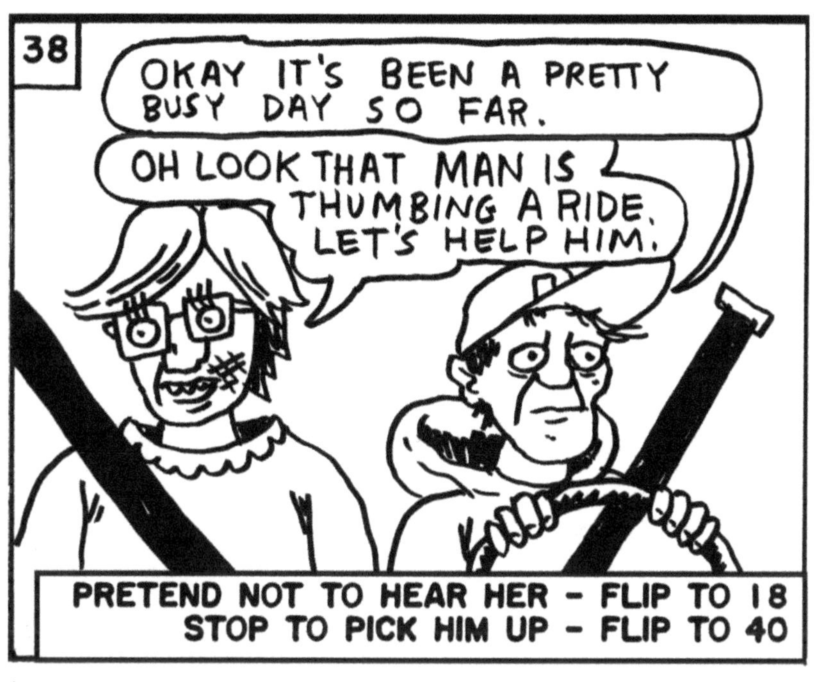

38
OKAY IT'S BEEN A PRETTY BUSY DAY SO FAR.
OH LOOK THAT MAN IS THUMBING A RIDE. LET'S HELP HIM.
PRETEND NOT TO HEAR HER - FLIP TO 18
STOP TO PICK HIM UP - FLIP TO 40

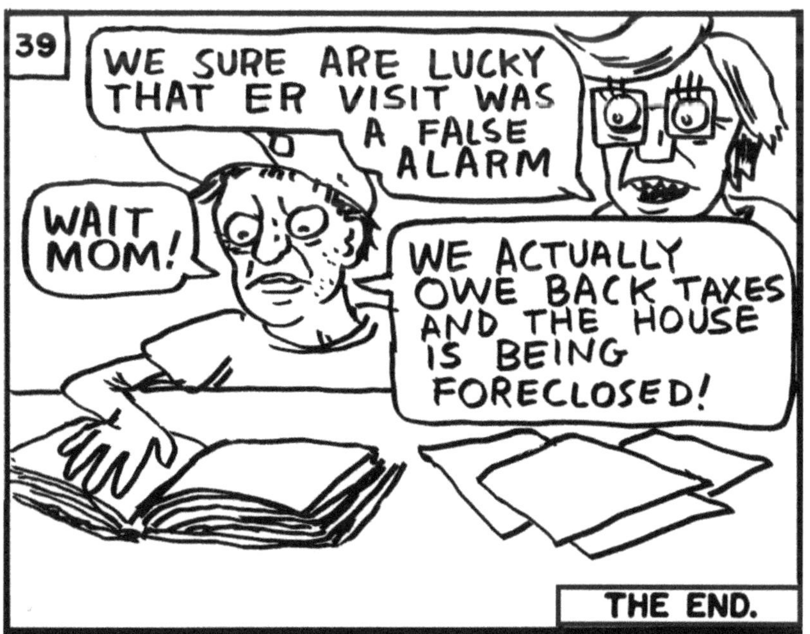

39
WE SURE ARE LUCKY THAT ER VISIT WAS A FALSE ALARM
WAIT MOM!
WE ACTUALLY OWE BACK TAXES AND THE HOUSE IS BEING FORECLOSED!
THE END.

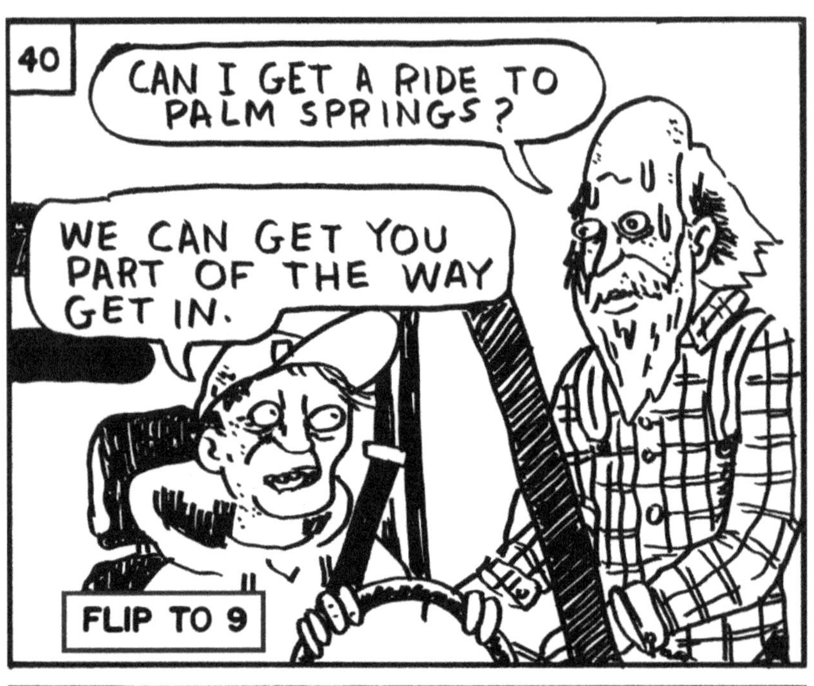

40
CAN I GET A RIDE TO PALM SPRINGS?
WE CAN GET YOU PART OF THE WAY GET IN.
FLIP TO 9

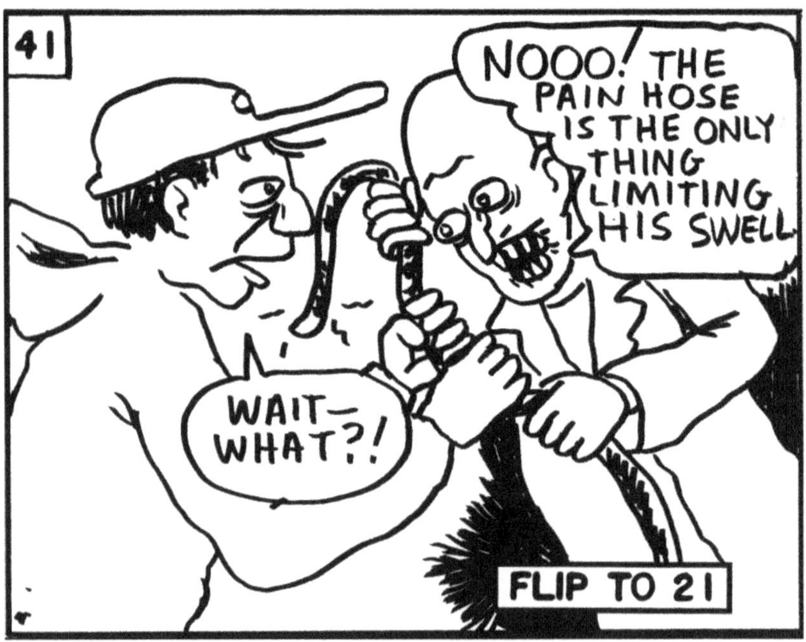

41
NOOO! THE PAIN HOSE IS THE ONLY THING LIMITING HIS SWELL
WAIT— WHAT?!
FLIP TO 21

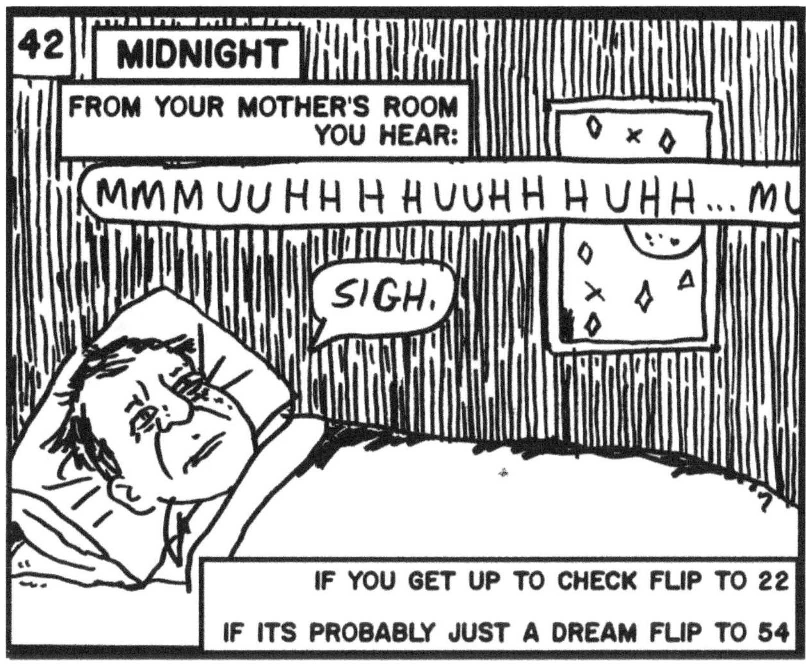

42
MIDNIGHT
FROM YOUR MOTHER'S ROOM YOU HEAR:
MMM UU HH H HUUHH H UHH... MU
SIGH.
IF YOU GET UP TO CHECK FLIP TO 22
IF ITS PROBABLY JUST A DREAM FLIP TO 54

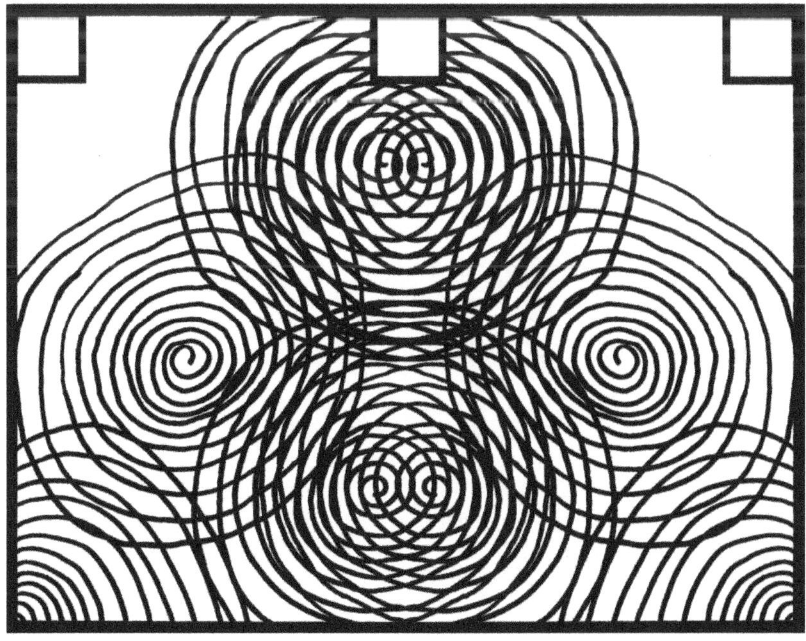

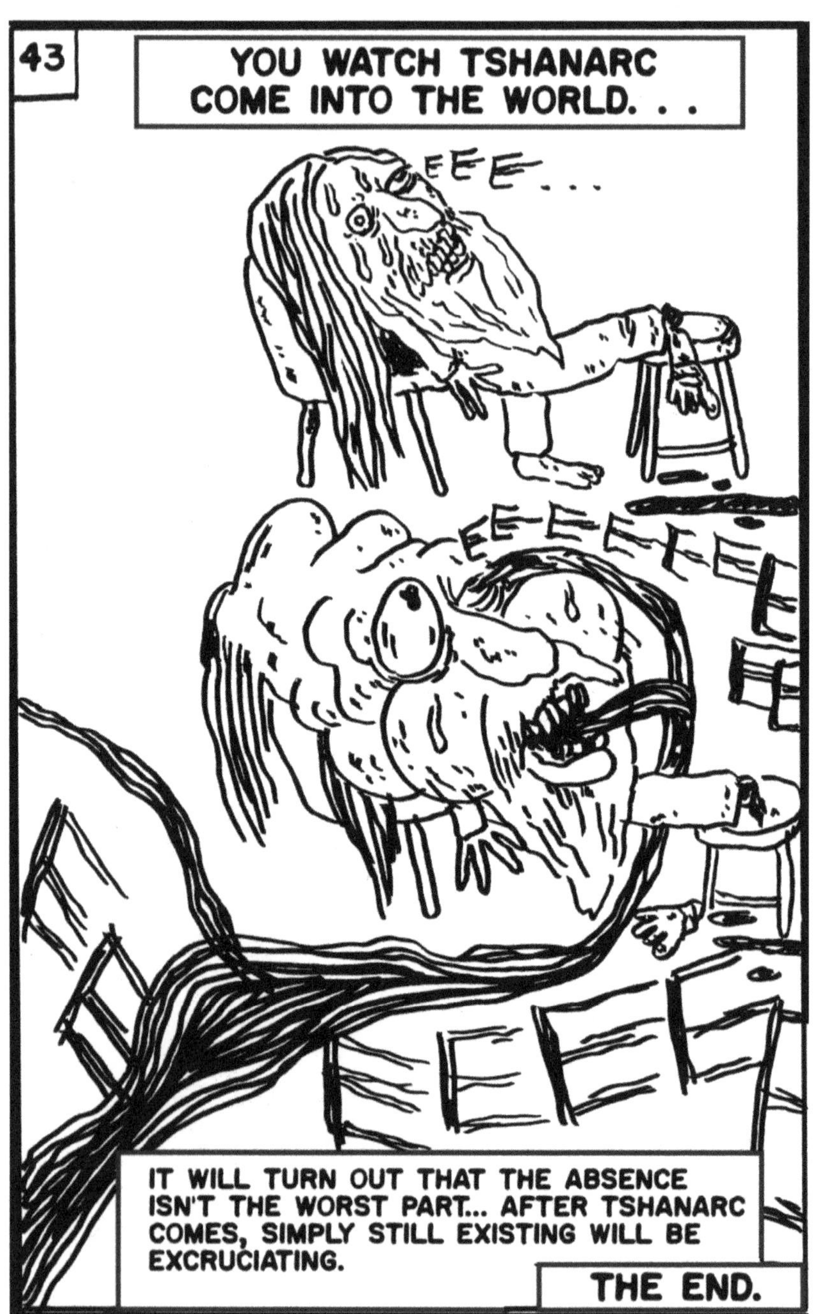

43
YOU WATCH TSHANARC
COME INTO THE WORLD. . .
EEE. . .
EEEEEEEEEE
IT WILL TURN OUT THAT THE ABSENCE
ISN'T THE WORST PART... AFTER TSHANARC
COMES, SIMPLY STILL EXISTING WILL BE
EXCRUCIATING.
THE END.

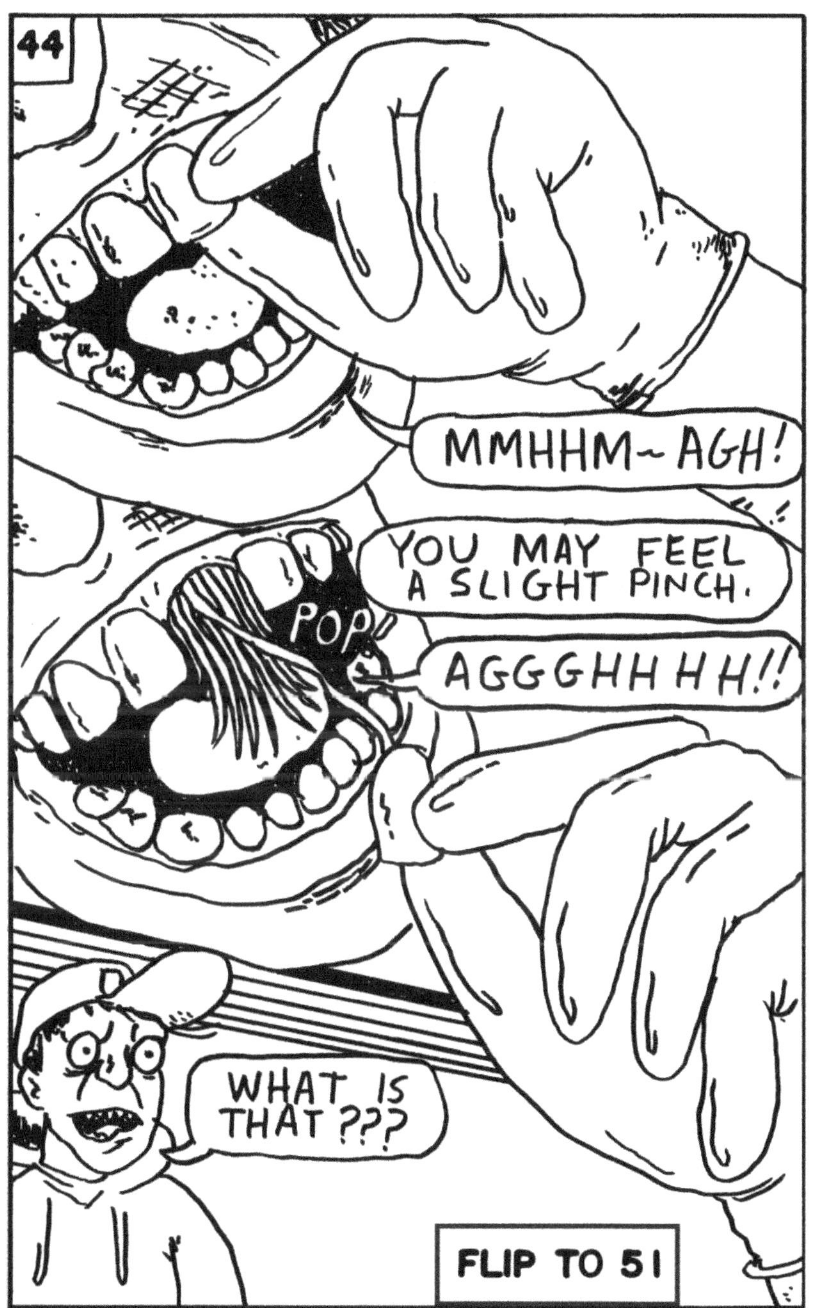
44
MMHHM~AGH!
YOU MAY FEEL A SLIGHT PINCH.
POP!
AGGGHHHH!!
WHAT IS THAT???
FLIP TO 51

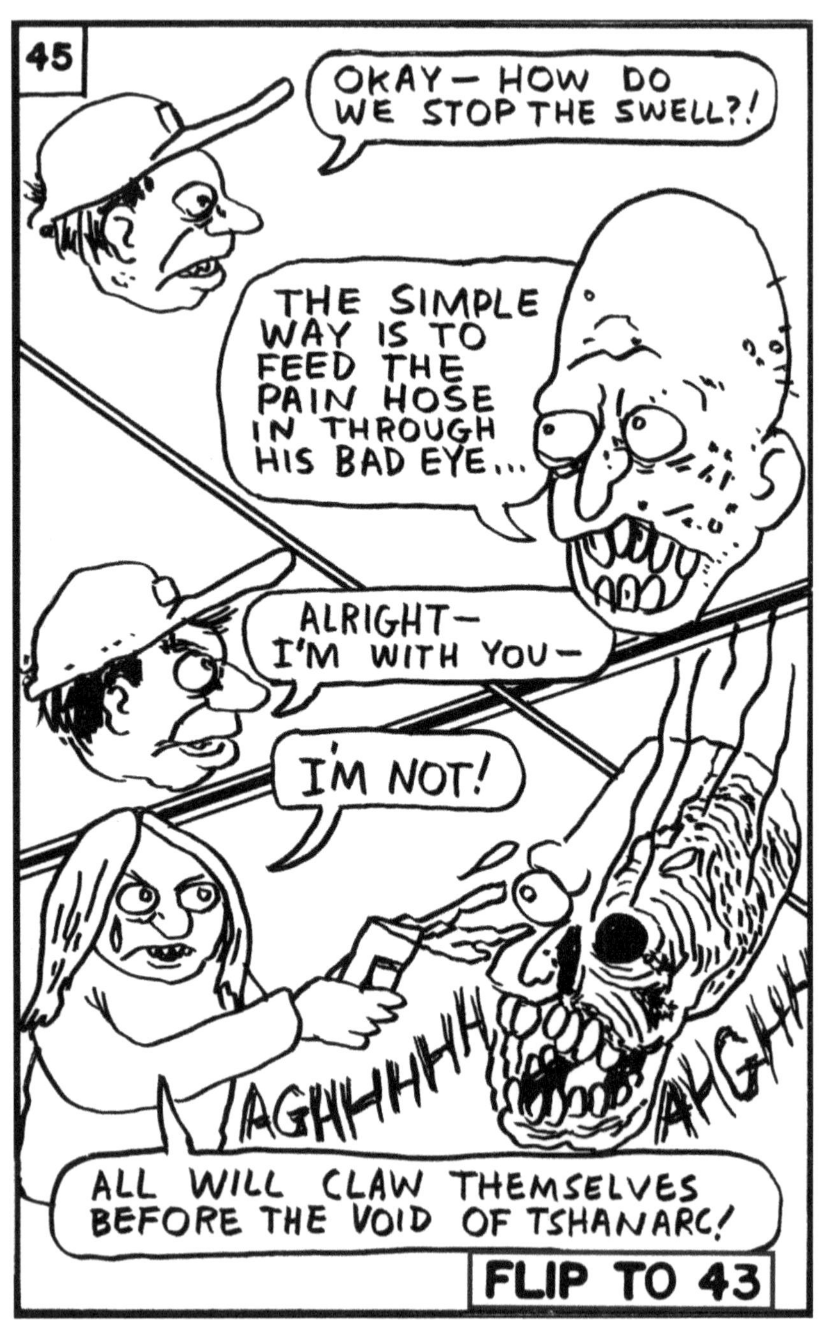
45
OKAY— HOW DO WE STOP THE SWELL?!
THE SIMPLE WAY IS TO FEED THE PAIN HOSE IN THROUGH HIS BAD EYE...
ALRIGHT— I'M WITH YOU—
I'M NOT!
AGHHHHH
AHGHH
ALL WILL CLAW THEMSELVES BEFORE THE VOID OF TSHANARC!
FLIP TO 43

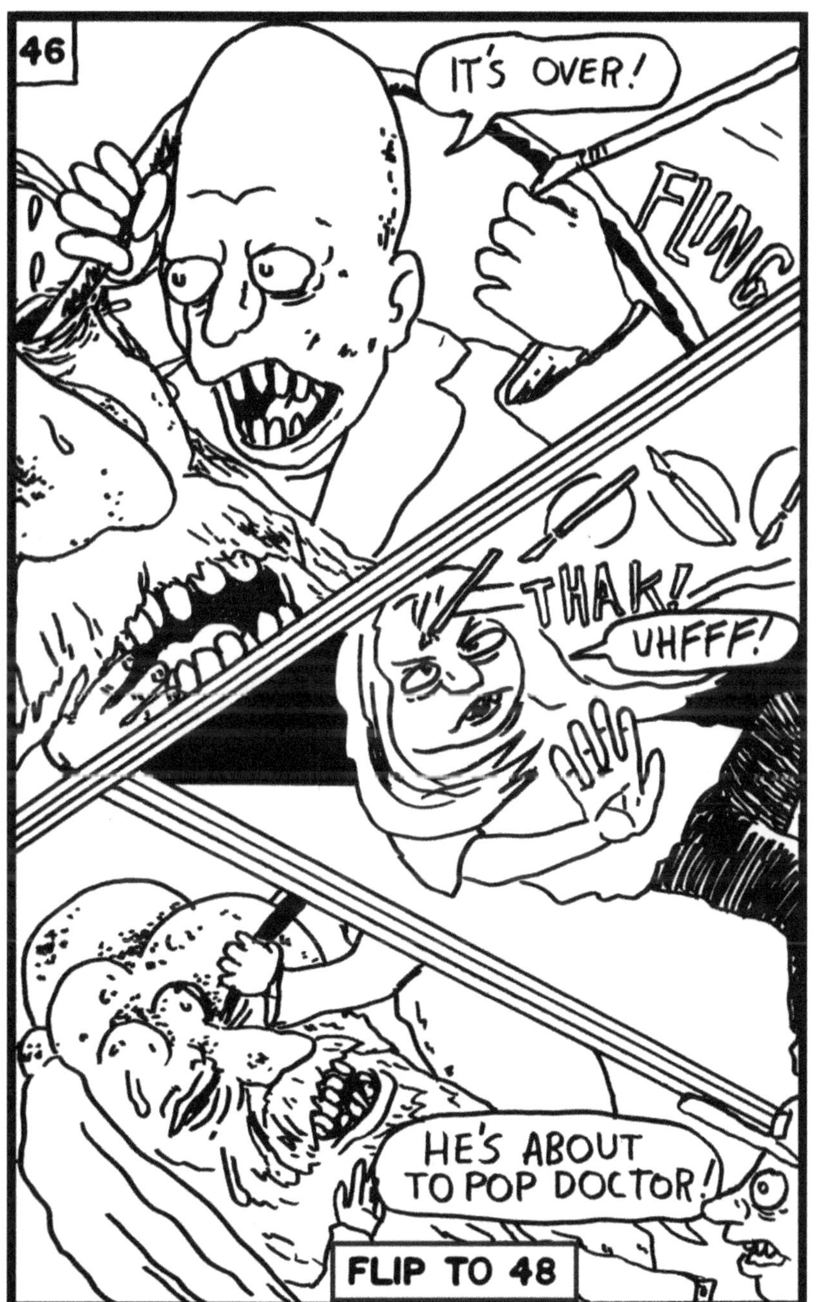
46
IT'S OVER!
FLING
THAK!
UHFFF!
HE'S ABOUT TO POP DOCTOR!
FLIP TO 48

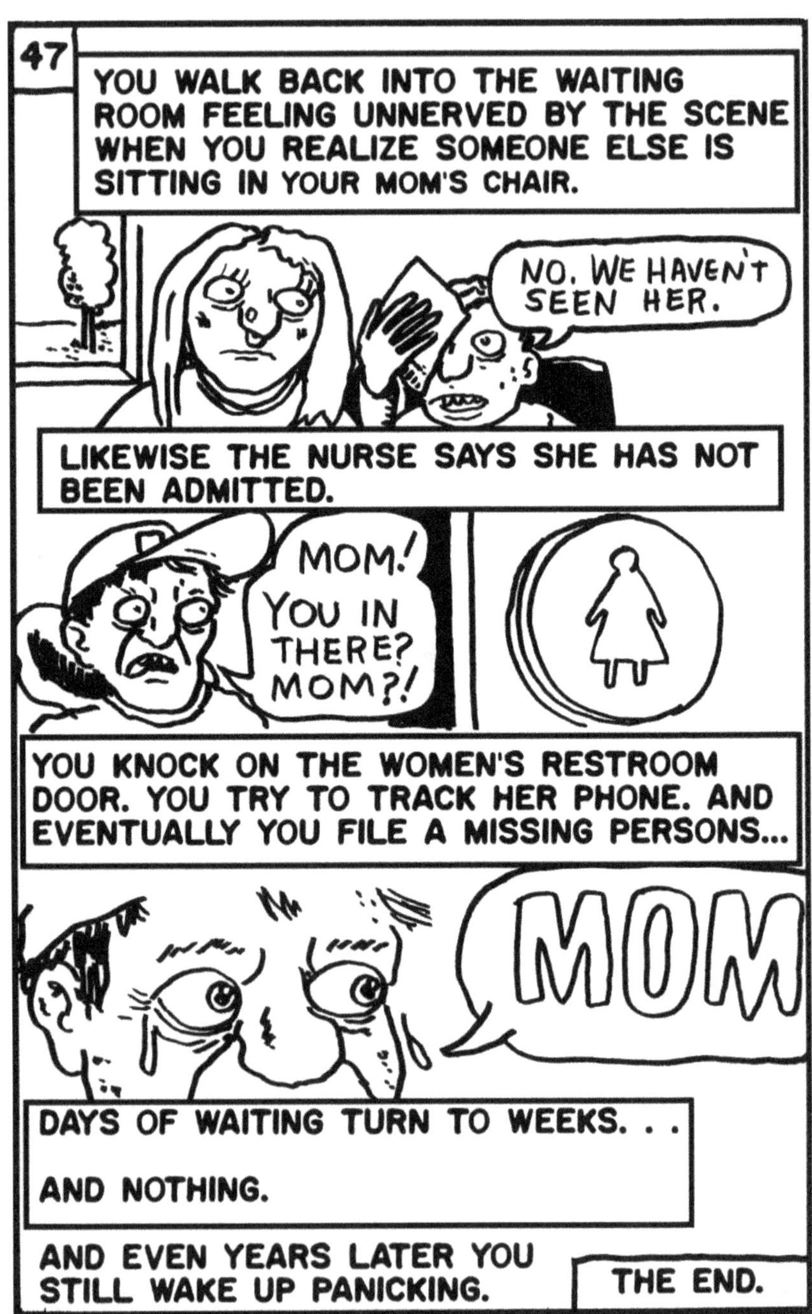

47
YOU WALK BACK INTO THE WAITING ROOM FEELING UNNERVED BY THE SCENE WHEN YOU REALIZE SOMEONE ELSE IS SITTING IN YOUR MOM'S CHAIR.
NO. WE HAVEN'T SEEN HER.
LIKEWISE THE NURSE SAYS SHE HAS NOT BEEN ADMITTED.
MOM! YOU IN THERE? MOM?!
YOU KNOCK ON THE WOMEN'S RESTROOM DOOR. YOU TRY TO TRACK HER PHONE. AND EVENTUALLY YOU FILE A MISSING PERSONS...
MOM
DAYS OF WAITING TURN TO WEEKS. . . .
AND NOTHING.
AND EVEN YEARS LATER YOU STILL WAKE UP PANICKING.
THE END.

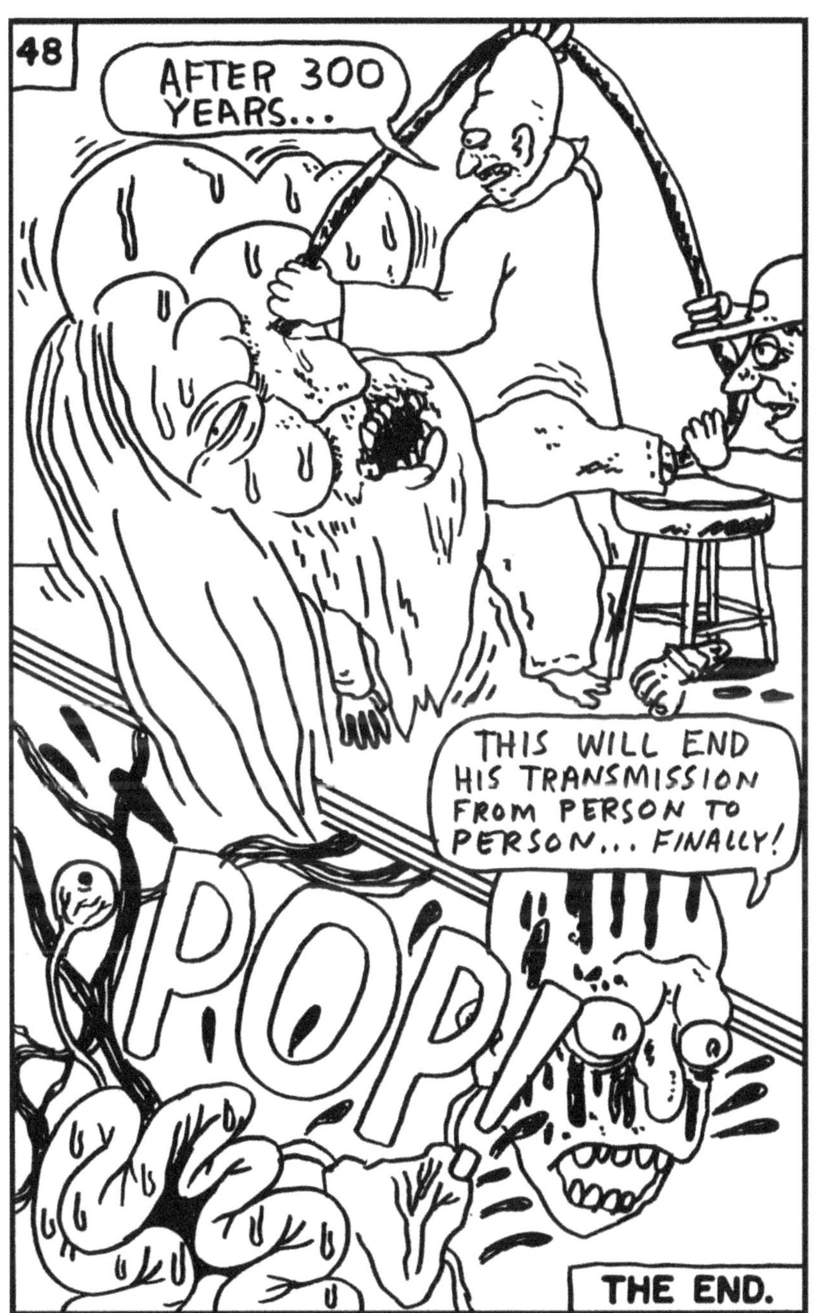

48
AFTER 300 YEARS...
THIS WILL END HIS TRANSMISSION FROM PERSON TO PERSON... FINALLY!
POP!
THE END.

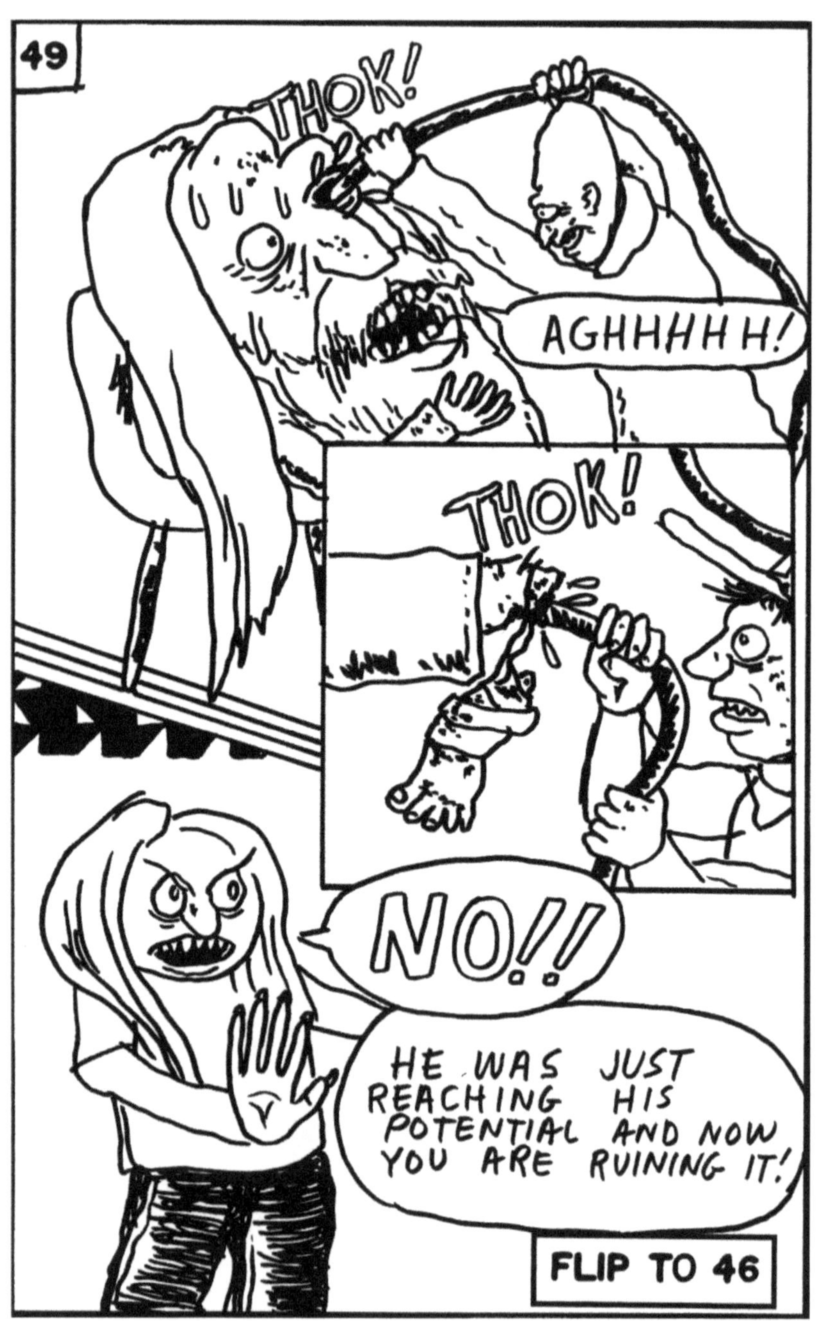

49
THOK!
AGHHHHHH!
THOK!
NO!!
HE WAS JUST
REACHING HIS
POTENTIAL AND NOW
YOU ARE RUINING IT!
FLIP TO 46

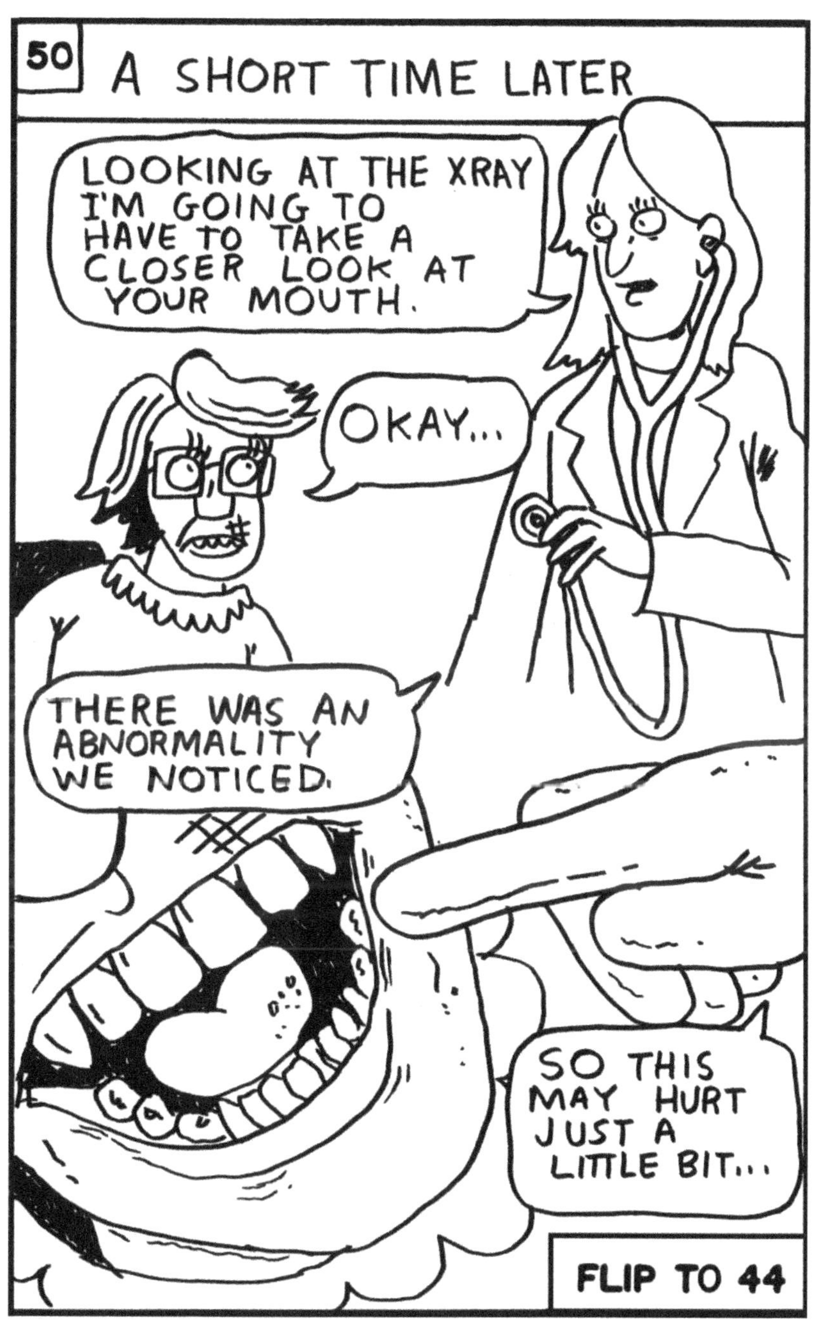

50
A SHORT TIME LATER
LOOKING AT THE XRAY I'M GOING TO HAVE TO TAKE A CLOSER LOOK AT YOUR MOUTH.
OKAY...
THERE WAS AN ABNORMALITY WE NOTICED.
SO THIS MAY HURT JUST A LITTLE BIT...
50
FLIP TO 44

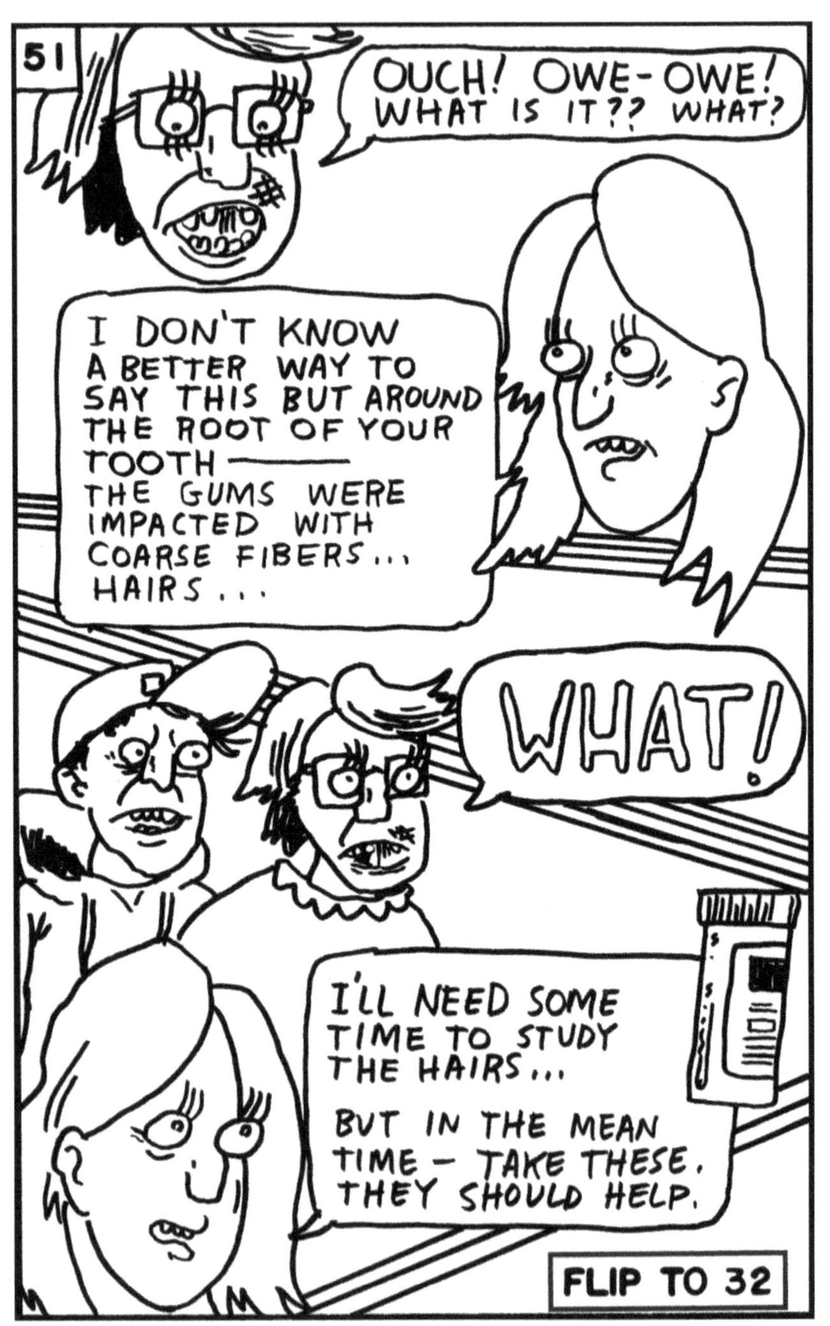

51
OUCH! OWE-OWE! WHAT IS IT?? WHAT?
I DON'T KNOW A BETTER WAY TO SAY THIS BUT AROUND THE ROOT OF YOUR TOOTH — THE GUMS WERE IMPACTED WITH COARSE FIBERS... HAIRS...
WHAT!
I'LL NEED SOME TIME TO STUDY THE HAIRS...
BUT IN THE MEAN TIME — TAKE THESE. THEY SHOULD HELP.
FLIP TO 32

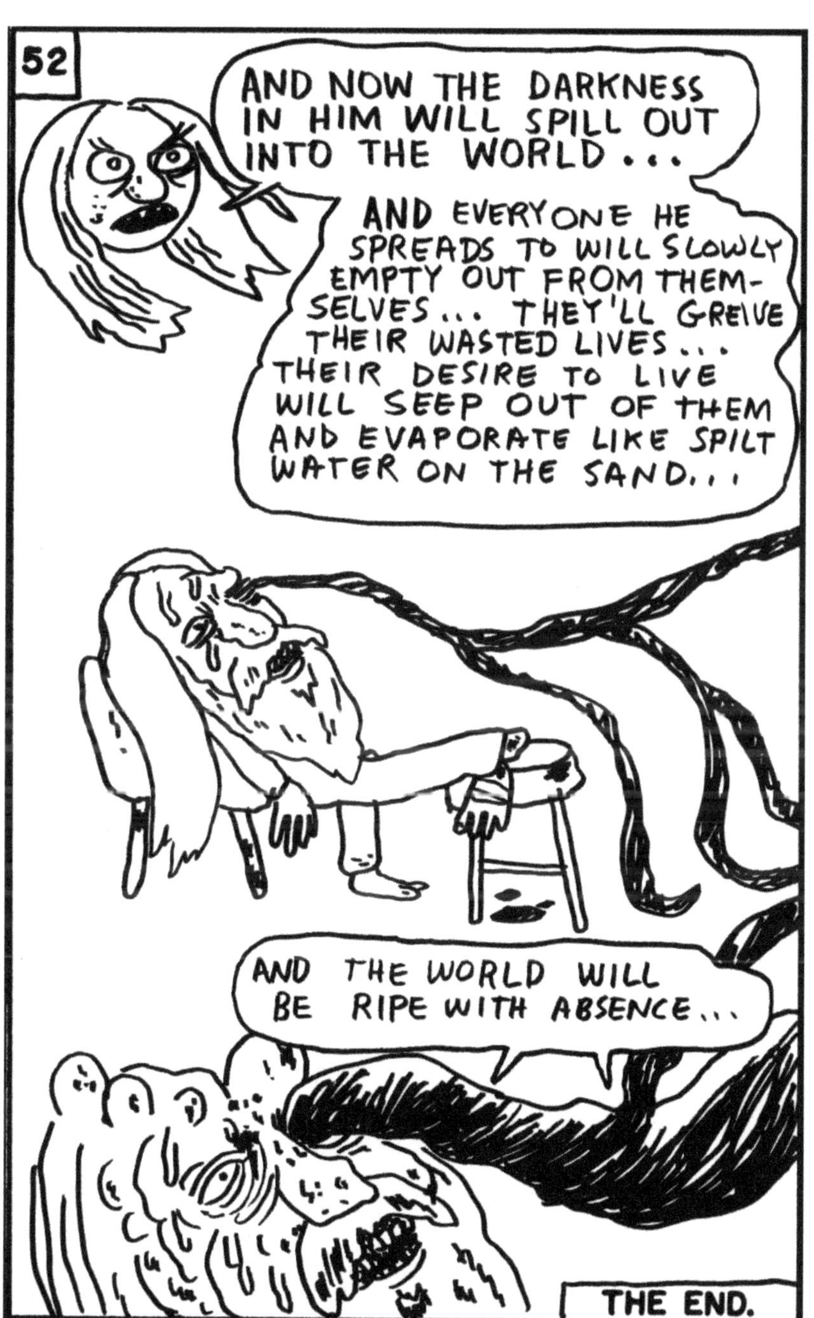
52
AND NOW THE DARKNESS IN HIM WILL SPILL OUT INTO THE WORLD...
AND EVERYONE HE SPREADS TO WILL SLOWLY EMPTY OUT FROM THEM- SELVES... THEY'LL GREIVE THEIR WASTED LIVES... THEIR DESIRE TO LIVE WILL SEEP OUT OF THEM AND EVAPORATE LIKE SPILT WATER ON THE SAND...
AND THE WORLD WILL BE RIPE WITH ABSENCE...
THE END.

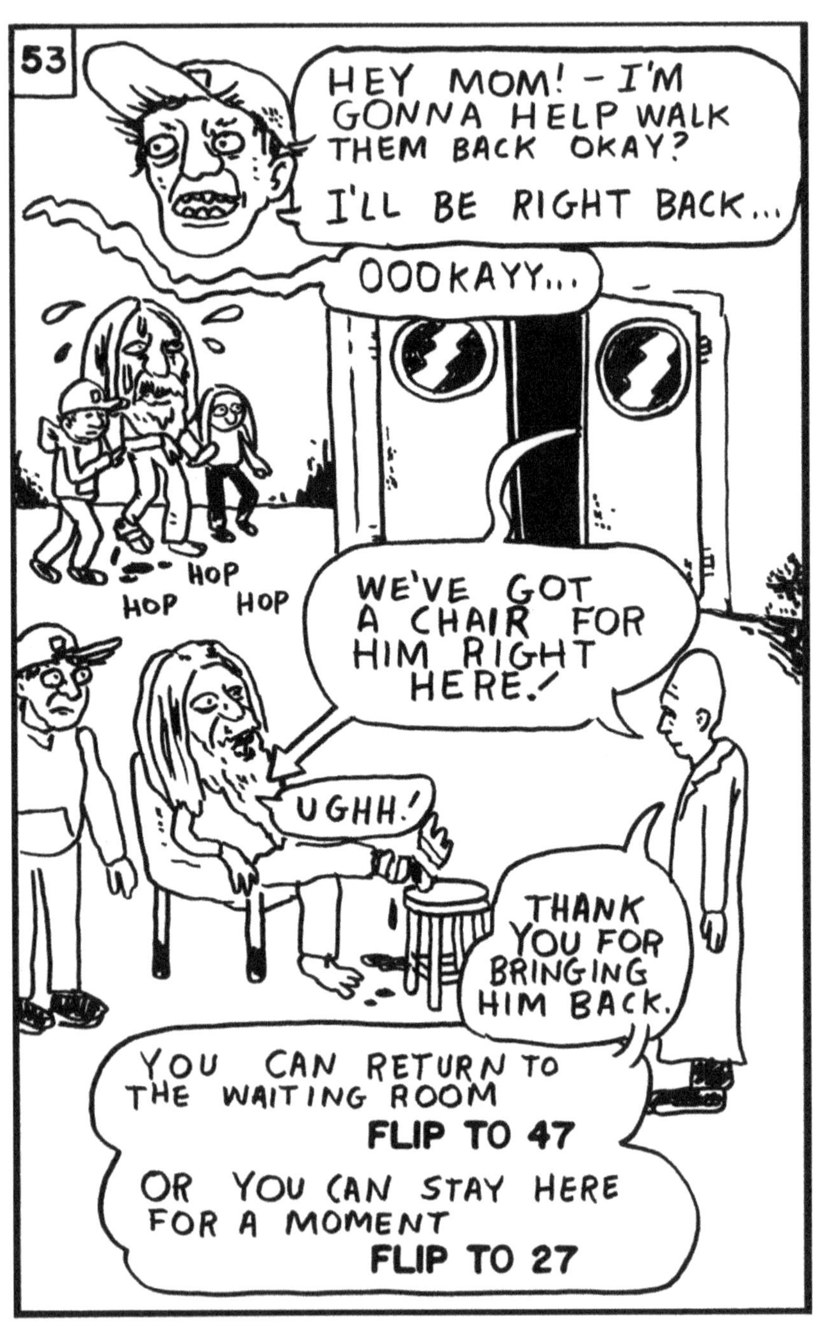

53
HEY MOM! - I'M GONNA HELP WALK THEM BACK OKAY?
I'LL BE RIGHT BACK...
OOOKAYY...
HOP HOP
HOP HOP
WE'VE GOT A CHAIR FOR HIM RIGHT HERE!
UGHH!
THANK YOU FOR BRINGING HIM BACK.
YOU CAN RETURN TO THE WAITING ROOM
FLIP TO 47
OR YOU CAN STAY HERE FOR A MOMENT
FLIP TO 27

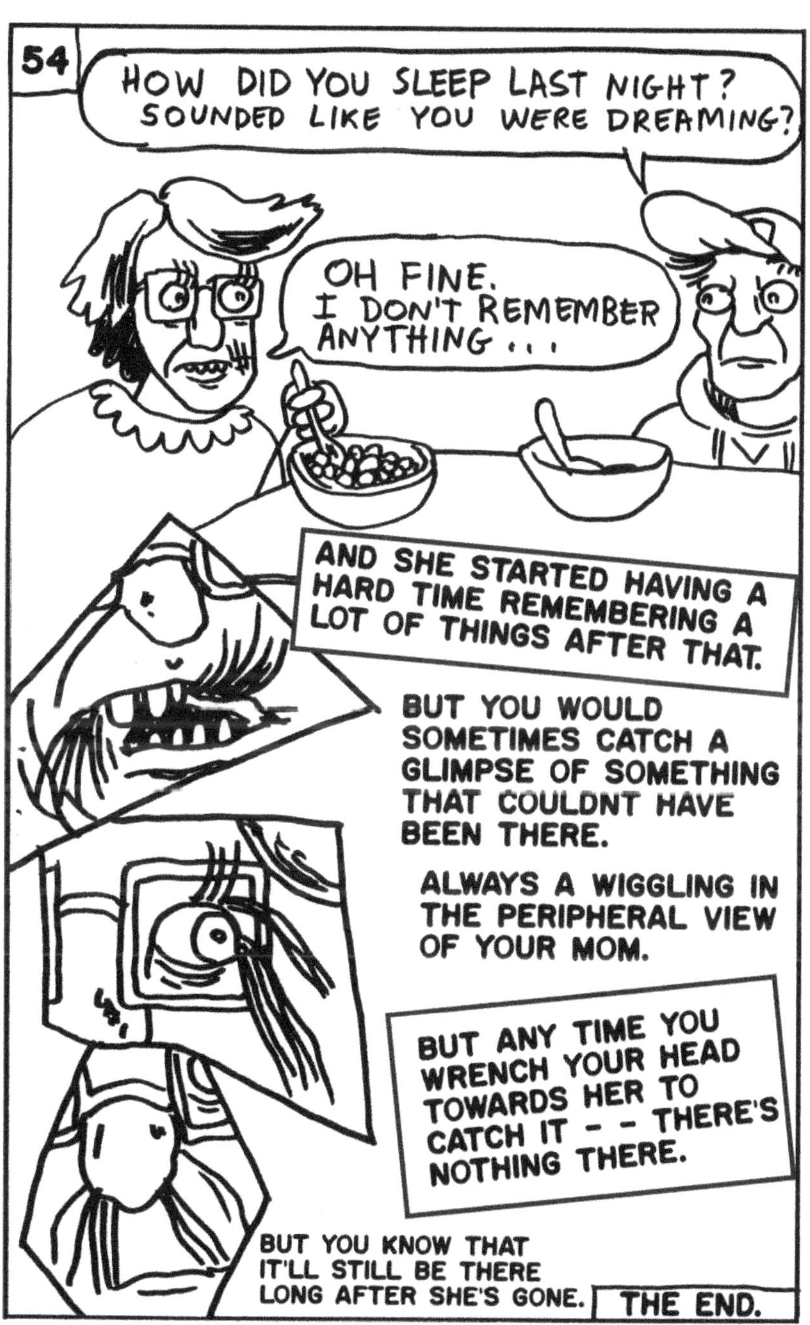
54
HOW DID YOU SLEEP LAST NIGHT? SOUNDED LIKE YOU WERE DREAMING?
OH FINE. I DON'T REMEMBER ANYTHING . . .
AND SHE STARTED HAVING A HARD TIME REMEMBERING A LOT OF THINGS AFTER THAT.
BUT YOU WOULD SOMETIMES CATCH A GLIMPSE OF SOMETHING THAT COULDNT HAVE BEEN THERE.
ALWAYS A WIGGLING IN THE PERIPHERAL VIEW OF YOUR MOM.
BUT ANY TIME YOU WRENCH YOUR HEAD TOWARDS HER TO CATCH IT - - THERE'S NOTHING THERE.
BUT YOU KNOW THAT IT'LL STILL BE THERE LONG AFTER SHE'S GONE.
THE END.

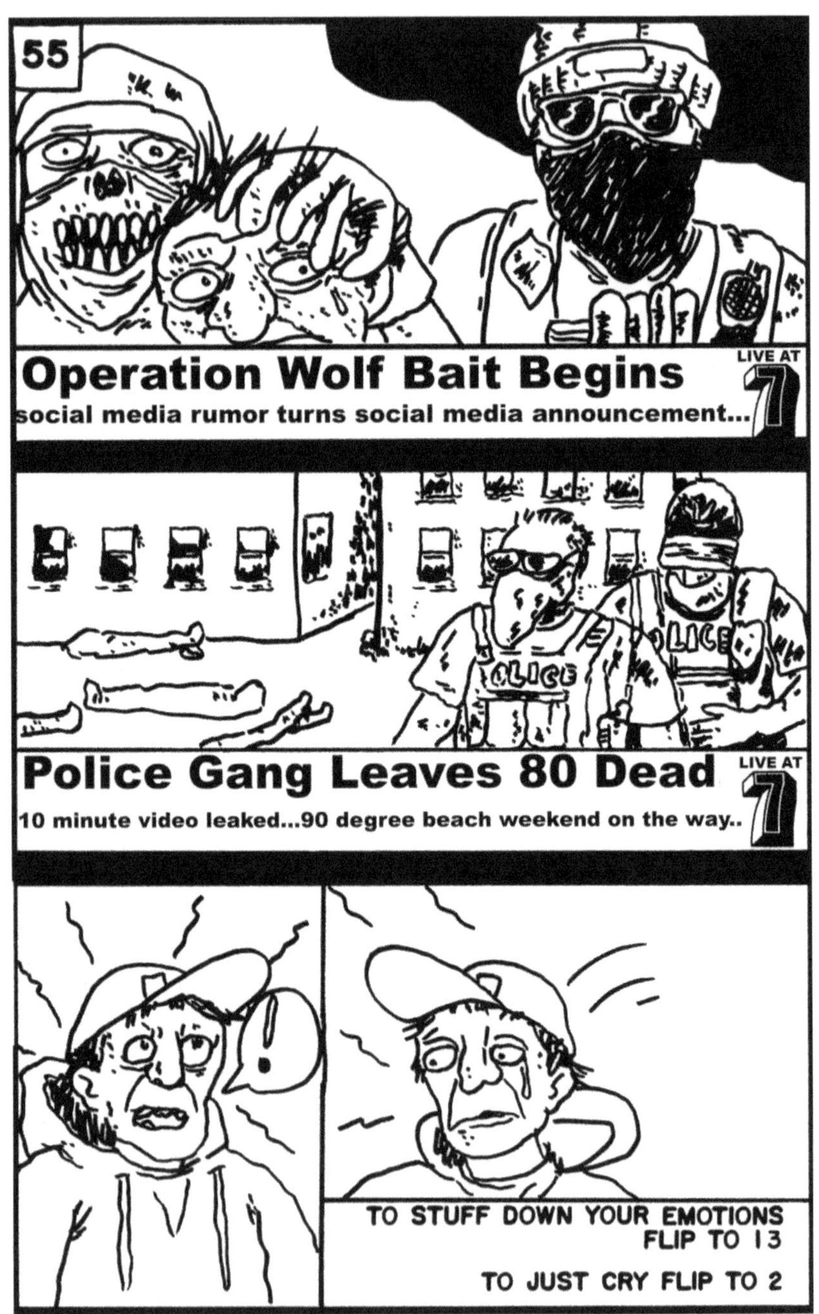

55
Operation Wolf Bait Begins
social media rumor turns social media announcement...
LIVE AT 7
Police Gang Leaves 80 Dead
10 minute video leaked...90 degree beach weekend on the way..
LIVE AT 7
TO STUFF DOWN YOUR EMOTIONS
FLIP TO 13
TO JUST CRY FLIP TO 2

56
YOU SIT FOR 20 MINUTES AND THEN GO LOOK AT THE VENDING MACHINE. ALL GARBAGE. ALL EXPENSIVE.

YOU SIT BACK DOWN . THE NURSE WHO CHECKED YOU IN NODS AND INVITES YOU TO COME BACK ON BACK.

SOON:

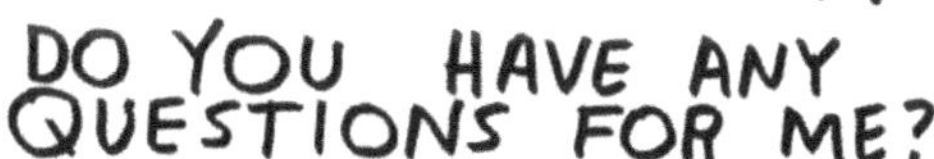

OKAY SO THIS ISN'T ANYTHING TO BE WORRIED ABOUT...

WE'LL WAIT FOR THE RESULTS BUT I EXPECT YOU'LL JUST EXPERIENCE TENDERNESS AND NEED TO KEEP TO SOFT FOODS....

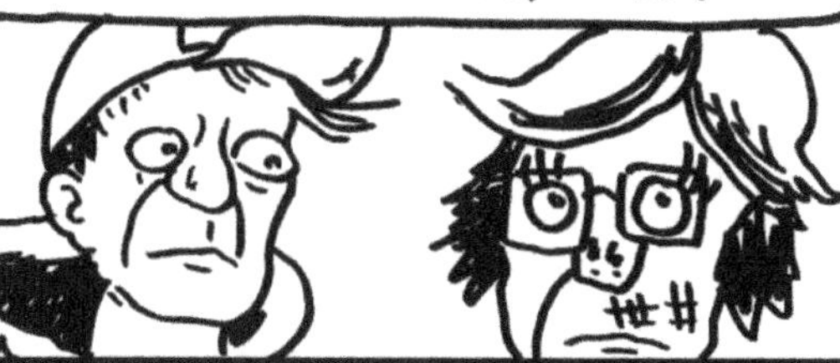

DO YOU HAVE ANY QUESTIONS FOR ME?

TO SAY "NO THANK YOU DOCTOR"
FLIP TO 6

TO ASK QUESTIONS FLIP TO 17

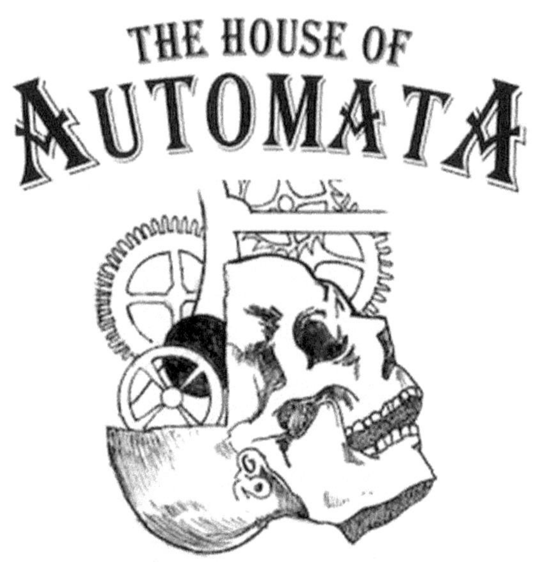

THE HOUSE OF AUTOMATA –
AN INTERVIEW WITH MICHAEL START

The House of Automata is an extensive automaton exhibition and restoration workshop in Scotland, UK. Within its walls, hundreds of antique treasures are either ready to entertain viewers, or awaiting reanimation by the deft hands of this family-run operation. In speaking with co-founder Michael Start, his love for his work is immediately palpable. Immersed in a world of mechanical figures — ranging anywhere from key-operated Parisian pigs that play trombone, to dolls which emerge from giant roses blowing kisses — who wouldn't be utterly captivated?

Zara Kand

ZK: *Would you mind giving us a brief history of automata art?*

MS: The history of automata is longer than you might think. Mythology is populated with automata and many examples are described in Homer's 'Odyssey' and 'Iliad', where the God Hephaestus created twenty Golden Tripods to serve at banquets, mechanical guard dogs, and a deadly throne that clasped to death those that sat in it — he made that for his mother.

Hero of Alexandria provides the first actual sketches and plans for automata around 2000 years ago, including archers and singing birds alongside dispensing machines and automatic doors. Prowess in automata making seems to pass like a baton across countries and civilizations throughout the last two millennia, with high points in the middle east and China, around a thousand years ago. More recently, in the 17th and 18th century, the Germans produced gilded mechanical automata based on classical and fantasy themes, including silver ships called 'Nefs' that would rock and roll down the dining table, stopping to fire their cannons. From 1750 to 1850 the baton passed to London where the English used lavish mechanical gifts, singing birds and automata laden clocks to expand international trade, gaining footholds to build their empire. Automata to this point had been objects of power, typically owned by Sultans, Emperors and Kings who desired to emulate the gods with the power of apparently bringing objects to life.

The French, from 1850 to 1920, mastered techniques to bring automata to the mass market as objects of entertainment, artistry and technology, incorporating music boxes from Switzerland and wonderful sculpture. Five or six families of artisans competed with each other to supply the world with automata via the great Paris Exhibitions that were held at intervals for nearly 60 years, buyers came from all over the world to Paris and automata were exported in the thousands.

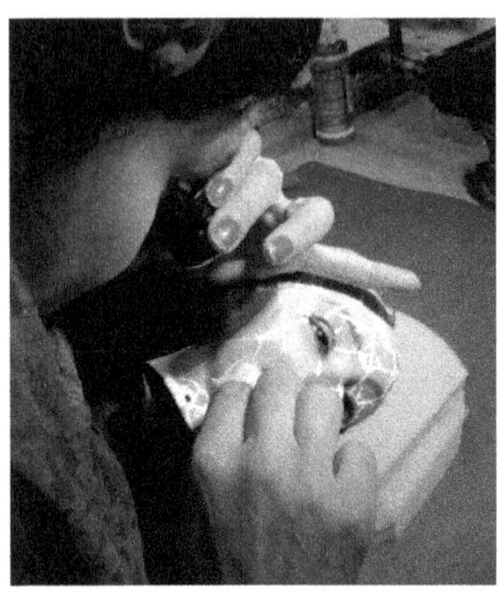

Maria sanding back the repaired cracks in this c.1880 Ball balancing automaton head

MS: I trained in Technical Horology in London and started my career as a clockmaker. Despite great success in this field, I was seduced by clockwork objects that dance, drink, or sing rather than just tell the time. A dealer in automata in London's Portobello Road market helped me to change direction, and then the skills of my wife Maria, a sculptor and painter, became vital to the workshop. This combination produced restoration work that stood up well in the commercial and museum sectors. We had found our niche.

ZK: *Who does your team consist of and what are each of your specialties?*

MS: The team at The House of Automata consists of myself, Michael, my horologist wife Maria, trained in fashion, painting and sculpture, and our youngest son Hector who graduated in Fine Art about five years ago. We also work with interns and other craftspeople who visit from institutions such as West Dean College of Restoration near London or Ecole Boulle in Paris. This keeps us in touch with modern thought on restoration and helps to prevent our approach becoming too insular.

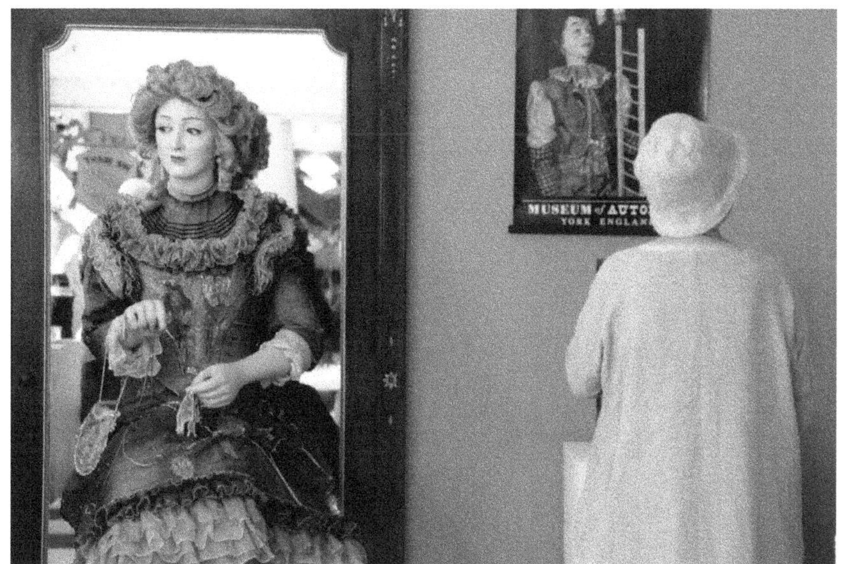

The Exhibiton of automata. Nancy, a life moving figure made in Paris c.1910 can be operated by push button.

ZK: *Can you share a bit about the technical process involved in restoring these mechanisms and how that might have changed over the last centuries?*

MS: Technically our process is a traditional one using the techniques and philosophy of clockmaking for the mechanical side and a conservative approach to the textile elements of an automaton. We experiment often with new glues, dyes, and solvents but we have consistently returned to the originals for the qualities they impart and the way they work seem to look and feel better. The two lathes used in the workshop are a 1890 Boley Swiss watchmaker's lathe and a 1958 Myford. Most restoration work is done using hand tools, and is recorded with drawings and notes in workbooks.

ZK: *How does the acquisition process work?*

MS: In a word, the Internet. When we started 40 years ago I would travel to France and buy automata in auction or markets, bring them back, restore and sell them in our central London shop. We moved to the Highlands of Scotland in 2002, cutting ourselves off physically from the market. At the same time the Internet took off and we now use internet search services and auction sites to find automata more effectively. Sellers also find us easily by the same route.

ZK: *As one of the few teams keeping these art forms alive amidst a culture increasingly prone to digital media, can you elaborate on why you feel this work is important?*

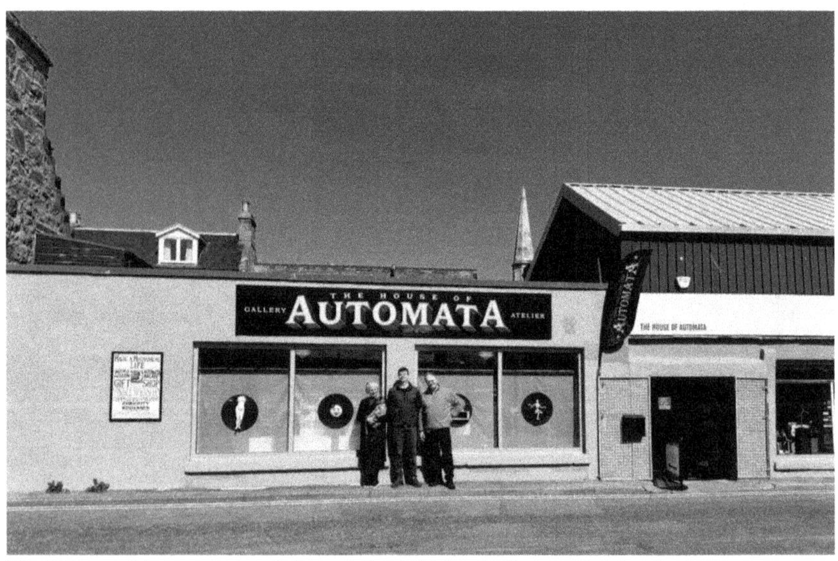

The House of Automata workshop and exhibition in Forres, Scotland

MS: Working with automata is important to me because it is a world I feel I can control. I have the same power over them as a surgeon does to people, yet automata have an infinitely longer life. The repetition of an automaton's movements is reassuring and each piece offers you a different 'take' on life. Nighttime in the museum surrounded by them is never scary, they stand or sit and wait for me to bring them to life.

ZK: *Do you feel you have made an impact on the way that people perceive the arts in general?*

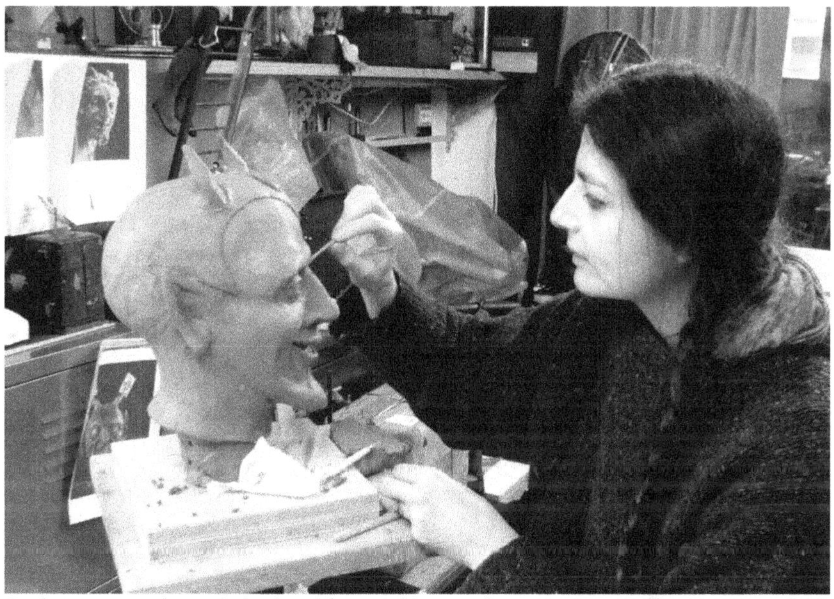
Sculpting a Mephistopheles head for moulding and a papier mache final product, filled with mechanism it will sleep and wake before producing playing cards from its mouth and the top of its head, based on an 1860s original.

MS: For many of our visitors, collectors, and supporters we have across the world I feel a responsibility to provide a sort of alternative reality to the one that our media portrays. It's escapism via physical objects rather than film or story. And the feedback we get from people is amazing.

ZK: *What is the strangest automaton you have worked on to date?*

MS: There is a subset of automata *Smokers* who inhale lit cigarettes and then puff the smoke out unexpected places. One extraordinary piece featured a seated man with a lady standing facing him: he slowly inhales on his cigarette as he leans back on his chair. From his trousers rise his impressive appendage; the surprised lady turns round and lifts her dress to sit on it ... at that moment a plume of smoke shoots up from the impressive member and she shoots up in alarm. It's hilarious and highly complex but is not on display in the exhibition!

ZK: *What have you found to be the most rewarding aspect of the work you do?*

MS: The most rewarding aspect of the work I do is that I can create my own world and populate it with mechanical people.

ZK: *Likewise, what are some of the challenges you encounter?*

MS: The main challenges I encounter are prosaically — the costs and responsibilities of operating a publicly accessible exhibition. In the workshop the challenge is recognizing our limitations, some of the rarest and finest work can only be done properly by further specialism, repeating processes to perfection and our restoration expertise is quite broad which means there are limits to what we can excel at.

ZK: *You are also an exhibition space, hosting events in which visitors can view these antique*

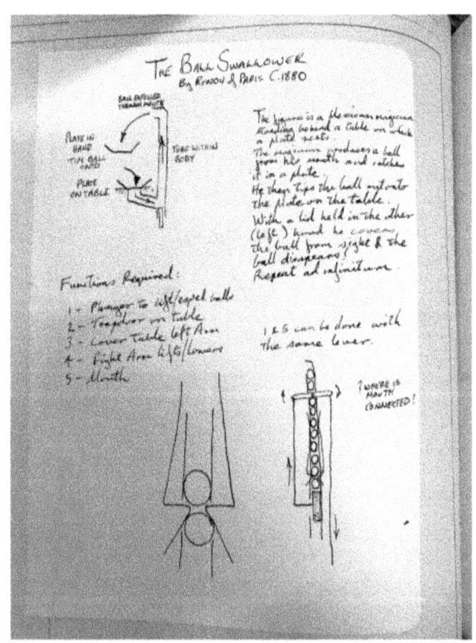

Page of notebook referencing the Ball Regurgitating automaton by Renou, c.1880. The Mexican magician produces brightly coloured balls from his mouth and placing them on a plate in front of him they disappear one at a time.

marvels up close in all their tangible glory. Can you share a little about the nature of these events? What tends to be the audience response to such sensory experiences?

MS: We open the exhibition to the public three days a week and on the last Saturday of every month we hold an 'Automata Salon'. This is a special show of automata in action for a seated audience which show rare and impressive automata working. We usually end with the Archer firing four tiny sharp arrows one after the other across the room. The shows have always sold out and are great fun.

ZK: *You've recently put out the book* 'Secrets of Automata'. *What was the impetus for this publication, and could you give us a feel for its contents?*

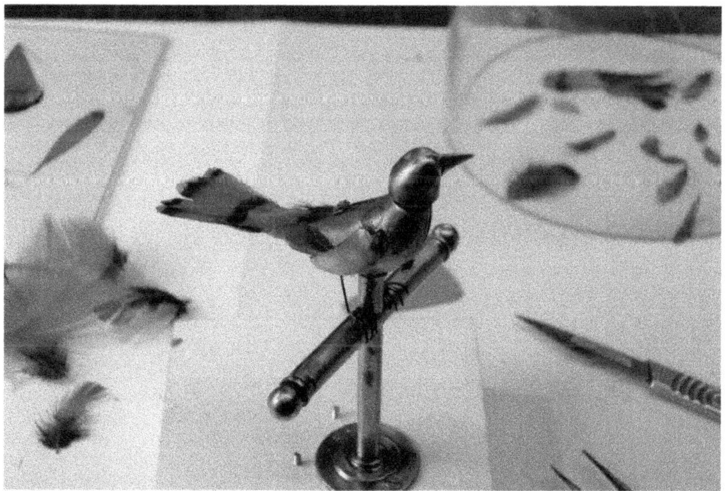

Feathering a mechanical singing bird

MS: *'Secrets of Automata - Ingenious Designs for Mechanical Life'* is a book I had to write. We often see modern makers designing movement from scratch, like reinventing the wheel. Nearly all of the movements and sounds of life and nature have been portrayed by automata makers in the past. Eating, walking, dancing, sailing, wind, and water all have a mechanical version, some of which are ingeniously lifelike. These mechanisms were often not recorded, designed to be hidden in the bodies or the bases of the automata they animate. I found that time and time again, I would open up an automaton and see lost secrets of mechanical design that were not recorded anywhere. So I compiled an eclectic mix of automata movements from waterspouts to tightrope walking, with birdsong in between, and documented the mechanical principles that made this happen with photographs and technical drawings of over two hundred mechanisms.

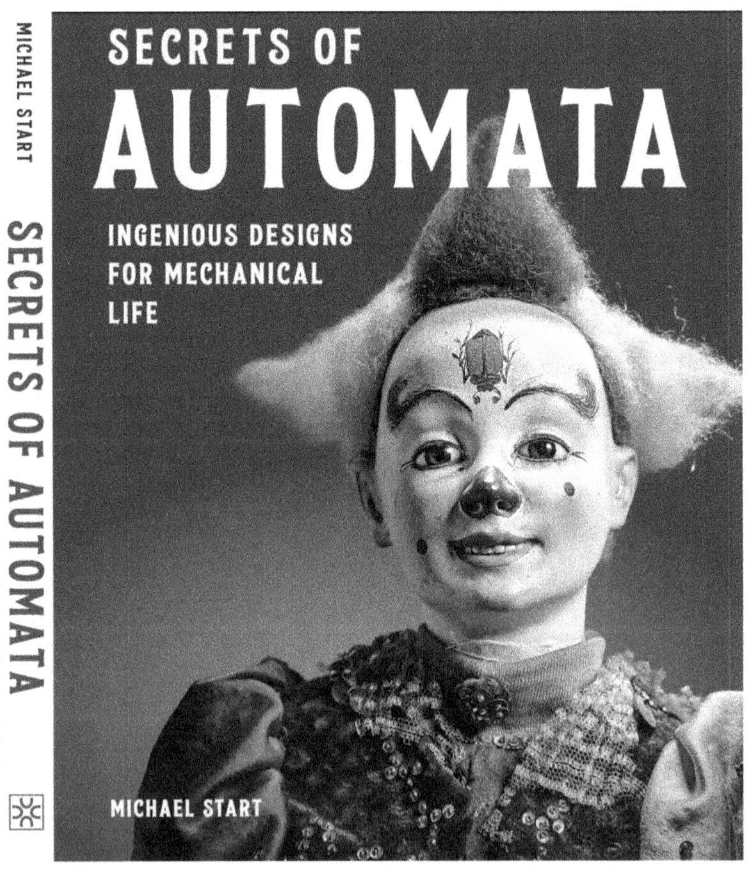

CHICKEN SOUP FOR ETERNAL DAMNATION
By Jean-Paul L. Garnier

Well, I'd done it now. I'd really done it. Always figured it was a possibility, and now it had happened. I was in hell. Hell with a capital H. Yep, I'd done it. If it was one thing in particular, or just a cumulation of little things, I couldn't say. And it's not like they give you a pamphlet explaining everything when you arrive. Unless, I guess, explanatory pamphlets aren't your thing. In that case they might provide one, or many. But I didn't mind pamphlets so much, so there weren't any. But something to read would have been nice. Didn't see any books though, just a big empty room. Not exactly the picture I would have imagined, but how would I have known what to expect, it's not exactly like I'd studied up on what to find in hell, or any of the alternatives. Not only was I naïve enough not to know why I'd ended up here, but I had no idea what to expect. Sure did feel like hell though. I would have thrilled to read an explanatory pamphlet. Boring, dull – not the exciting fire and brimstone, but thoroughly uninviting and mundane. Nothing to do but sit there, so I sat. Sat long enough to be bored out of my gourd, and then sat some more. They really couldn't have provided less to do. Nothing to look at. Not even a smell to the place. It was as blank as blank could be. And I knew damned well this was hell, but didn't know why I knew. I knew nothing, my mind was empty, and that in and of itself made it hellish. Completely without stimuli, boring as can be.

I spoke to fill that vast silence, and nothing came out. My mouth was as empty as the room. Tried to stand up since I'd been sitting for God knows how long, but I couldn't. Seemed that part of hell was designed to thwart every want, need, or desire. Nothing happened. No one came. By then I was hungry and bored out of my skull, it really was hell. And it stayed that way for longer than I can remember.

I tried lying on the floor to sleep but couldn't. And no matter what position I tried it was like there was pieces of gravel under me, even though I kept sweeping the floor with my hands. As I was repositioning for the thousandth time, a door appeared in the wall and a man wearing khakis and a light blue t-shirt entered the room carrying a clipboard.

"We're ready for you, sir. Please come with me. Right this way."

He was reading off of a script and had a practiced, saccharine tone. Very corporate.

"Really? Where are we going?"

My voice sounded this time but was scratchy from disuse.

"Why, to the waiting room, of course. Right this way."

Waiting room? Then what the hell was this? What the hell, indeed. My knees wobbled as I got up while the man gestured to the door. When I entered the room he motioned to some chairs in the corner and exited the way he had come in. The door disappeared as soon as he was through it.

The room looked much like the waiting room in a dentist office, but with no receptionist. It was virtually empty except for the chairs and a small table between them. I guessed I was supposed to wait some more, but for what, I could not say. Under the table in a small wicker basket were two magazines. Both identical back issues of *Highlights Magazine*, yellowed with age, complete with a peeling sticker with some doctor's name and home address scratched out with fading pencil. Wouldn't be my first choice but finally it was something to read. Before coming to this place I would, and could, read just about anything. My home was always filled with books that I thought that I'd get around to reading eventually. Even in the shower I'd find myself reading the backs of the shampoo and conditioner bottles, or a cereal box in the kitchen, I'd read anything that was put in front of me. So, *Highlights Magazine* it was. Normally it would have been my absolutely last choice of magazines, but it was there and so was I. And since this was a "waiting room" I supposed that they would make me wait. For what? God only knew. Or perhaps the Devil only knew. Who knows. Reluctantly but obsessively I picked up the stale back issue. Nothing but smarmy articles and an already finished crossword puzzle. Read it cover to cover, twice. A shampoo bottle would have been preferable. It couldn't have taken me more than twenty minutes to suffer through the poorly written and uninteresting pieces and ads in the magazine but my butt was starting to go numb as if I'd been sitting there for hours. I tried to reposition myself in the chair but could not budge. So, it was back to the magazine for round three. I grabbed the other identical issue in hopes that it would somehow be different, but there was no variation except for the name of the subscriber sticker on the front.

After three more reads I couldn't take it anymore. I would have torn the magazines to pieces for want of something to do, but as little comfort as it had brought I kept thinking about leaving the next victim of the waiting room with even less to do than I had been provided. It might be hell but there was no reason to be a jerk.

The wait was getting to me and I still didn't even know what I was waiting for. Frustrated, I read through the magazine again, cover to cover. By now I had nearly memorized the thing. My head felt like it was falling off with boredom and discomfort but I couldn't bring myself to take yet another pass at the rag.

Sitting there not reading was even worse, almost. I would have given anything for one of Ballard's novels, or anything really, something to pass the time in a world other than this, in contemplation. Nothing but white walls to occupy me here, and the damnable ancient back issue of *Highlights*. There wasn't even bricks to count, just bare smooth white walls. They stretched time into even longer intervals, giving nothing, devoid of personality.

A door materialized and the guy in khakis entered again, big smile dripping with an eager to please falsity.

"Oh, good, you're still here."

As if there had been an option to leave. I didn't answer with anything but a truly bored look.

He continued, "Good, good, very good."

I wasn't following him but figured his words were designed to annoy.

"Please follow me, right this way. And please, do bring the magazines, if you like."

Hard pass. Regardless of what waited on the other side of the door that hadn't been there a moment ago. I took my time getting up, figuring there was no hurry to be led to yet another waiting room, the next hopefully with different magazines, but his offer to take them didn't leave me much in the way of hope. He never stopped with that saccharine smile as he gestured for me to enter before him. The door led to a long blank hallway and it made me uncomfortable to be followed through the passage that was so narrow no two people could stand shoulder to shoulder. And the longer we walked down the hall the longer it seemed to become. I couldn't be sure how long we walked, but it felt like fifteen minutes or more.

Finally, we reached a door and my guide nudged by me to open it, but he did not enter.

"This is your room, sir. I won't be joining you as it's been designed specifically for you, and we value privacy."

With that he turned and left and somehow managed to vanish from the hallway within seconds. Reluctantly I entered and the door automatically shut behind me. At first I had a difficult time seeing, as the fluorescent lights were overly bright, but within a few minutes my eyes adjusted. As my vision returned I couldn't believe my eyes. Perhaps I wasn't in hell at all? On one side of the room sat an overstuffed armchair next to a small end table. It looked comfortable too, despite the tacky upholstery, but it would have fit right in at my apartment back home. On the other side of the room the wall was fully lined with bookshelves, complete with library. And next to that was a milk crate full of LPs and a portable turntable. Oh boy, did my spirits lift! I don't know what all the waiting was about but apparently it had been worth the wait. A comfy chair and all I could read, perhaps this was heaven.

I tested out the chair with a pat of my hands and indeed it was a cozy one. I sat for a minute and took a deep breath, collecting myself. Yes, this would do nicely. Getting back up I approached the shelves to make my selection. Starting at the top left shelf in the case on the right I perused the titles and my heart sank. I said it out loud because I couldn't believe what I was seeing, as if somehow speaking would undo the reality of it, "The complete works of Glen Beck, yuck!" This certainly wasn't heaven! Or maybe it was someone's idea of a joke. When I looked at the next shelf down I knew it wasn't. The complete works of Bill Cosby. Couldn't even bring myself to say it out loud this time. It was wrong. It was cruel. But it also sparked a curiosity in me. A morbid curiosity. Wondering how bad it could get, I continued to scan the bookshelves. Bill O'Reilly, Palin's biography, Reader's Digest abridged novels, Dan Bongino, Barbara Bush's biography, Triggered, the complete James Patterson, all of the Left Behind books, it went on and on. An orgy of bad taste. A virtual who's who of those who had corruptly bought their way onto some bestseller list, you know the ones with the little cross next to the title. Ironic to choose the symbol of Christianity for such devious game playing with money, numbers, and perception. There were hundreds of books that I, or no one in their right mind would want to read. I'd never been so defeated and unhappy around bookshelves. Was I being haunted by ghostwriters? But I held onto hope and scanned the titles, futility.

The last two bookshelves were filled completely with *Chicken Soup for the Soul* books. A perfect punctuation to my disgust. And it brought to mind a forgotten dream where I had written a book called *"Chicken Soup for Eternal Damnation,"* which was now starting to look all too prophetic. Even if I could bring myself to read all this schlock it would be worse than rereading the dead magazine that I now regretted leaving behind. It was sick.

With the bookshelves a total waste of space I looked to the crate of LPs fearful of what I might find. Thank God they weren't audiobooks, I guess. But it wasn't much better than the titles on the shelves, it was as if someone had transplanted every unwanted thrift store dusty stack of vinyl with a careful ear for everything I never wanted to hear. Streisand and Kristofferson, Frampton Comes Alive, Jazzercise workouts, Sing Along with Mitch, I couldn't even bring myself to say the band names, there were so many among my least favorites. But I kept digging in a frantic hope that something listenable had slipped through the cracks.

At the very back, the last album was a battered old copy of a CCR record. Finally, something palatable, no matter how overplayed and not high on my list, having heard it countless times before. It was something anyway. Almost with relish I clicked the turntable on and reached for the album to slide it out of its sleeve.

And the sleeve was empty.

So, I listened to the motor of the turntable running, the white noise the only bearable entertainment to be found. Until it clicked off on its own, never to turn on again.

I still didn't know what I'd done to end up here, but one thing was for sure. I was in Hell.

SEXUAL DISTANCING – AN INTERVIEW WITH CAM GIRL MORGAN LEE

Sex work is one of the oldest forms of work in recorded history. What happens when this form of labor merges with technology? Does our relationship with technology alter our sexuality? And how do sex workers protect their mental and physical health? At *Electronic Brain* we aim for open and earnest conversations about topics which are prevalent in our society, but remain taboo subjects for open discussion. Pornography has been at the heart of many first-amendment cases, often paving the way for what artists and writers can get away with, and it is often an indicator of how society's mores change over time. We spoke to cam girl Morgan Lee about her thoughts on these subjects, where human sexuality is headed, the politics of labor, and the motivations behind those who hire sex workers.

Jean-Paul L. Garnier

JPG: *What was your motivation for going into this line of work, and if you could, perhaps give us an example of your background in this type of work?*

ML: I've done this twice in my life and the first time was in college and the main motivation was having a little extra income, I was putting myself through college with two jobs and still not able to quite meet the financial needs of where I was in my life and so, at that point I was on Chaturbate and a friend of mine recommended that I do it. It was just kind of a fun side. I've also been somebody that's been very sexually open. So, it was a very quick and easy way to make ends meet. Round 2. Same mentality, post COVID, I had been laid off from my job at the beginning of the pandemic and needed to make some money. And knew that was a quick and easy way to make money, as a lot of people did during that time. And it was just something that I was familiar with, something that I was comfortable with, again still being a very sexually open person, somebody who is really good at talking to people and chatting and flirting. I'm in sales as my main job and the pipeline between those two things is actually, I think, quite easy. It's all customer service. It's chatting, making sure people are happy, and it was a really easy transition.

JPG: *Aside from financial reasons were there other motivations tied into that?*

ML: I tend to lean on the voyeuristic side of sexuality. There's always been a little bit of me that likes being an exhibitionist. There's an attention that I kind of crave that sex work, or camming, definitely scratches.

JPG: *Does that fulfill a different need than in more personalized sexual exchanges?*

ML: Entirely.

JPG: *Can you elaborate on how that's different, if you're comfortable with that?*

ML: I think it's different in a lot of ways. I guess I should preface this with that I'm also polyamorous. Maybe I just have a slutty brain. But, you know when you come home and you see your partner, even if you have a great sex life, you have a little bit of an expectation. Somebody who is a little bit needy or is a little bit of a perfectionist, it's really nice to have a whole gauntlet of men telling you that you're hot everyday. It's really good for your mental health, in my opinion. And it's also validating in a way that's different. You can come home and be like, I'm sloppy and I had a bad day and your partner can be perfect and make you dinner. Or you can also just post a picture of your ass on the Internet and have a bunch of men tell you that you're really hot and say that they want to send you money about it. That's validating in a way that I don't think that anything else could really verify.

JPG: *You mentioned having done this at several different periods of your life. Has that response to this type of validation changed over time for you?*

ML: I think that validation is a little bit cyclical. There's times where it's just like, hell yeah, this is awesome. There's times that it's like this is something that is very mentally healthy for me. This is something that is fun. This is something that I enjoy. This is something that I find sexually, emotionally and even physically fulfilling. And then there's other times where it becomes a burden. And in that regard, I think it's very much like any other job. There's those days where you make a good sale, or you get a good contract, or you make the perfect garden for somebody, whatever your job may be. And then there's the days where it's the most emotionally draining thing you can do to wake up and see ten messages. And I don't think that it's any different than any other job in that specific regard of some days you're super stoked on it, and other days are just like, oh my God throw me off a bridge.

JPG: *What do you think is the motivation behind your clients engaging in this sort of exchange, beyond just sex and masturbation?*

ML: One of the things that I think was both the highest motivator of my job and one of the main reasons for me hitting burnout in that job was the loneliness. My background is actually in psychology and I feel like it's very easy to become a fake therapist. I feel the same way about bartenders and hair stylists, sex workers—all of us should actually have an honorary master's degree in psychology, if not a doctorate. But one thing that I found regularly, the way that I made the most money was to send videos.

It was the same video to every guy. Obviously I don't have time to customize every single video, but to my top clients I would roll over in a cute little negligee, puffy eyed, not looking cute, no makeup on, not having my hair done or anything. And roll over and just send a video saying "good morning, baby" and send that to them on Snapchat. I got more money from that than any of the most graphic, most pornographic videos that I ever sent. I was specifically working mostly with straight males, but I think the male loneliness of wanting to wake up next to somebody and having that video sent to them at 6:30 in the morning, that would guarantee me like $600 a day. Like I said, I was doing it for money, obviously great money, but also emotionally taxing to realize how many men are that lonely. And how disconnected we are as a society that people are willing to send me $20 every morning to not even see my tits. Just to see cleavage in a negligee, me and my bed in my half painted, floor unfinished shitty bedroom. It was both a motivator and the reason I wanted to stop because that takes an emotional toll of realizing how disconnected we all are.

JPG: And do you find that that's a different set of motivations when dealing with women or trans clients?

ML: I unfortunately haven't had the chance to work with a lot of women clients. Trans clients, I wouldn't say that I've worked with a ton. I did work with a lot of clients that were questioning their gender and or sexuality. A lot of them used me as a personal therapist, as somebody who was open-minded as well as obviously sexually open in a lot of ways. I had a lot of clients that would show me pictures of themselves, males dressed in women's clothing that were on the spectrum between cross dressing or trans questioning. A lot of them didn't even know where they were on that spectrum. Again, falling into that therapist, psychologist, accidental job of "I want to root you on. And yeah, you look hot," and them sending me more nudes than I was even sending them. That was actually very common.

JPG: *Do you think that clients were helped in discovering their identities in that way, and on the inverse of that, what did you learn about how you identify through those exchanges?*

ML: It's hard to know where any of those clients ended up because I was obviously not a clinical psychologist, keeping data. I hope they're all doing great. I hope they all were able to come out in whatever way that they needed to. But that's kind of under the umbrella of sex work, being people's unofficial psychologist. I don't know how any of them are doing. I haven't followed up. I stopped doing sex work after about a year of it, last round, so I don't know where any of these people are now. I think that my personal experience with it is still a little burnt out because again, a psychologist is equipped with all of this knowledge on how to avoid burnout. How to manage all these situations, how to have time on, time off. And in sex work it's really funny, because you want to promote yourself and you want to hustle, and really if you don't stay on all the time you lose viewers and you lose clientele. And so even if I'm only gonna use this one website, you have to promote yourself through Snapchat, TikTok or Instagram. At the end of the day you find yourself always on and then you get home and just want to not have sex. I've been having fake sex with people all day, and then when you get home, it's just like, "no partner, sorry. I'm over it." One of the roughest things that's not really spoken about is how much our own sex lives suffer from doing it for work. And I assume that construction workers also don't want to come home and renovate their garage.

JPG: *How often does cosplay and or role-playing enter into the requests from clients?*

ML: The market for it is very significant. I never engaged that much because it's an area of expertise that I didn't really know. I know that there are a lot of great sex workers out there that are into a myriad of different cosplay activities. Even with the dom/sub switch scenarios, a lot of people were a lot more intense about that than I ever really felt myself fitting into. I would engage in some. I definitely felt that it was easier to fall into sub. Because then I had a dom telling me what they wanted me to do, but I also had a lot of men that wanted me to dom them. I've never been fully immersed in this. Even though I'm a little comfortable domming in personal life, doing it professionally I always had a little bit of imposter syndrome. And some of those guys really did need an actual dom and I don't think my imposter syndrome was completely unfounded. But yeah, a lot of guys wanted a lot of intensity that I don't know that I was ready to give them.

JPG: *And with the clients, do you think they were discerning enough to identify when you were outside of your comfort level, like if you were experiencing imposter syndrome? For instance, is that something the client is paying enough attention to pick up on, or is it just that their focus is around their particular need at that time?*

ML: No, those guys are a little relentless. I feel like when you're online, you are just this object more so than the objectification of women generally in sex work. I think that's one of the things that separates those divides of the sectors of sex work. But I think a lot of these guys are like, no, you can do it, you can learn, which almost seems encouraging. But in retrospect, and after meditating on it a little bit, you realize that these guys just don't want to pay the girls that actually know what they're doing. So, they try to find the girls that are newer and aren't super confident and try to work them into what they want them to be. Which has its own psychology too, for sure. But yeah, I feel like a lot of the guys were just, "Oh, you're new. We're just gonna straight up take advantage of you," which I don't know how that relates to sex work in person, per se, but it definitely seems like it's easier to take advantage of somebody on the Internet, just like you can yell at somebody on Facebook a lot different than you can yell at somebody in real life. I think that that comes through a lot in online cam work.

JPG: *So, obviously in S&M culture power dynamics are a big part of the puzzle. But because this exchange is not faceless but removed through the technology, how much do you feel that those power dynamics were engaged in and how do you navigate your comfort level in that? For the client, how much of it is about power for them versus just sexuality? When it goes into a place that is more about power dynamic than it is about sex, how do you guard your own feelings and navigate it within your own comfort level?*

ML: I think a lot of it is power dynamics, especially with the veil of the Internet. A lot of guys feel like they have more power than they do, and then going into S&M stuff it's really hard to say no, but also there's this awesome protection of just not responding to a message, whereas physical sex workers are in a situation, they're physically in front of somebody who could cause harm to them, whereas I could just delete and block. Which makes a huge difference, and I think that's one of the biggest differences in the different sectors of sex work.

People are bullies online and they can treat you however they want. They can say whatever dirty things. You can say, hey, "I specialize in X,Y and Z." And they're like, "No, but I want you to do this." And you're like, "I don't do that." And you get all these, nasty messages or pleas like, "can you please do this? Can you please do that." Or "fuck you for not doing this? Fuck you, you're a slut." What do you mean? I'm a slut? Obviously, I am. I'm naked on the Internet. But you're not allowed to call me a slut when you just paid me $10.00 for a video of my pussy.

JPG: *What are your thoughts, and this is both personally and professionally, on the giving versus receiving of fantasy scenarios?*

ML: I think that is very specific to each worker. I worked with people that wanted to have a lot of fantasy, and I don't think that is something that I specialized in. I was definitely in it for more of a "quick get your rocks off." I was working on a site that was known for more of a connection base if you will.

JPG: *A girlfriend experience type of thing?*

ML: Girlfriend experience, very chat oriented. A lot of conversations. A lot of fucking nerds, if I may, that wanted to talk out these elaborate experiences. Whereas I'm just trying to put my pussy on the Internet and get $10 per picture. But there's definitely need for that out there. The amount of people that really either wanted the human connection that "good morning, babe, how are you," down to people that would write literally twelve paragraphs a day describing what they wanted to do to me. And sometimes it was hot. Sometimes it was terrifying, sometimes it was somewhere in between that I'll use the all-encompassing "exciting" for that. And you can kind of tell how people's actual lives are. You can tell who has a wife and they're dissatisfied and want to get their rocks off real quick. And the people that are bordering on incel and need this weird, long story. To maybe start edging?

JPG: *In your experience, what was the proportional breakdown of just wanting to get off versus elaborate fantasy?*

ML: I would say it was probably 25% elaborate fantasy, 25% rocks off. And 50% lonely men looking for connection.

JPG: *What's the strangest request that you ever received?*
ML: I told you about Knife Man.

JPG: *You said, "Knife Man," but you didn't elaborate on that? I can only imagine where this goes next.*

ML: Knife Man was definitely the most elaborate storyteller that I worked with. He was also one of my highest paying clients. He wanted storytelling, and that's when I was like, I don't really think I can do this, and I told him, "You know, love you, buddy. But I don't have time to invest. And I'm also not a creative writer." He would write these gorgeous, actually pretty fucking hot scenarios. And I'm just not a writer. I felt like a guy responding to a woman in a traditional sense of, "cool babe." But he was very into S&M and had a lot of scenarios of fucking me with knives, which is why I call him "Knife Man." It was a lot of slow build up and some of them are traditional things like pouring hot wax on my body while I'm tied up. And almost every scenario started with him fucking me with the base of a knife. After sliding the entire knife over my body, so I don't know if I'm going to be harmed or not. And I think this is actually, now that I'm saying it out loud, an important part of sex work. People that might be a little divergent in any way shape or form are able to talk through fantasies that they can't do in person. Because even in an S&M club rubbing a knife over somebody and having that person not know if they're going to actually be harmed physically or killed is a lot. Online, it's safe. I had a VPN, as far as he knows I'm working in England. But yeah, the fantasy was almost always the same—rubbing a knife against my neck, against pretty much every main artery and then turning the knife around and fucking me with the handle until I cum. Then he would never finish the story of what he wanted to do after. Which is always fascinating to me. It didn't get me off. Not my thing. But again, he paid well just to write these stories to me every day. He should probably be in porn writing rather than paying girls to listen to his stories. That's the standout of all of my clients.

JPG: *Let me process that for a minute.*

ML: And again, I think that's why part of sex work, especially online sex work, is super healthy. There's a lot of people that have a lot of things that they can't tell, a therapist might actually send you to a place if you tell them that. He was a successful business guy and he would come home and just want to write these stories, but he wanted to share them with somebody and he would pay girls online to listen to them and engage in them. I don't know what that means from a psychological perspective. I only have my bachelor's degree in child development. I don't have a degree in human sexuality and adult psychology. But there was something going on with that guy for sure. But I hope that he takes a girl out and fucks her in a very normal and healthy way. Because he's able to have these fantasies online for money.

JPG: *When it comes to these sorts of fantasies that are shared in these scenarios, is it often a high degree of specificity, like what you've just explained, or is there, for lack of a better word, more of a pedestrian angle—vanilla sex, for instance?*

ML: It was all over the place. There was a lot of vanilla sex with guys just wanting to be like, "Hey, do you want to cam real quick, in live-time? And I will tell you how to get naked in front of me while I jack off." And I would charge them for 30 minutes and it took 10. But then there was also the opposite side of the spectrum of these guys that want me to write novels back about these almost *Story of O* level experiences of S&M. There was also everything in between. The most filler, and I did see this a lot, was people that had recently had a kid and/or had been married for a while, that wanted a third, but weren't ready to commit to physical engagement with another person. So, I regularly just shook my ass online for a couple that would pay me to explore how they might feel having a threesome, from a safe distance where the physical fears are gone, like disease, STIs etc. Also the removal of the physical intimacy, that's a little debatable… But for the most part, it was a safe way to explore what they might want. It was a lot of guys in that "I might want to leave my wife… Let me see how I actually feel... Am I still a sexual being? How do I feel about cheating without physically cheating?" Which I don't know how

I feel about that line, but I understand that it is a little easier for people to fuck somebody on the Internet versus in person and their partner's interpretation of that also being very different.

JPG: *So, in my understanding it was a large percentage of this being almost a trial run for potential Poly relationships.*

ML: The medium was, I would say 70%, then there was the outliers on the crazy and the needy. And the middle was guys trying to just jack off. Or people trying to figure out how to open up their relationships. And that might be site specific for the site that I was on.

JPG: *Where do you draw the line with request and at what point do you find an exchange to be inappropriate, and if so, how then do you handle it? You mentioned blocking people before but if it hasn't quite gotten to that level, for instance....*

ML: That definitely took me a minute to realize, like with any job. And going through this with my current job, it's really easy to say yes to everything and then it's really easy to quickly feel overwhelmed. And that's when I started telling people this isn't my expertise, find a different girl. And a lot of people would request, for a decent amount of money, very specific requests. At first I was trying to take all of them. And then realized I don't have the time or capacity for this. And also, I don't have expertise in this. Find something you do better, just like any other business. If you're a cobbler, you don't necessarily know how to fix a belt just because you work with leather. And it took me probably three months to learn how to say, "this is what I'm good at and this is what I'm not."

JPG: *And did you ever find that there were certain requests that perhaps initially you were being accepting of that were having negative repercussions for you, in a mental health way, that you had to define different boundaries for as the work went on?*

ML: Definitely, the amount of guys that are immediately like, "you're just a fucking whore, you should die." Textbook incel responses are definitely prevalent. I, luckily was smart enough to immediately block, block, block. But it still takes an emotional toll to read that.

JPG: *Roughly what percentage of these scenarios did you find that the clients are coming from a misogynistic place?*

ML: The website that I was working on in both circumstances, pretty low. I would say 3%. It was not as much of a problem as I think a lot of people think it might be.

JPG: *What are your thoughts on the porn industry being democratized? For example, moving away from big industry with mafia ties to people being able to create and distribute it from home with nothing but a phone?*

ML: I think there's pros and cons. I think that all of us should have personal integrity and control over our own bodies and how we want to sell them. In whatever interpretation you want that to be. The best reference to look at is the music industry. In the 90s, we all got to listen to the same music and there was something that was great about that. We all listened to the same song and got to relate to that. But everybody was manipulated over it. And now, with the advancements in technology, there are bands that are on the Billboard top 10 that have never had a record deal because you can produce your own shit and put it on the Internet. And that comes with its own set of problems. I think for the most part it's for the best because it cuts out a lot of manipulation and a lot of the mob shit. I don't think any John should be making money off of a woman. And I think that it does offer a lot of empowerment for anybody to be able to do sex work online. That's something that we're talking about for online sex work that isn't even soon to be in the conversation about physical sex work. What does that actually mean for the girls that are on the streets? What does that mean for strippers? How many strippers are still paying out 75% of their nightly income to the DJ's and the house? That's a conversation that needs to be had at every level of this industry because it means something significantly different for all of us.

JPG: *As someone that hasn't done in person sex work, do you think it gives a different sense of agency, to not have a pimp scenario for instance, or something like cocaine introduced to lower inhibition and things that the pornography industry traditionally did in some eras as a form of manipulation? Do you think it's provided a greater sense of agency for people in sex work?*

ML: I think that still falls very much into where you are in the sex work umbrella. It's very different depending on where you're at. Some of us benefit, whereas I think everybody else is almost suffering but everybody thinks that it's better because of the people that don't have that.

JPG: *You mentioned getting back into it during COVID and layoffs, do you think that pornography was drastically altered by the social distancing of COVID, similar to the rise of popularity in pornography during the HIV crisis as a safe sex alternative? And does this mean we're moving into an era of sexual distancing?*

ML: I think that sexuality is changing a lot. I question where sexuality is going. I feel like 50 years ago if we were married and you saw another woman, you might cheat on me with her. And it's so easy to not do that and just masturbate to OnlyFans and throw her $20. I don't know how much of that is about safety, per se, I think that the AIDS crisis is a really good reference to ponder.

That's something I actually would love to sit and write about personally.

JPG: *Now that sexuality and technology are so intertwined for many people, especially in these forms of sex, at least in the business angle of sexuality, where do you think that notions of sex and sexuality will go from here? What do you think the future of sexuality is, how will sexuality change on account of how differently we're interacting with it than we have in the past?*

ML: I think that it'll very much mirror how everything else is changing in light of technology. There's a lot of conversations about autism spectrum disorder becoming more prevalent because of how online we are all the time and we're not having these human interactions. And the way that we respond to each other, the way that we interact with each other has all changed with technology. Being able to send a thumbs up emoji instead of saying, "hi, thank you for your response, I really appreciate you." I think that sex work is just going to forever mirror current culture. I feel like we're all becoming a little bit more concise in our communication. I think that we are all cutting a lot of culture out of our communication and our lives in general, I mean I'm guilty of this. I feel like porn, as well as everything else in our generation, has come to scrolling to the good part, to just fucking cum. And all of us, especially with social media and the Internet, have become so dopamine addicted because of so much stimulation with online culture. We all want the immediate. When is the climax gonna happen? I feel like that is very much reflected in the porn industry as well.

JPG: *In relation to that, do you think that this has altered and changed the nature of how fantasy works for people?*

ML: Oh, entirely. I mean, fucking fast forward to the cumshot. None of us want the story. Twenty years ago, renting a porn from the video store, it would be an hour video. Who has an hour to watch a video of sex? Who masturbates for that long? Who wants the buildup and the story of so and so coming over, whatever the setting may be, whether it's aliens or a stepbrother or whatever. I don't have time for that. Show me the fucking cumshot compilation. I need to get off in less than 5 minutes, and I feel like that is changing culture of—we just need to get going. And I don't think that's going to change, it's only going to get worse. But on the flip side of that, the Instagram person in me that spends entirely too much time scrolling, has noticed a lot of girls posting about smut. Specifically fairy smut, and I don't know what I did to my algorithm to make that as much of a thing as it is. So, girls are going back to reading smut. I don't know where that lies within the general Pornhub cum compilation side of what I just said, but it does seem like there is almost this revolution against that too. Sit and read smut. And it's having a little bit of a revival, in a weird way. I don't really know where culture lies in that, I'm definitely still on the five minute let's go side of things.

JPG: *How has engagement with technology, both personally and professionally altered your sexuality, if it has?*

ML: I don't know if it has. I am just on that cusp generation of, I've always had access to online porn. So, I think I've always been in that generation of instant gratification.

JPG: *Switching gears to the political arena. Most of our readers will probably have at least been vaguely aware of Project 2025, which we are seeing unfold in front of us today. In Project 2025, there is a potential attack against pornography. What do you think are the motivations of the architects of Project 2025 for potentially criminalizing certain forms of sexuality, including pornography?*

ML: I think that it's a bunch of fucking hypocrisy. If you look at the guys that are behind all of this, most of them have some weird sexual deviancy, and I use that term lightly because I think that all of us in this industry would be considered sexually deviant. But a lot of the guys that are poo-pooing any kind of sex work are the people that are actually keeping us employed. Pornhub in 2020, during Trump's first term, published a bunch of really great data, which I still love. I love Pornhub and will pay for my subscription to them. Everybody that wanted to ban trans people, and ban trans porn, it turns out that those were the states that had the most people watching those types of porn. I think that is exactly what's happening. The scariest thing about all of this, like with any kind of change in sex work, we have to be worried about human trafficking at all times and I know that all these people have this soap box about being anti human trafficking and all those laws actually just harm sex workers without actually stopping human trafficking, where it actually should be stopped. These laws are all very convoluted and tied into two laws in one. I'm really worried about what 2025 is going to do for the sex work community. In further perpetuating, pushing those, especially the sex workers that are in person, further down. Also if they ban online sex work how many of us are going to have to go to physical sex work and how much more is that going to be criminalized? And how much did this turn into a teacher with a side gig all of a sudden becoming a criminal? A felon. Losing their job. And that's already been happening a lot just because of people's sexual prudence. But 2025 is only going to make all of that worse, while all of these motherfuckers have escorts who are protected because they're fucking a senator instead of a John that runs the Ford dealership in their local town.

JPG: *If there was one thing that you would want or hope for people to understand about sex workers, what would that be?*

ML: That it's work. At the end of the day, sex workers, no matter where you are under the umbrella, whether it's stripping or camming or physical, actual, you know, giving blow jobs in a fucking alley—everybody's like, oh my God, you're exploiting your body—talk to a fucking construction worker. Most sex workers are smart enough to take precautions like using condoms to prevent STIs and HIV. A lot of sex workers that are physical are taking things like Prep and other drugs that have been developed to prevent HIV transmission. We have a lot of ways of being a lot safer around our work, and then you compare that to "Dean" across the street, going and climbing up an electric pole. He is putting his body in a lot more danger than any sex worker is, any guy that's working in Caltrans, the death rate of that type of work. Any guy working in the trash industry is putting his life in more danger than any sex worker. And so, let's take their religion out of work. We're all doing what we need to do to pay our rent or our mortgage and feed ourselves and our families. And I don't know, my titties are on the Internet, your back got blown out from lifting a piece of equipment that was too high. You got hit by a fucking tractor, how is this any different, work is work, we're all doing what we need to do to survive under capitalism?

JPG: *Back to the democratization of pornography for a moment. Twenty-five or so years ago, there was an attempt to unionize in the pornography industry, when it was more of an industry than individual workers. It was for healthcare reasons because of the spread of HIV and various diseases. And ultimately, this unionization, if I remember correctly, was shot down. Now that as an industry it's been democratized and is more in the individual's hands, do you think there is a greater or lesser stigma against the health care issues surrounding sex work and how might we be able to address these things as a culture to make it safer for sex workers?*

ML: I think in general, we're all more downtrodden. And I don't mean that with sex workers, I mean that with everybody. What person that's working radio broadcast has healthcare? What person working at a small business has healthcare? I think that the ideal that healthcare is a human right has continued to degrade since then. There have been some great movements. Star Strip Club in West Hollywood, they're the first unionized strip club in California. I know Portland has had a lot of unionized strip clubs. I think those are all great strides. I think that unionization is great, but I think in general unionized anything has been degraded significantly over time, and all of us have come to this beaten down, downtrodden idea of we don't get things like health care or benefits anymore. And I actually feel like strippers specifically, which is what I call the middle tier of sex work, they're in person but not on the streets, underground. They're the ones really holding all of us up and I think if you look at union history in general across all areas of work, like looking at electricians, plumbers, these people that have traditionally been very union forward—strippers are very much picking up the slack and carrying through the fact that we need to look back at the Wobblies and we need to look back at what work history was and actually protecting ourselves and God bless them for that. I think they're doing more work for the blue-collar sector of America than any actual blue-collar factor is.

JPG: *And back to tech for a moment, a site like OnlyFans for instance, which is just the tip of the iceberg in platforms for this kind of work — are the tech companies behind this doing anything to protect sex workers and respecting their boundaries?*

ML: No, not at all. And actually, I feel like they're almost as bad as having a John. For example, I mean I was on "find my girlfriend," we'll call it that for now. Their payout system is an abomination. You have to have $500 in your account to get your payout. If you have $500 and $5 comes in after that, you cannot cash out. I know a lot of girls have had similar problems with OnlyFans. I know similar girls have had problems with Chaturbate and other websites that are popular, and that's ultimately why I stopped doing it, even as a side hustle, because I'm just not getting my fucking money. These guys are paying me in earnest and I cannot cash out until I have $500, but I should be getting a weekly payout.

JPG: *Do you think this is a form of gamification to keep people coming back to the work?*

ML: I think it very much is.

JPG: *And lastly, what warnings or advice would you have for someone that's considering getting into sex work, particularly for young people?*

ML: Have your strong boundaries written out before you walk into the position. What are you comfortable with? Are you a dom? Are you a sub? Are you OK with going into these long extensive storytelling scenarios? And even going into porn, one of the best pieces of advice that I read is you can walk in with your boundaries, but you also need to know when your boundaries are allowed to be crossed, which is the secondary thing of, I will only do vaginal. And then you're not making enough money, and how much money is your ass worth? And to have that in the back of your mind. you know, do I wanna do gay porn? I don't know. Is it worth $500? No. Is it worth 1000? Yeah. And really have those boundaries, honestly, written out in your journal of—what am I OK with? What will I do? And just like any other job, avoid burnout. What is my work schedule? When do I respond to Snapchat? Do I even have a Snapchat? Do I just tell guys I am on this site and this site only, and really deciding how much you want to engage with the job.

JPG: *Is there anything you feel like I missed that should be discussed? Or anything you wanted to say that you haven't had the opportunity to?*

ML: I mean, do it. Try it. There's a lot of money. Take care of yourself while you do it. But I will say that with this industry and any other, and honestly in retrospect, where I'm at in my current job position, which is not in sex work, I have had an easier time setting up those boundaries in sex work than I have in any corporate position.

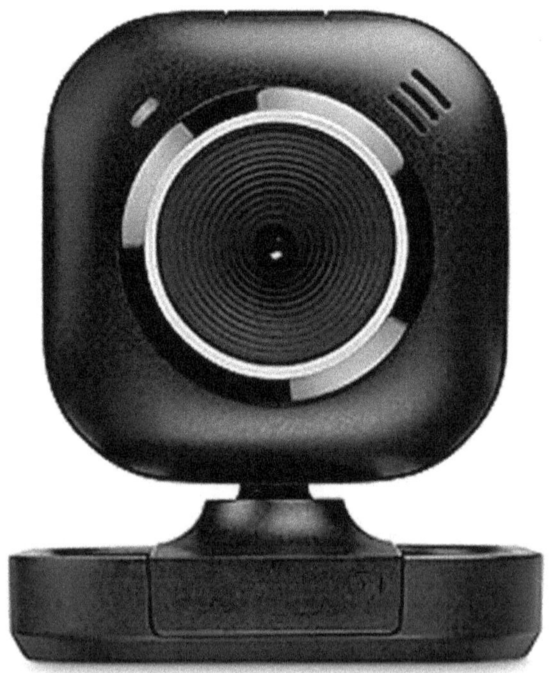

CARE OF YOUR ELECTRIC SHEEP
By F. J. Bergmann

Welcome, New Owner! Your Electric Sheep™ Companion Robo-Animal, Lawn Care Management System and Home Defender™ Security Perimeter Patrol has been designed for the ultimate in ownership satisfaction. Please follow all instructions below for maximum function and enjoyment.

1. *Coat care*
Static cling can be prevented by a grounded metal collar—we recommend stainless steel. Be sure to use a non-conducting leash. Stains may be removed easily with non-aqueous cleaning solvents. Do not immerse. Never allow your Electric Sheep™ to enter a bathtub or other body of water, with or without you. Sunken spots in the fleece should be filled in with steel wool, dryer lint or sustainable/renewable-forest-product excelsior, and non-aerosol-spray-painted to an appropriate hue of Owner's choice.

2. *Companionship*
Your Sheep will readily learn to come when you call its name and perform simple tricks such as ball retrieval. Do not use inflatable balls! Do not reach into Sheep's oral cavity. Your Sheep is programmed to be very cuddly. Only under-tail duct should be used for recreational activity; see 3b, below.

3. *Sustenance*
a) Any vegetal or cellulose matter ingested will be ejected from Sheep's under-tail duct in due course (usually within 5–7 days) as neatly compacted pellets, suitable for animal feed, stove fuel, or composting. Warning: pellets may be inconsistent in size or composition—not recommended for recreational drug manufacture.

b) Feeding non-vegetal substances is not recommended and may void warranty. In case of accidental ingestion of non-vegetal material, turn off switch located inside throat passage (first folding back the Lawn Care/Home Defender™ fangblades) and schedule non-routine maintenance by an approved facility. In case of accidental severing of body parts, turn off switch as soon as practical. If body part can be recovered, refrigerate while transporting to medical facility. Do not allow your Sheep to stray beyond the established perimeter of property. If Sheep is allowed to develop a taste for living flesh, warranty automatically becomes null and void.

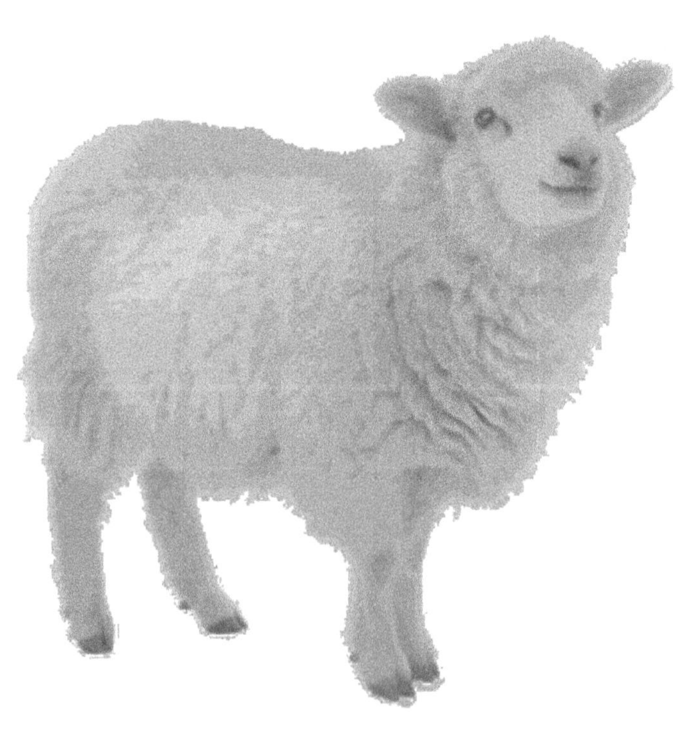

CONTRIBUTOR BIOS:

Michael Alan a.k.a. Michael Alan Alien is a born and raised New York City artist creating progressive drawings, paintings, public art, performance art. He creates daily both publicly and at his studio, immersed in the fine art world, with roots in the underground street art movement of the 80s/90s raised on punk music.

His work has been featured in over 600 publications, books, and media sources, including the New York Times film and in print, Vice, NBC's Today Show, the New York Post, American Artist, Art 21, Art Forum, Art+Auction, GQ, Architectural Digest, Vogue, Marie Claire Italia, ArtNet News, The Huffington Post, Bomb Magazine, Frank 151, the Village Voice's "Best in Show," The Creator's Project, The Gothamist, TimeOut New York, Harper's Bazaar, Frame, Animal, Hyperallergic, Curbs and Stoops, Bust, NY Art News, FAD and many more. http://michaelalanart.com/ - @michaelalanalien

F. J. Bergmann is the poetry editor for Weird House Press and *Mobius: The Journal of Social Change* (mobiusmagazine.com). She lives in Wisconsin and fantasizes about tragedies on or near exoplanets. Her work has appeared in genre venues and places that should have known better. She is a Science Fiction & Fantasy Poetry Association Grand Master and a Writers of the Future winner. She likes to ride horses. She is pretty sure she'd like to ride unicorns, if only they'd cooperate. She thinks imagination can compensate for anything.

Michael Todd Gallowglas is a hybrid-author (with mainstream and alternative publications), storyteller, and educator from Northern California. He has written over 20 books including novels, short story collections, poetry collections, and non-fiction books. He holds a Bachelor of Arts in Creative Writing from San Francisco State University, a Master of Fine Arts in Fiction from Sierra Nevada College, and a Master in Fine Arts in Poetry from the University of Nevada Reno, Tahoe. His traditional storytelling show at Renaissance Faires, Celtic Festivals, and geeky conventions has mesmerized audiences for over thirty years. When not writing, Gallowglas is an avid gamer, enjoys ballroom dancing (swing, blues, and tango are his favorites), and adores coffee. Lots and lots of coffee. https://mtoddgallowglas.com/

Jean-Paul L. Garnier is the owner of Space Cowboy Books bookstore and publishing house, producer of Simultaneous Times Podcast (2023/25 Laureate Award Winner, 2024 BSFA, Ignyte, and British Fantasy Award Finalist), and was the editor of the SFPA's Star*Line magazine from 2021-2025. He is also Editor-in-Chief of Electronic Brain magazine. In 2024 he won the Laureate Award for Best Editor. He has written many books of poetry and science fiction. https://spacecowboybooks.com/

Jenna Hanchey (she/her) is a land-based mermaid who listens to what the birds carry on the wind. Her fiction and audio narration are BSFA-nominated, and work to explore grief, imagine possibilities, center intimacies, and engender hope. Her nonfiction writing examines how speculative fiction can imagine decolonization and bring it into being, while her own fiction tries to support this project of creating better futures for us all. Follow her adventures at www.jennahanchey.com.

Zara Kand is a painter, mixed media artist, and freelance writer for prominent arts publications. She is also a curator and private painting instructor. She was raised in Europe and has lived in the US for the greater part of her life, creating art since a wee toddler. Having been featured in numerous international publications and US galleries, her work is often referred to as dreamy and emotional, with dark and psychological undertones. http://zarakand.com

Jardine Libaire has written novels (including WHITE FUR, and YOU'RE AN ANIMAL) and nonfiction books (including THE SOBER LUSH); has worked on artist collaborations like GOLDTWINZ; and co-wrote the film ENDINGS, BEGINNINGS. She is co-editor of the new zine PO Box Outer Space. The Mojave

Desert is her home these days, a little compound in the middle of nowhere with Earth Angel, Jackpot, Neil, Venus, Antares, Kate, Jupiter & Loverman.   https://fleursdumalsyndicat.com/ @jardinelibaireprojects

Walker Mettling is a printmaker and cartoonist in Joshua Tree California. Since 2010 he's run a gonzo all ages comics micropublishing experiment and edu-excit-o-tainment project called the Providence Comics Consortium. walkermettling.com

Pablo Ramírez (reprinted from the program of his 2022 solo performance, "Golosa: An Excessive Recital in Overabundance"

Hola! My name is Pablo Ramírez and I am an actor, performer, and poet from Los Angeles, CA. My work manifests itself in the form of solo performance shows. Through the use of persona, humor, narrative, and poetry, I often engage in topics of Latine masculinities/femininities, my queerness, fatness, and grief. I author most of my scripts as a way of blending theoretical frameworks and stage aesthetics. I am not, however, a stranger to performance of literature and often partake in traditional theatrical artistry.

RedBlueBlackSilver is an American musician who focuses on instrumental soundtrack music, with a particular emphasis on using the techniques used in sound therapy (binaurals, solfeggio, etc.) to accentuate the listener's experience. His music can be heard in Desert Oracle Radio, Simultaneous Times Podcast, and in several documentaries. He believes that musical enjoyment is a combination of conscious and unconscious factors, and that musicians have an opportunity to increase their influence over the unconsciously perceived aspects of their music.
https://redblueblacksilver.bandcamp.com/

Peter Schutes is the nom de plume of a prolific and acclaimed novelist. As Peter Schutes, the author writes hardcore adult erotic fiction such as *The Slaves of Rome, Small Cockpits and Big Hangars, Muscle Bottom, and The Gospel of Priapus*. Writing in the style of vintage pulp authors from the 1960s and 1970s, Peter lovingly recreates the look and feel of dirty bookstore paperbacks. He lives in Los Angeles. You can read many of his stories on his world wide web page at peterschutes.com

A∴ A∴ Ron Sheppard. A Nebraska native, Sheppard now calls Joshua Tree, California home after living in DC, NYC, LV and LA. Living inside nature has greatly influenced his practice over the past decade in JT; a relationship he never experienced within metropolitan jungles or, ironically, even amongst farmlands of his upbringing. Sheppard is a painter, illustrator, sculptor, performance artist, writer, musician, and tattooist. He exhibits nationally and internationally, with lasting impacts from residencies in Vienna (KEX), Yokohama (ZAIM), and Kanazawa (Ge-Shuku). As the son of an artist, he began exhibiting in the Midwest from the age of 13. https://aaronsheppard.com/

Michael Start is a trained Horologist who specialises in Automata restoration at The House of Automata in Scotland. The museum which he set up adjoins the workshop and has Europe's largest public display of antique automata with over 200 automata, many of which can be seen working.
Michael's work has been featured in TV restoration programmes for the Discovery channel and feature films like Scorsese's 'Hugo'.
Michael Start is also the author of 'Secrets of Automata' a unique reference book which reveals classic designs for mechanical life for the first time.
He also runs a Fleas Circus. https://thehouseofautomata.com/

Other Titles from

Space Cowboy Books

Books:

Human Voices, Alien Conversations – James Machell

Electronic Brain #1 – Various Authors

Entropocene – Jean-Paul L. Garnier

The Enigmatical Sphere of El Chupa-Ku – Juan Manuel Pérez

Space Exploration: Strange New Worlds – John C. Mannone

One Way & Other Stories – Miriam Allen deFord

Life During the Lazarus Age – Robert Frazier

Dreaming of Autonomous Vehicles – Jaroslav Olša, Jr.

The Future is Brief – Jean-Paul L. Garnier

Wave IX – Various Authors

The Martians – Emilie Procházková

Mexicans on the Moon – Pedro Iniguez

Another Time: Time Travel Stories 1942–1960

Complete Poems 1965–2020 – Michael Butterworth

Simultaneous Times Vol. 3 – Various Authors

Simultaneous Times Vol. 2.5 – Various Authors

Simultaneous Times Vol. 2 – Various Authors

Simultaneous Times Vol. 1 – Various Authors

Garbage In, Gospel Out – Jean-Paul L. Garnier

Betelgeuse Dimming – Jean-Paul L. Garnier

Future Anthropology – Jean-Paul L. Garnier

www.spacecowboybooks.com

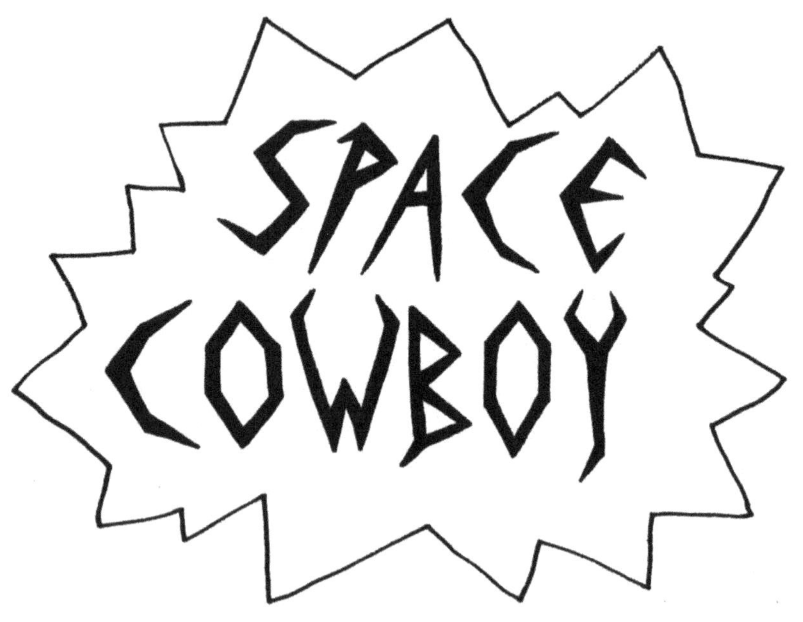SPACE
COWBOY